EIGHT

EFFECTIVE PROBLEM SOLVING

───

STRATEGIES FOR A WORLD THAT WILL DEMAND INNOVATION

DAVID PARSONS

The principles and strategies of this book are summarized in a companion volume: *Educating Problem Solvers*. The education book starts with education chapters of this book found in *Part IX*. Each principle is then summarized, including each of the strategies and a smattering of the supporting argument.

Washington, DC.

ISBN 9781475278378

Version 1.5

www.EffectiveProblemSolving.com

To Nora, Emerson, Desmond, Frank, Alexandra, and Annabelle, the future of our family.

Table of Contents

v

Eight Principles of Problem Solving

#1: *MENTAL MODELS ARE NOT REALITY* ....*PAGE 44*

Guard against overconfidence, confirmation bias, and the Einstellung effect, where we assume that solutions to problems we have encountered in the past are equally applicable to a new situation.

#2: *BE WILLING TO REFRAME THE PROBLEM*........................ *PAGE 80*

Effective problem solvers monitor their progress toward a solution. They question whether the problem representation they have chosen is actually moving them in the right direction. Is it adequately exposing the landscape of possibilities? Are the rules and procedures associated with the representation getting results? If not, effective problem solvers are willing to reframe the problem.

#3: *SEEK UNDERSTANDING THROUGH EXPLORATION* .... *PAGE 105*

Problems have a structure that needs to be discovered and explored. We cannot know in advance where the hard parts of the problem are hiding or where we might find the opportunities for great solutions. Problem exploration requires the discipline and the imagination to move from one aspect of a problem to another, from one perspective to another, to discover the pitfalls and possibilities.

#4: *CREATE MAPS OF COMPLEX PROBLEMS*........................ *PAGE 147*

Problems are made up of interrelated parts. Even on the most complex projects, the relationships among the parts of the problem can be mapped in such a way that participants in the problem solving effort can find their way about.

#5: *THE PERFECT IS THE ENEMY OF THE GOOD*................ *PAGE 177*

The perfect is the enemy of the good. Goals often require compromise. Markets require negotiation.

#6: *MANAGE THE PLANNING FALLACY*.............................. *PAGE 192*

We underestimate the time it will take to complete tasks, and we overestimate the benefits that will accrue. This is true even when we undertake tasks where we have experience on comparable tasks. Set firm intermediate goals. Look to experience to test and challenge projections.

#7: *EMPLOY MINIMUM NECESSARY CONTROL*.................... *PAGE 203*

In order to reduce the probability of unwanted side effects, the meta problem solver gets things done with the least control that will achieve his objectives.

#8: *THE REAL WORLD MAY FIGHT BACK*.............................. *PAGE 219*

Problem solving occurs within a framework of established relationships among people and organizations. These relationships form a structure that resists change.

Acknowledgments

As I think back about influences on this book, I must start with my uncle, Don Parsons, who encouraged my fascination with things mathematical. In college, I was fortunate to encounter several professors who introduced me to the mysterious question of how we think. My roommate, Dick von Briesen, and I enhanced our college experience with numerous offbeat projects, some of which called on his skills as a locksmith. We learned together the value of teamwork.

As you will find in the pages of this book, my architecture thesis advisor, Jerzy Soltan, encouraged me to grapple with the process of design with his undying emphasis on exploration. Brad Dunham, a professor of mathematics from IBM, encouraged me to apply principles of natural selection to computer-based architectural design.

At the firm of Building Systems Development in San Francisco, its founder, Ezra Ehrenkrantz, inspired many young architects to challenge the way buildings are built. I was fortunate to be one of those. John Wade brought me to the School of Architecture & Urban Planning of the University of Wisconsin–Milwaukee. I am in his debt for involving me in an interdisciplinary seminar that studied the way we think from the perspective of linguistics, psychology, philosophy, and education. This group introduced me to the work of Marvin Minsky and Roger Schank.

I am deeply grateful to Joe White for many years of partnership at Syncon Corporation and Andy Siprelle at Simulation Dynamics for challenging me to tackle problems that were at the limit of my reach.

As for bringing all of this together into a book, I have needed extensive support and criticism. None was more important than the review of an early draft by Margaret McDonald. She was unrestrained in her criticism. I have come to learn that such guidance is as valuable as it is difficult to get. My sister-in-law, Ellen Kriegel, gave a later draft a rare read that combined editorial and substantive corrections. Tom Schrader and Jeff Griffith have been through two drafts, giving me substantial encouragement and food for thought. Doug Parsons,

Acknowledgments

Steve Preston, Kathy Powell, Jeff Snell, Eric Bartelt, Mardi Lewis, and Don Neuman have also provided thoughtful feedback.

Through all of this, through forty-six years of this, my wife, Jutta, has been my cheerleader, coach, manager, and team doctor. None of these things would have happened without her support.

Preface

As a kid, I used to love the challenge of brainteasers. My uncle gave me a subscription to *Scientific American*. My only real interest in it was Martin Gardner's monthly column called "Mathematical Games." In college, my roommate and I spent as much time on various screwball projects as we did on course work. Our crowning achievement freshman year was constructing from heavy paperboard an object called the intersection of five cubes. We had a navy surplus sonar control unit; built a search light from airport runway lights; and dabbled in geodesic structures à la Buckminster Fuller.

I was drawn to architecture not as an artist or an engineer, but as a puzzle solver. I liked fitting things together. In graduate school, I became interested in the process of design - not just doing it, but thinking about how to do it. This included dipping my toe in the water of computerized design. My thesis advisor, Jerzy Soltan, challenged me to be aware of my design approach. Far from stultifying creativity, Soltan's method was to look at problems from many angles, opening up opportunities for innovative solutions. Through the years since then, I have often returned to the question of how problem solving actually works. These musings have been stimulated by an eclectic range of projects, by coworkers and by a select group of high impact authors. Some projects dealt directly with the question of how problem solving of a particular sort should be organized.

Over the last ten years, in fits and starts, I have reviewed these projects and the many notes that have recorded my thoughts as I worked. In this book, I have tried to sort out what all of this adds up to. What is the nature of problem solving? Is there a structure that underlies problems? Does the work we do in school prepare us to solve problems that occur in the real world? In short, what lessons have I learned?

I have finally given a name to the common denominator of a life of projects and thinking about projects: *meta problem solving*. Meta problem solving is the set of conscious measures we take to monitor and control our problem solving efforts.

A core premise of this book is that we are powerfully guided by our mental models of the world. These models are purpose driven. They are not only powerful organizers of the information available to us, they are powerful filters, excluding every input considered extraneous.

Generalized mental models, or frames as I will call them, are functional things that have problem solving capabilities like calculation and logic attached to them. They are specifically designed to be manipulated. For all their power, mental models have serious flaws leading to overconfidence and error. The problem solving principles I propose in this book can be employed to monitor problem solving and reduce errors inherent in the problem solving process.

Who is this book for? My starting point was to pass on what I have learned to my children so they can guide the education of their children. When I think about what the world will be like in the 2030s and onward, I am certain that the effective people will be the meta problem solvers, those who are disciplined to explore each new problem with an open mind and fresh ideas. In the process of developing the principles in this book, I have looked at the state of education, wondering where learning these principles would fit in. I am heartened by the trends in problem-based learning and related theories that de-emphasize teaching and put learning in the hands of the student and her curiosity. I review the prospects for learning the eight principles in *Part IX*.

So here we are, me writing and you reading, somewhat separated in time and space. My bet is that we are very different people in our passions and our capabilities. Since the lessons in this book grow out of my experience, our challenge will be to translate these lessons into principles useful to you - not an easy task. I will do my best to draw general conclusions from specific examples. However, the largest part of this burden will fall on you. Your mental models of the world are very different from mine. Only you can sort through this material and integrate it into your way of thinking.

Introduction

Human activity is a pandemonium of problem solving. We are constantly trying to improve our world, or at least maintain and repair it, so it will function to our liking. These efforts, the thrashing about of seven billion people, interact to create a dynamic kaleidoscope of action and reaction.

The eight principles presented in this book make up a supervisory scheme that problem solvers can impose on themselves. I call this scheme *meta problem solving*, since its principles combine to create an awareness of our problem solving efforts *from above*. In adopting the principles, we are creating an alter ego that looks down upon our struggles to solve problems. Meta problem solving monitors and controls our problem solving efforts. The eight principles recognize the potential fallibility of the mental models we invoke to organize our thinking. They call for the discipline to explore a problem without allowing premature conclusions to limit our exploration. We can mitigate our tendency toward bias and overconfidence by being aware of it. We must create alternative solutions with an open mind, much as a jury admonished by a judge not to form conclusions until the evidence is in. We must seek good solutions but not be trapped in a quest for the perfect. We must allow good solutions to emerge from our explorations, not lock ourselves into preconceived notions.

A central concept in my argument for problem solving principles is the *frame*. I adopt the central thesis of Marvin Minsky's frame theory.[1] He argues that the building blocks of cognition are not minute and unstructured elements, but rather more elaborate data structures that model the systems we are thinking about. He calls these structures *frames*. We have a lightning-fast ability to match situations we encounter with one of the thousands of frames we have in our mental filing system. With each new problem we encounter,

---

[1] Marvin Minsky, "A Framework for Representing Knowledge," *Artificial Intelligence Memo No 306*, Massachusetts Institute of Technology, Artificial Intelligence Laboratory, 1974.

the frame we call up guides us in collecting information to build a situation-specific mental model. These models provide an explanation of the dynamics of a situation and allow us to predict the outcomes of alternative courses of action.

Problem solving requires self-criticism in order to overcome the natural overconfidence that framing instills. To be self-critical is to criticize our ideas, not ourselves. It is one thing to think about problem solving outside of the context of solving an actual problem, such as while you are reading this book. It is another to be aware of the pitfalls of problem solving while being engaged in it. To do this, we must find ways to stand outside of the framing and representation system that so naturally shapes our ideas.

The art of taking tests gives us an apt example of meta problem solving. Tests challenge two levels of knowledge and skill. First, we are tested on what we know and on our ability to solve problems. Second, we are tested on our ability to take tests. On the first front, there is little students can do in the short term to improve their knowledge of the various subjects prior to exams, perhaps study lists of likely College Board vocabulary words. On the second front, however, students can learn a great deal in the short term. We could call it *meta* test taking. Rule one: manage your time. Rule two: categorize questions, moving through the test quickly, then cycle back to spend remaining time where it could be most productive. Rule three: always guess when the odds are in your favor. The common thread to these rules is awareness of where you are and what you are doing. You must monitor your progress, not getting lost in the moment. Your most important tool is a watch.

Meta problem solving is a purpose-driven instance of metacognition, a branch of cognitive psychology introduced by John Flavell, a psychologist specializing in childhood development. In 1979, he wrote "Metacognition and Cognitive Monitoring, A New Area of Cognitive-Developmental Inquiry."[2] This short article, appearing in *American Psychologist*, launched metacognition as a new branch of

---

[2] John H. Flavell, "Metacognition and Cognitive Monitoring, A New Area of Cognitive-Developmental Inquiry," *American Psychologist*, October, 1979.

cognitive psychology. Flavell defined metacognition as: *knowledge and cognition about cognitive phenomena.*

As esoteric as metacognition may sound, thoughts about thoughts are an everyday occurrence. Consider the last time that you could not remember the name of a person. You knew that you knew the name, but you could not come up with it.

Flavell argues that thoughts about thoughts are no different from other kinds of thoughts, except that the objects being considered are thoughts.

> *… metacognitive experiences are especially likely to occur in situations that stimulate a lot of careful, highly conscious thinking … in novel roles or situations, where every major step you take requires planning beforehand and evaluation afterwards; where decisions and actions are at once weighty and risky; where highly affective arousal or other inhibitors of reflective thinking are absent. Such situations provide many opportunities for thoughts and feelings about your own thinking to arise and, in many cases, call for a kind of quality control that metacognitive experiences can help supply.[3]*

The ability to think about our own thoughts develops in childhood later than the ability to think about other kinds of things. Flavell determined that at about age five, children begin to realize that their mental representations are distinct from the real world that they represent.

In my own experience, metacognition played a major role in my survival as a youth soccer coach. When my son was seven years old, he played on a soccer team. This was before I started coaching. The scene at games was chaotic on the field and overenthusiastic on the sidelines. The fathers had a way of going a bit overboard both in rooting their youngsters on and in kibitzing the referees.

One sunny Saturday afternoon, one of the mothers came over to a group of miscreants, including me, and offered the opinion that we were being obnoxious and would we please stop. Later, when I had time to reflect, I realized that she was right. We were out of control.

---

[3] Ibid., p. 908.

Shortly thereafter, I was approached to become the coach of my son's team for the following year. With this prior experience fresh in my mind (as it is today), I offered the opinion that I was not cut out to be a coach, not because I lacked soccer knowledge and skills; this was the common denominator of most parent coaches at that time. My concern was about temperament.

After further reflection, I decided that I could manage my behavior at soccer games, as long as I knew how I wanted to behave. I coached my son's teams and later teams for fourteen years. Before every game, I considered the kinds of situations that I might encounter and how, after the fact, I would like to have behaved. I was surprised at how easy it was to maintain my awareness of the situations as they unfolded. I was monitoring my own emotions and actions, on the lookout for telltale signs of impending meltdown. I often advised neophyte coaches to forget about acting naturally; this can only lead to trouble.

For me, meta coaching went beyond awareness and monitoring of my sideline behavior. There was also considerable planning involved. A major stumbling block for coaches in youth soccer is the common rule that all players must have a minimum of 50 percent playing time. Coaches go into a game with the best intentions, but at crunch time, they revert to playing all of their best players, without regard to the playing time of the others. When a weak player goes onto the field for a strong player, both of them know the consequences: a weaker team. The parents of both players know this as well. As a result, coaches delay the substitution of the weaker player, and at the end of the game, it may not happen at all. Only a clear plan of substitution can overcome this quandary. The solution is for pairs of weaker players to share a position. Each knows that he will play half of the game. The substitution has a neutral effect on the strength of the team. An indirect consequence of this approach is that the coach will focus on training these players for that position to improve overall team competence.

Meta coaching props can also serve a purpose. One day I observed the calm demeanor of another coach, aided by his conspicuous accessory at games, a lawn chair. At the time, coaching from the sidelines was against the laws of soccer, although the specter of coaches exhorting their teams was common. I brought a lawn chair to my next game and spent considerable time sitting in it. This was a tangible reminder that I was to observe and enjoy the game, not to be obsessively controlling. The lawn chair became a permanent part of my soccer coaching persona.

Meta coaching is about monitoring and controlling coaching. Because it requires little knowledge of soccer skills and tactics, it is eminently teachable in a short period. *Meta coaching* bears the same relationship to *soccer coaching* as *meta test taking* bears to *test taking*.

Our destination in this book is a set of principles for effective problem solving. To get there, we need to build an understanding of the relationship between the real world of problems and our mental models. From this, we can explore the ways that mental models can fail us and then prescribe principles that will improve our effectiveness. For each principle, problem solving strategies are proposed. Part IX explores the challenge of integrating effective problem solving principles into the way we teach.

Figure 1 divides the problem solving cycle into four phases: framing, exploring, deciding, and acting. Framing connects the real world to our mental models. Exploring generates alternative solutions. Deciding sets our course of action. Acting connects our mental models back to the real world. The diagram locates the eight problem solving principles within this model. The first eight parts of the book draw the connections between each of the eight principles and the challenges of problem solving.

In Part I, *Mental Models are Not Reality,* I put my own spin on Marvin Minsky's frame theory. Frames provide us with a template for understanding how systems behave and for predicting how they will react to change. Framing a problem charts a landscape of potential solutions that we can explore. As we build situation-specific mental models, we come to believe in them as accurate stand-ins for the real world.

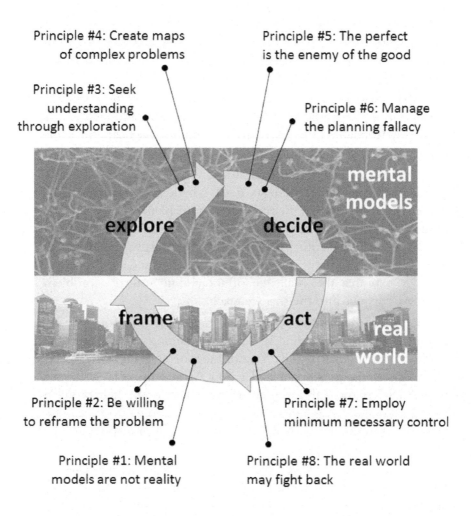

Figure 1: Problem Solving Cycle

We can confuse our mental models with the world that they represent. As a consequence, several factors undermine our effectiveness as problem solvers. Among these, I discuss overconfidence, confirmation bias, overemphasis on early impressions, and the Einstellung effect, where we assume that solutions to problems we have encountered in the past are equally applicable to a new situation. Several strategies are presented to overcome these weaknesses.

In Part II, *Be Willing to Reframe the Problem*, I argue that effective problem solvers monitor their progress toward a solution. They question whether the way they have chosen to frame a problem is moving them in the right direction. Is it adequately exposing the landscape of possible solutions? Are the rules and procedures associated with the frame getting results? The ability to reframe a problem relies on understanding that there are many ways that a problem can be framed.

Part III, *Seek Understanding through Exploration*, stresses the importance of fully comprehending a problem before committing to any aspects of a solution. Problems have a structure that needs to be discovered and explored. We cannot know in advance where the hard parts of a problem are hiding or where we might find the opportunities for great solutions. Problem solving itself has a structure that likewise must be mapped out before early steps commit us to the wrong path. To explore a problem, we must be able to hold it up to the light and view it from different angles, to form multiple representations much as an architect looks at a building design in plan, elevation, and perspective. Our mental models can impede this kind of multifaceted exploration. As rapidly as we frame a new situation, it is hard work to put that frame aside in favor of another, and then another. Once a frame takes hold, it rapidly grows roots; it becomes our reality. Problem exploration requires the discipline and the imagination to move from one aspect of a problem to another, from one perspective to another, to discover the pitfalls and possibilities.

Part IV, *Create Maps of Complex Problems*, emphasizes the importance of capturing the structure of complex problems in a map that charts the interrelationships among the parts of the problem. The strategies presented here are rich in detail, perhaps as complex as the problems they are intended to map. They will require perseverance of the reader.

Part V, *The Perfect is the Enemy of the Good*, uses this old political adage to stress that problems in the real world do not have perfect solutions. The aspirations of multiple stakeholders must often be integrated, calling for compromise on all sides. Limited resources force us to set priorities. Limited time requires that we accept the best solution available when we would like to continue searching for better. We must seek a balance between the investment in exploration recommended in Principles #3 and #4, and the potential benefit that will result from a solution that is good but not perfect.

Part VI, *Manage the Planning Fallacy*, proposes strategies for overcoming our inability to predict the costs, quality, or schedule of courses of action that we undertake. These strategies emphasize reliance on experience with similar problems rather than on predictions grounded in current knowledge of the roadblocks that might be encountered.

Part VII, *Employ Minimum Necessary Control*, urges problem solvers to guard against unintended consequences by minimizing the changes that they make. This is particularly meaningful in areas of regulation and control where the actions of the problem solver are likely to stimulate unforeseen countermeasures.

Part VIII, *Recognize the Intransigence of Established Relationships*, addresses the quandary of unintended consequences. Problems exist within a fabric of existing relationships. Much like ecologies in the natural world, changes in this fabric bring on a rebalancing of the rest. Innovative solutions are particularly likely to stress existing relationships. To guard against the intransigence of established relationships, we must first search them out. We can then apply several strategies for coping with their resistance to change.

Part IX, *Educating Problem Solvers*, looks optimistically at the potential for students to learn the eight principles in school. Schools need to prepare us to think about problem solving. If the test taking and soccer coaching examples given above are any indication, teaching such principles would require relatively little investment in time, since they are layered on top of subject-specific knowledge and skills. The challenge is that for problem solving principles to take hold, we must apply them to real problem solving situations. For example, teaching test taking methods would not be effective without the pressure of performance on important tests. Meta coaching is only useful when the coach understands the real need for it.

Ironically, extracurricular activities provide rich opportunities for solving real problems. Sports, music, debate, and drama all require performance. Students prepare, perform and then evaluate. There are many opportunities to relate curriculum content to real problems. Science fairs are a good model. Scenarios where students are required to explain subject matter to others draw them into a deeper level of understanding. The audience can be peers, parents, younger students, or the public.

PART I   *Principle #1: Mental Models are Not Reality*

Problems exist when we can imagine a world that is better. This imagining takes place in our minds. We create and manipulate mental models of reality. We model the world as it is and as it could be. Our minds are well adapted to creating these models; they are the foundation for building predictions of how the world will turn and of the consequences of our actions. For all their power, mental models are flawed. They often guide us to see only what we want to see. They can imbue us with overconfidence. To combat these shortcomings, we need to maintain awareness that our mental models are not, in fact, the real world itself. They are highly selective models that may miss crucial details. As we confront problems, we may be under the illusion that we have seen it all before. But each real world situation brings its own unique considerations.

Problem solving Principle #1 calls for us to monitor our problem solving efforts with a critical eye, to recognize that mental models are not reality. We must employ self-conscious strategies to guard against overconfidence and our tendency to seek out information that confirms our preconceived assumptions.

Chapters 1 through 4 describe mental models as tools that we use to predict how the world will behave and how the world, in turn, will react to our actions. Chapter 5 gives several examples of frames that dramatically failed to capture essential real world characteristics. Chapter 6 describes several factors that underlie our tendency toward overconfidence. Chapter 7 presents strategies for better aligning our mental models with the reality that we intend them to comprehend.

Chapter 1 Mental Models

Our ability to solve problems relies on mental models of problem situations. They are purpose driven, much like tools in a workshop. The knowledge that they capture enables us to understand, explain, predict, and control the world we live in.

In the 1960s, the rapidly expanding capacity of computers ushered in the field of artificial intelligence. At the same time, the field of cognitive psychology was taking root. A core question in both fields was how the human mind represents reality. Marvin Minsky had a unique perspective on mental processes, having been the founder of the Artificial Intelligence Lab at MIT. In the early 1970s, Minsky developed the *Society of Mind Theory*, where he attempted to explain how intelligence could be the product of the interaction of non-intelligent parts. In 1974, Minsky published a paper titled "A Framework for Representing Knowledge."[4] He criticized contemporary cognition theories built on what he called *minute, local, and unstructured* building blocks. He called for a more structured view of how we think. Exhibiting a measure of modesty, he explained that he was trying to bring together several of these issues by *pretending* to have a unified, coherent theory. Minsky summarized his thinking as follows:

> *Here is the essence of the theory: when one encounters a new situation (or makes a substantial change in one's view of the present situation), one selects from memory a structure called a Frame. This is a remembered framework to be adapted to fit reality by changing details as necessary.*

---

[4] Marvin Minsky, "A Framework for Representing Knowledge," *Artificial Intelligence Memo No 306*, Massachusetts Institute of Technology, Artificial Intelligence Laboratory, 1974.

A frame is a data-structure for representing a stereotyped situation, like being in a certain kind of living room, or going to a child's birth-day party. Attached to each frame are several kinds of information. Some of this information is about how to use the frame. Some is about what one can expect to happen next. Some is about what to do if these expectations are not confirmed.

Minsky's goal was to build a theory that would set a direction for the development of artificial intelligence. I combine Minsky's frame notion with the central position given to *prediction* by Jeff Hawkins and Eugene Meehan. (We will meet these gentlemen in the next chapter.) Our ability to control the world - to act - to solve problems - relies on our ability to predict the consequences of our actions. Our ability to predict grows out of our understanding of how systems work. Frames embody this knowledge. We use frames to generate representations of specific problem scenarios. Once a representation is loaded with information that describes the situation, we are able to use the representation to explore alternative outcomes and choose a course of action.

Chapter 2   Prediction Machines

Problem solving is grounded in our ability to predict the behavior of the world around us and the consequences of the actions we contemplate. The human mind is designed to make continuous predictions of future events.

One day my four-year-old granddaughter asked me to describe how to catch a crab. I explained that you go out on a dock, or maybe in a boat, where you think there might be crabs in the water. You tie a piece of meat - I thought *chicken neck* would seem gross - to a string and lower it into the water. You hold the string lightly in your hand, and when you feel the string wiggling, it means that there may be one or two crabs nibbling at the meat. Slowly, you pull the string up until you can see if a crab is there. You bring the crab near the surface of the water. Then you take your net, slip it into the water, and swoop it up from under the crab.

Nora declared, "Then you have to put a lid on the net." In an instant, she had visualized the crab climbing out of the net. She had never seen a live crab. Yet she effortlessly created this scene in her mind and played it forward, predicting what the crab would do.

This ability of the human mind to predict what will happen next is at the heart of human intelligence. Jeff Hawkins made a fortune as the developer of the Palm Pilot. He has dedicated his post-Palm Pilot years to investigating how the mind works. His seminal work, *On Intelligence*,[5] presents his model of the functioning of the neocortex, the part of the brain that makes mammals so special, and humans more special yet. His core idea is that the neocortex is made up of *invariant representations* of all aspects of the world that we experience. These representations are generalized. For example, we remember a

---

[5] Jeff Hawkins, *On Intelligence* (New York: Times Books, 2004).

person's face as a single model, not as a particular view or combination of views. We are able, in ways not fully understood, to use this model not only to recognize a person from various views but also from partial views and from views we have never seen before. Our memory is filled with these representations. In fact, our memory is these representations. We use them continuously to predict what will happen next. When what happens does not match our prediction, the difference gets our attention. For Hawkins, prediction and action are closely linked. According to Hawkins, Nora's visualization of the crab climbing out of the net is what the most recently developed components of the brain are designed to do – to predict what is going to happen next.

> *The brain uses vast amounts of memory to create a model of the world. Everything you know and have learned is stored in this model. The brain uses this memory-based model to make continuous predictions of future events. It is the ability to make predictions about the future that is the crux of intelligence.*[6]

Consider the following scenario that occurred several summers ago at my brother's beach house. As I enter the workshop, a room chock-full of beach paraphernalia, I spot a bright red two-string kite. I am instantly transported back to my youth, when I was infatuated with controllable kites. I had mail ordered a two-string kite from Seattle. It was huge, or maybe I was just smaller. The kite had a trapezoidal shape, with each corner cut off. The surface of the kite was heavy paper. I reinforced the edges with cloth tape. There were four basswood struts for the main frame and two perpendicular struts for the triangular tail fins. The kite required a lot of wind to fly and a long tail for stability. I made an elaborate wooden spool for the two heavy lines that connected my hands to the two support points on the front of the kite.

All of these memories of the kites of my youth come back to me readily. Beyond these images, I remember the process of flying the kite: setting it on the ground so that it would not blow away; unrolling the lines, keeping them untangled; then running to the kite to

---

[6] Ibid, p. 6.

prop it up in a certain way for the takeoff. Then I would go to the operator end of the lines and prepare for takeoff. After a long wait, the wind would build. I would back up quickly, and the kite would rise off the ground. Standing there in my brother's workshop, I feel the kite in my hands as it tilts from lying on the ground to vertical, then the takeoff. I feel the pull on my hands, and my response as the kite turns on an angle and I tug on the appropriate line to get it vertical. Then it soars. I take it to the left and dive it toward the ground. At first I am cautious, completing the dives well above the ground. As I gain confidence, I bring it down close to the ground and guide it horizontally, moving across the wind and then heading into it. As the kite slows down, I turn it up to gain altitude and speed. Usually the flight would end in a daring dive gone awry. I had tape and additional sticks to do field repairs. Finally, either the wind would subside or the kite would be broken beyond field repair or it would be dinnertime. I would wind up the lines and make my way home.

I am certain, there in my brother's workshop, that I am not actually remembering any specific day from my youth, or even a specific kite. I am reconstructing. I am building a simulation. I am able to construct from my memories a model of Rock Creek Park, of a kite, and all of the ancillary gear, including myself. I can then apply my knowledge of the sequences of actions and events that would ensue. The model in my mind has just enough information to allow me to create this moving picture.

I look at the kite in the workroom. It looks nothing like the kites of my youth. This kite is made from rip-stop nylon fabric. The structural members are round plastic struts with rubber connectors that bend but do not break on impact. The kite string is much lighter and stronger than what I remember. Yet, I can look at this kite and imagine flying it. I don't mean *imagine* in some general way. I mean that I can create a picture in my mind of the steps required to fly the thing: more than a picture, a moving picture. The kite strings have fabric straps on their ends, one red and one green. I can feel the kite in my hands through the straps. Mind you, I am still standing in my brother's workshop.

The purpose of these mental feats is clear. I am contemplating taking this kite out for a test drive. To decide whether to move

15

forward into this activity, I want to know how it will turn out, so I simulate it in my mind. This is what we do all the time. We imagine the consequences of our actions, both good and bad. This ability to predict outcomes is what makes us such able problem solvers. We are prediction machines.

I ask myself whether I can fly the kite alone, or would I need help. The critical step is the takeoff. It is somewhat tricky to get the kite airborne without someone holding it in the air. But I did this many times as a youth.

More questions. Is there enough wind? Is the beach too crowded? What is the direction of the wind? Wind direction could be a showstopper if it takes the kite over even a few people sunning themselves near the breaking waves. Why speculate? I will answer these questions soon enough.

So off I go to the beach, kite in hand, but in my mind, it is already soaring across the sky.

We are constantly predicting what is going to happen next. There are several reasons for this. First, we compare our predictions to what actually happens in order to detect if the world is as we expect it to be. Second, we predict what is going to happen in order to plan our own actions. Looks like it might rain, I will take an umbrella. Third, we predict the consequences of the actions that we contemplate. How else would we be able to decide what to do? *Our ability to predict is the foundation for our ability to act.*

Eugene Meehan was a political scientist with a lifelong interest in how knowledge in political science should be pursued. Among his twenty-seven books is *The Thinking Game: A Guide to Effective Study,* where he examines the role that knowledge plays in human activity. His book *Explanation in the Social Sciences, a System Paradigm*[7] presents his core idea, that the purpose of knowledge is prediction.

Here ... we define purpose in terms of two fundamental needs or requirements: first, the need to anticipate future events so that behavior

---

[7] Eugene Meehan, *Explanation in the Social Sciences, a System Paradigm* (Homewood Illinois: The Dorsey Press, 1968).

can be adapted to them; second, the need to control future events... so that man can become something more than a servile prisoner of natural forces.[8]

Meehan equates knowledge with the systematic explanation of events. For Meehan, knowledge is captured in mental constructs, generalized models that capture the key elements in a class of real world phenomena, the relationships among the elements, and their rules of behavior. He calls these mental constructs *systems*.

Meehan and Hawkins have tackled the question of how we solve problems from very difference perspectives, yet their models of knowledge and action are remarkable close, including their focus on *prediction* as the central purpose of intelligence.

So where do predictions come from? Hawkins emphasizes our ability to remember sequences of actions, such as the singing of a song. But our ability to predict is much more powerful than remembering sequences. *Predictions come from our understanding of systems.*

---

[8] Ibid, p. 19.

Chapter 3   Systems

In order to solve problems, we must be able to predict the outcomes of our actions. Our ability to predict grows out of our understanding of the world. Thinking in terms of systems stresses a focus on a set of elements, their properties, and interrelationships. An understanding of these system characteristics allows us to predict system behavior. System descriptions can be specific to a single real world situation, or they can be generic, describing the elements and relationships that govern the behavior of a class of situations.

This chapter lays the groundwork for discussing the mental models that we use to navigate the waters of problem solving. The essence of the systems view is that we house our knowledge of the world in the form of systems. Understanding systems is the foundation of our ability to predict. Systems thinking provides a structure for understanding the components of a complex experience.

Consider the word *system*. Most nouns divide the universe of things into two groups, those things that the word refers to and those that it does not. *Automobile, fork,* and *sunset* each defines a set of things. The word *system* is different. We can look at anything as a system. Commercial advertising has proven this point with such products as *nail polish systems*. When we use the word system, we are invoking a way of looking at a thing. We are asking the listener to consider the thing as a whole and to consider its parts. We are looking for understanding of how the parts interact to dictate the behavior of the whole. If I say *look at that bicycle*, you are free to consider the bicycle in a manner of your choosing. You may fancy the color scheme, the implications of the tire width, or the ample saddlebags. But if I say *look at that bicycle system*, I draw you into considering the elements of the bicycle and how they function together.

You think that there must be something special about this particular bicycle for me to have called attention to it as a system.

To look at a part of the world as a system is to try to understand the relationships among its parts and to understand how the assemblage of parts behaves under certain circumstances. A systems model is a functional thing that we build to capture our understanding of a physical or social phenomena. Our need for understanding is targeted. For example, as drivers, we only need to know certain things about the systems that make up our cars. We need to know how to operate it, not how to fix it, manufacture it, ship it, or sell it. People with these different obligations would have entirely different models of a car as a system.

The purpose of understanding a system is to be able to predict its behavior. To drive a car, I must know that turning the top of the steering wheel to the left will cause the car to turn left. I understand; therefore, I can predict. Use of the word *system* is designed to focus on the understanding of a phenomenon as a set of dynamically interrelated parts. People certainly do not have to use the word system to understand systems. I am using it here to focus our attention.

In order to be effective problem solvers, we must be able to predict the outcomes of our actions. The ability to *predict* is grounded in our ability to *explain*. When we see that flipping a certain switch turns on the lights in a room, we can form an explanatory link between the two events. Flipping the switch causes the light to go on. We understand the switch-light system sufficiently to predict what will cause the light to go on. If I now want to turn on the light, I can predict that the action of flipping the switch will cause the light to go on. Beyond that, I know from my experience that there will not be unintended consequences from this action. No alarms will sound, and no disturbing smells will result. This knowledge is functional in that it supports a specific action. My knowledge, derived from observing that the light goes on when I flip the switch, does not support other light-related actions such as repairing the behind the scenes electrical system that actually makes the one event cause the other.

If I am asked to explain the operation of my car or of the lighting system in my house, I must ask (or assume) what the purpose of the explanation is. What is the questioner trying to predict? If she wants to operate the vehicle or the lights then a *black box* explanation will be appropriate. Throw switch A, and thing B will happen. There is no need to explain or understand the chain of cause and effect *under the hood*. Can I explain the operation of my car? Yes, sufficiently to operate it.

A system description breaks a system down into a set of elements and their relationships. But the elements and the relationships that we choose to describe are a function of our purpose. If our task is to operate the lights, we don't care about the internal components of a light switch or the color of the switch or the wiring that connects the switch to the light. These facts are not relevant to turning the lights on and off.

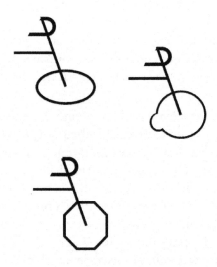

Figure 2: Bicycles

Look at the illustration in Figure 2.[9] What do you see? I hope you see three bicycles with peculiar front wheels. Are you imagining

---

[9] Adapted from Edward de Bono, *The Mechanism of Mind*, (New York: Penguin Books, 1969) p. 150.

the behavior of these bicycles? Can you feel what the ride would be like, maybe the feeling of the seat as the bump in one of the wheels hits the road? You certainly are having no problem filling in the rest of each bicycle in your mind: the seat, rear wheel, and pedals. We have a model of bicycles in our minds as a system. This model goes well beyond simply being able to identify an object as a bicycle. It allows us to inspect a bicycle we have never seen before to determine whether we would be able to ride it. Maybe the tires are flat. Maybe it is locked. We use this system model to predict what it would be like to ride each of the aberrant machines in Figure 2 and what would need to be changed to make the system work as we would like.

We instinctively understand the world in terms of the behavior of systems. This understanding is the foundation for predictions of the course of events and of the consequences of our actions. The ability to predict events allows us to choose among alternative courses of action - in short, to solve problems. The real world outside of our minds has no inherent subdivision into components. We create models of the world; we impose a structure where we define the elements in a manner useful to our thought processes. We think of the systems – the buildings, corporations, bridge clubs, and human relationships – as being *out there* in the world. That is an illusion. Actually, we create them in our minds in the form of *frames*. A brief semantic note: when we use the word *system*, we are referring to something in the real world. When we use the word *frame*, we are referring to something in our minds.

Chapter 4   Frames

Frames are generalized mental models of real world situations. Frames embody our understanding of systems and their behavior. When we encounter a new problem situation, we use a frame as a template for organizing our perception of the problem. Frames guide us in collecting information to build representations of specific instances of the class of systems that the frame comprehends.

The purpose of generalized mental models, what we will be calling frames, is to produce representations that predict how a particular system, real or imagined, will behave. The frame specifies the elements of a system that we need to know about in order to make these predictions. Frames not only model the structure of systems but also capture rules of behavior, transformation, and decomposition. These rules are what we call *understanding* or *knowledge*. As discussed in Chapter 2, Meehan and Hawkins see the function of knowledge to be prediction. Frames are used to generate representations of specific problem situations so that the understanding embodied in the frame can be applied. To say that we know how to solve certain problems is to say that we know how to frame them. We know what information we need to collect in order to build a problem solving representation, and we know what rules to apply to the representation to get to a solution.

Hawkins focuses on frames that capture the essence of a specific situation or object. For example, we have a model of Jane's face that allows us to recognize her from many angles, lighting conditions, and combinations of glasses and hats. The *Jane's face* frame not only allows us to distinguish Jane from her friends but also to evaluate her mood and energy level.

22

Meehan's *system paradigm* emphasizes more generic models that capture general rules of behavior, allowing us to create representations of new situations. As we enter a house we have never been in before, we use our generic house frame to guide our expectations of what is coming next. We look for certain components of the house to fill in our representation of it. We note the elements that are unexpected, a bathtub in a bedroom, for example. Hawkins would say that when we leave the house, we will have constructed our first *invariant representation* of the house. Not only do we have generic house frames, we have frames for individual houses. Each time we reenter this house, we will have more refined expectations about what will be there. We will notice that the furniture has been rearranged or that there is a different smell in the air.

People with different purposes may frame a situation in very different ways. For example, I was drafted to be the treasurer of the housing cooperative where we live in Washington, DC. Part of the treasurer's responsibility is planning for the repair and replacement of facilities owned in common by the cooperative. One such facility is a sewage pumping station. In order to get an idea of the costs that we should anticipate, I arranged to meet the contractor that maintains the system. I went down to the pump house to take a look in advance of our meeting. The pumps, there were two of them, were original equipment, installed thirty-five years ago when the development was built. I have some experience with industrial equipment, and to my eyes, the pumps were beautiful. I could make rough sense of the setup, inferring that there must be a large tank below the shed. The pumps would be activated when the level in the tank reached a sensor near the top. The pumps would alternate. Having two pumps makes a lot of sense, allowing operation to continue if one of them fails. Then Dave, the contractor, appeared at the door.

He took me through the history of the system since he came on the scene fifteen years ago. For the first ten years, he worked with Jack, one of the residents who had managed the co-op from its inception. Jack was a stickler for maintenance. Dave did routine maintenance on the system four times a year. Jack would meet him and review the condition of the equipment. During the fifteen years, Dave had rebuilt one of the pumps. That was the only major cost. I asked how long the pumps would last. Forever, he said. They just have to be rebuilt from time to time to the tune of six thousand dollars. It would cost maybe fifty thousand to replace the whole system.

Between Dave, Jack, and me, we have three rather different frames for this system. I came to the situation with a fair layman's understanding of pumps and controls. From the meeting with Dave, I learned what I needed in order to create a reasonable projection of costs going forward. I combined this with cost projections for a dozen other facilities at the cooperative to get a rough picture of cash required for repairs over the next thirty years.

Jack had developed a good understanding of how the system should operate and how to detect when it was struggling. He would visit the shed on a regular basis to do some simple tests and call Dave to the site when something seemed awry. Dave had the knowledge needed to assess problems with the system and carry out repairs. Jack's knowledge was based entirely on his experience with this system. In the words of Hawkins, Jack's invariant representation of the pumping system served to guide his attention each time he came down to the shed. He probably did not spend as much time admiring the construction of the pumps as I did. He would look for telltale signs of dysfunction, run some brief tests, and listen to the sound of the pumps. He would be aware that during power outages, the tank would accumulate sewage with a potential for overflow into the local creek. Dave's knowledge was both specific to this system and also generic, fortified by work that he does on several similar systems and many others with similar components.

The role of frames is to generate representations of problem situations. We construct these representations to allow us to predict system behavior and take action to control it. The different frames of Jack, Dave, and me reflect our different problem solving responsibilities.

Frames embody our knowledge of the behavior of systems. In the case of the bicycle, the elements – wheels, frame, handlebars, pedals, brakes and gear system – define a coherent whole. We understand the relationships among the elements. These relationships add up to a behavioral model of the whole system. Some frames model systems as a kit of parts and rules of assembly. That is, we understand the elements and their relationships and can put them together in a wide variety of ways. Such is the case with piano melodies. And such is the case with our next scenario.

I was at my desk on the third floor of the Old Dodge Warehouse in Georgetown when Ezra phoned from San Francisco. "Could you go to Memphis tomorrow to work with the Alodex people on a site development schedule?"

"Of course. But you realize that I don't know anything about site development, right?"

"That's OK. They know about site development, they just don't know how to construct a schedule."

This was in May of 1969. I had started at Building Systems Development (BSD) that January. A week before the above phone call, Ezra had paid a visit to the Washington, DC, office. Ezra Ehrenkrantz was the president of BSD. He was in from the San Francisco office to sort out some personnel upheavals. Ezra had that charismatic ability in a one-on-one meeting to be completely absorbed in what you were saying and what you felt. I first met him when he popped up on the third floor space where four of us worked. When he came to my desk to introduce himself, he noticed that I was working on a schedule diagram – a lovely thing on yellow tracing paper. I noticed that he noticed, but we didn't discuss it. It became apparent later that, at that moment, I became the BSD scheduling expert, even though that diagram was my first effort to draw up a construction schedule.

The afternoon after Ezra called, I did what I could to study up on what the Alodex project was all about. They were a wholly owned subsidiary of Holiday Inn, created to develop single-family housing using 'systems' construction. BSD was working on the design of modular housing units that could be largely factory assembled. Alodex was ambitiously targeting East St. Louis for its first major development.

The next day, I was off to Alodex headquarters in Southaven, Mississippi, a southern suburb of Memphis. I had one day to work with several of their management people to develop the schedule. The purpose of the schedule was to add credibility to a proposal for funding from the U.S. Department of Housing and Urban Development.

I set up in a meeting room with a large white-board on one wall. A daylong parade of middle-aged Southern-speaking business guys came through to answer my questions.

I think I could train an eighth grader to do the job that I did. Maybe the age would be a problem, but I was only twenty-six, a virtual eighth grader to the Alodex people. The scheduling frame was an ironclad guide to extracting the information I needed. A schedule is made up of tasks. We needed to know one *internal* property of each task: How long does it take to perform? We needed to know one *external* property of each task: What other tasks have to be performed before the task can start? With this information, I could build a schedule, compute how long the project would take and map out the critical path. The one area of judgment was the level of detail: How big should the tasks be? This being my first time doing an actual schedule, I was intrigued by how the questions that I asked stimulated so much discussion among the Alodex guys. Does this go before that? Can't that task overlap a bit? On and on. I didn't have to know anything. It took people a while to get the hang of what I was after. They may have started out thinking that I actually knew something about their business – that there were right and wrong answers to my questions. Once I convinced them that *they* were the experts, the answers began to flow.

As the day wore on, the puzzle pieces started to fit together. Eventually I filled the whiteboard with activities and their interrelationships. I reviewed the schedule with each of the participants to see if the whole picture made sense to them. Then I was gone.

Critical Path Method (CPM) analysis describes a process as a set of interrelated tasks. Each task has one or more other tasks that must be completed before the task in question can start. Once time estimates are given for all of the tasks in the network, a critical path can be determined. This is the linear series of tasks that determine the length of the overall schedule. A delay in any task on the critical path will delay the project. Other tasks parallel to the critical tasks may have slack. Slack indicates that delay in non-critical tasks will not delay completion of the project. In the real world, relationships among tasks are often more subtle than simple precedence. Tasks may somewhat overlap. CPM, at least as I practiced it at the time, requires that task relationships be described as clear and simple, even if they were not in reality.

In this case, the frame was a prototypical way of describing tasks and their relationships. The representation was the actual CPM diagram that I built using the frame to collect information from the people who knew what they were doing. The CPM analysis performed on this representation predicted the overall project schedule and the tasks that were critical. Slack associated with completing all other tasks was also calculated. The diagram shown partially in

Figure 3 is a partial view of the end product. Everyone seemed satisfied with the day's efforts. The only real challenge was to get the Alodex staff to realize that they were the real experts, not me.

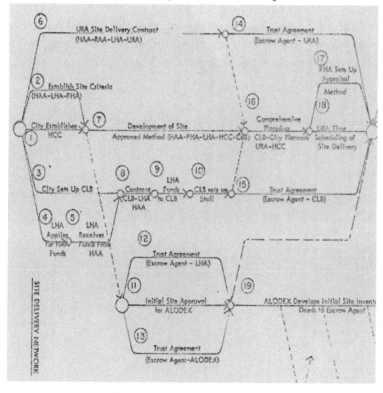

Figure 3: Alodex Site Development CPM Chart (partial view)

Frames are generalized mental models that we use as a starting point in problem solving and decision making. When confronted with a situation, we intuitively call up a frame to guide our collection of information. Our knowledge about the class of situations is attached to the frame. We use this knowledge to comprehend what is going on – to understand the situation as a system. Once we build the situation specific mental model, it provides the basis for predicting the outcomes of alternative courses of action. Often, as with the Alodex example given above, the frame includes detailed rules for analyzing the situation.

It is common when multiple people are engaged in solving a problem for their frames to be quite different, reflecting their experience and their different purposes. Problem solving Principle #1, that models are different from reality, calls on the problem solver to be aware of the central role of framing and that the mental representations that we derive from frames are different from reality and are probably different from the frames of others.

Chapter 5   The Fallibility of Frames

The purpose of mental models is to predict the course of events both with and without our intervention. We construct frames of situations in order to assess alternative paths that we might take. The cases described in this chapter illustrate frames that have failed to capture essential aspects of the real world situations they attempt to model. This undermines their predictive power, leading to bad decisions.

Case 1: Explosion

When we distort frames to fit our goals, bad decisions result, as illustrated by the following case. In March of 1962, a college senior - we will call him John - returned from a spring break trip to Florida with a stash of firecrackers. He did this in the knowledge that at Harvard, possession, let alone use, of firecrackers was grounds for expulsion. John and another student, Dave, decided that it would be a good idea to light off one of these units within the confines of the dormitory. John was a pre-med student headed for Harvard Medical School. Dave was also planning on graduate school. These trajectories could be substantially altered if the possession or, heaven forbid, use of these devices was discovered.

They selected an M-80 from the box of assorted firecrackers under John's bed. They took it into the bathroom and contemplated the possibilities. They considered flushing it down the toilet, but several edgy roommates sagely suggested that this could damage the plumbing system. I mention the consideration of this option as evidence that John and Dave were capable of considering possible consequences. They decided to run water into the bathtub and submerge the M-80 by tying it to a fork. M-80's are known to be waterproof. At this juncture of the story, we can only speculate on the nature of the frames that each of these two geniuses was operating under. As we will see, their mental models must have been significantly at odds with reality. It is safe to say that their take on the situation was shaped in large part by their desire to experience what they imagined would be a stimulating event.

The other roommates cowered in an adjacent bedroom as ignition approached. John lit the fuse, and Dave dropped the fork with attached M-80 into the six inches of water. Tile walls surrounded the tub on three sides. The perpetrators watched from several feet away as the fuse made bubbles that rose to the surface of the water. The explosion was deafening. It propelled the six inches of water to the ceiling, followed closely by the porcelain finish that had coated the bottom of the bathtub. As the water fell back into the tub, newly exposed steel gave it the look of a muddy lake.

In the immediate aftermath, John raced to his room, grabbed the box of firecrackers, and spirited them to his car in a remote parking lot. The noise was so loud that the conspirators assumed that dormitory staff would come knocking in a matter of minutes. Try as they might, they could not conjure a reasonable explanation for the state of the bathtub. However, as the minutes and hours passed, it was apparent that the incident had not been reported. This opened the door to the weightlifting mishap scenario, or the science experiment gone wrong scenario. It took two months for the students to repair the bottom of the tub with epoxy, all the while deflecting the curiosity of the weekly cleaning people.

It would be easy to credit this adventure to blatant stupidity, but it is worth digging deeper to consider how distorted a mental model can become under the influence of craving. What was the frame of mind that these students could have created to not realize the risk they were taking? They must have imagined that no damage would be done to the bathtub, that there would be a manageable noise well contained within their dorm suite, that some water would be splashed about, and that all would have a good time. These predictions were in the service of their craving for fun and excitement.

Was this an anomaly? Were these students temporarily deranged, or is it common that our mental models are so at odds with reality? The examples below suggest that college students do not have an exclusive right to self-delusion.

Case 2: Mental Models and Large Projects

The saga of the Sydney Opera House gives us an example of wishful thinking on a grand scale. In January of 1957, Premier Joe Cahill of New South Wales, Australia, announced that Jørn Utzon was the winner of the Sydney Opera House design competition. The project was estimated to cost $7 million ($53 million in 2010 US dollars). Construction was estimated to take four years. The funds were to be largely supplied by a lottery that would run during construction until the $7 million was raised. By 1961, the cost estimate was up to $18 million; 1963, $30 million; 1965, $40 million; 1967, $85 million; and the final bill for construction in 1974 was $102 million. The opera house had taken seventeen years to build from the time the winner of the competition was announced. All the while, lotteries were being staged to try to keep up with the expenditures.

How could the initial forecast of construction cost and time be so at odds with reality? In the mid-twentieth century, design competitions for major projects encouraged creativity over practicality. Competition organizers concealed the identity of competitors, eliminating their experience and expertise as a factor in selecting the winner. Design submissions were purely conceptual, without supporting detailed analysis or cost estimates. On reflection, we must say that the process worked. Only by deluding the public about the cost of the project could such a daring and impractical solution be selected. The result, after many years of political and engineering travail, was an architectural landmark.

Our interest in this project is the capacity of the human mind to form a mental model so at odds with reality. These were not college students pulling a stupid prank. They were teams of architects, engineers, and politicians that wanted to believe in a vision. Wishful thinking seems to be the norm on major projects. The Big Dig, Boston's major tunnel project, was estimated to cost $2.8 billion in 1982. It ended up costing $8 billion in 1982 dollars. Denver International Airport was estimated to cost $2.8 billion. The final bill was $4.8 billion. Also, such overruns are commonplace in military procurement. The F-22 fighter aircraft project was initially to provide 750 aircraft at a total program cost of $26 billion, or $35 million each. Final program costs were $62 billion for 171 aircraft, a cost of $361 million each. In each of these examples, participants have a strong interest in believing the most optimistic vision of the problem, however at odds with experience that might be. *Part VI, Manage the Planning Fallacy*, digs deeper into this phenomenon.

Case 3: Wrong Lessons From Experience

The dark cloud in the blue sky of success is the difficulty in knowing what you did right. What were the keys to success? It is human nature to attribute success to one's own actions. We tend to ignore other factors that may have played a critical role.

My first experience in building and operating a manufacturing plant was a smashing success. In 1984, my partner, Joe White, and I decided to jump feet first into building a factory. We built the plant on schedule and on budget. It produced what our customers had specified, and we made a serious profit. Going in, we knew virtually nothing about processing cheese whey. It turned out to be challenging but doable. We felt that we just had a knack for this stuff.

The logical next step was to build an adjoining plant to refine lactose, a by-product of the first plant. How hard could that be? The plant would cost twice what the first plant cost, but the projections indicated a decent profit. We didn't anticipate a drop in the lactose market, or the difficulty of achieving projected lactose yields, or the finicky state inspectors who had issues with the design of the centrifuges that were an integral part of the process.

Going into the first project, we knew how little we knew. We were wary, and we were conservative. Emboldened by the success of that project, we entered the second with a more optimistic view. We thought we knew what we were doing. Unlike the first project, we did not have customers committed in advance. This was not an oversight; it was just a different marketplace. It turns out that having a committed customer with a long-term purchase agreement was the single most important component of the first project. The first time around, we were very suspicious of the claims of equipment manufacturers. On the second project, we were overly inclined to their unrealistically optimistic projections.

We humans are an odd mix of being risk averse and yet overly optimistic. We have a palpable fear of regretting the results of the actions we take where risk is involved.[10] Yet we are incorrigibly optimistic that we know what we are doing.[11] In this case, over optimism resulted from framing grounded in one successful experience. Our mental model of the first project emphasized matters that were under our control. We made good decisions about the scope of the project, jettisoning components that diluted its return on investment. We were successful at selecting equipment suppliers. We managed the construction process and plant start-up. We modeled the process to verify the claims of equipment suppliers. While considering the second project, we felt that we could perform all of these functions even better than on the first project. We could only benefit from our experience. However, this egocentric frame minimized the differences between the projects, as illustrated by the following three factors:

A central issue in both projects was yield: the amount of raw material flowing into each plant was predictable, but how much finished product would be produced and how much would be lost in the process? We failed to consider that the potential for waste was very different between the first and second processes.

Both projects used state-of-the-art equipment unfamiliar to us. The claims of the suppliers on the first project were largely testable and proved to be valid. Critical claims of suppliers on the second project proved unreliable. We had not considered that state food inspectors might not approve a critical component.

On the first project, we had a firm four-year contract for purchase of our product. No such arrangement was possible on the second project. We based our financial projections on what we considered a conservative price for commodity-grade lactose, with nothing but upside for production of pharmaceutical grade. As if on cue, as we started production, the floor dropped out from under the commodity lactose market, proving our projections far too optimistic.

---

[10] Daniel Kahneman and Amos Tversky, "The Psychology of Preferences," in *Scientific American*, Vol 246, No 1, 1982.

[11] Colin F. Camerer and Daniel Lovallo, "Overconfidence and Excess Entry: An Experimental Approach," in *Choices, Values and Frames*, edited by Kahneman and Tversky (Cambridge: Cambridge University Press, 2000).

These are but a few examples of the fallibility of frames. At the heart of this fallibility is our natural tendency to have confidence that our mental models accurately describe reality. We use past experience to build mental models of new situations. This is the essence of framing. Yet, as illustrated in the cases above, we must guard against our selective memory of the factors that caused past successes.

Chapter 6   Confirmation Bias, the Einstellung Effect, and Overconfidence

Mental models are powerful tools that allow us to predict the consequences of our actions. Our extensive toolkit of frames enables us to build representations of problem situations rapidly and intuitively. Frames house our knowledge of the world, poised to be applied to each situation we encounter. This capability is the essence of human intelligence.

Powerful tools often come with the danger of misuse. When we frame a problem, the resulting mental representation becomes our reality. We are typically unaware of the process of framing, and once adopted, a mental model can be difficult to shed. Since a frame guides our collection of information, we tend to confirm assumptions about the problem that are built into the frame. Confirmation bias can perpetuate the use of an ineffective mental model, dulling our senses to what might otherwise be obvious shortcomings.

Confirmation Bias

When a problem confronts us, we scan our vast store of frames to find a match for the initially recognized characteristics of the situation. James Reason, a professor of psychology emeritus at the University of Manchester, has specialized in the study of human error. Reason argues that we are susceptible to triggering inappropriate frames by matching characteristics of the present situation to superficially similar past experiences.

A knowledge base that contains specialized "theories" rather than isolated facts preserves meaningfulness, but renders us liable to confirmation bias. An extraordinarily rapid retrieval system, capable of locating relevant items within a virtually unlimited knowledge base, leads to our interpretation of the present and anticipation of the future to be shaped too much by the matching of regularities of the past.[12]

Juries provide an apt example of the tendency to form conclusions based on early evidence. Judges ask jurors to listen to evidence presented on both sides of a case and keep an open mind until the last arguments are made. But can this really be done? Raymond Nickerson, an experimental psychologist at Tufts University, thinks not.

The judge's admonition to maintain an open mind during the evidence-presentation phase of a trial seems designed to counter the tendency to form an opinion early in an evidence-evaluation process and then to evaluate further evidence with a bias that favors that initial opinion. Whether jurors are able to follow this admonition and to delay forming an opinion as to the truth or falsity of the allegations against the accused until the jury-deliberation phase is a matter of some doubt. It is at least a plausible possibility that individual jurors (and judges) develop their personal mental models of "what really happened" as a case develops and continuously refine and elaborate those models as evidence continues to be presented. To the extent that this is the way jurors actually think, a model, as it exists at any point in time, may strongly influence how new information is interpreted. If one has come to believe that a defendant is guilty (or innocent), further evidence that is open to various interpretations may be seen as supportive of that belief. Opinions formed about a defendant on the basis of superficial cues (such as demeanor while giving testimony) can bias the interpretation of inherently ambiguous evidence (Hendry & Shaffer, 1989).[13]

---

[12] James Reason, *Human Error* (Cambridge: Cambridge University Press, 1990) p. 2.

[13] Raymond S. Nickerson , 'Confirmation Bias: A Ubiquitous Phenomenon in Many Guises" in *Review of General Psychology* 1998, Vol 2, No 2, pp. 175-220, 1998, Educational Publishing Foundation. p. 192.

When we form a mental model of a problem, we are in the position of a jury; we are the finders of fact. We build an initial sketch of the problem situation that guides us as we fill in the details. We construct this initial sketch by matching salient characteristics of the situation to one of the multitude of frames we have mentally on file. Given a choice, we would rather act as pattern recognizers, searching out the frame we have in our mental file that best fits the situation, rather than trying to construct a frame from scratch. Once we have selected a frame, we look for information that confirms its validity.

Nickerson is unrestrained in his concern for the effects of confirmation bias:

If one were to attempt to identify a single problematic aspect of human reasoning that deserves attention above all others, the confirmation bias would have to be among the candidates for consideration. Many have written about this bias, and it appears to be sufficiently strong and pervasive that one is led to wonder whether the bias, by itself, might account for a significant fraction of the disputes, altercations, and misunderstandings that occur among individuals, groups, and nations.[14]

Studies of problem solving in many contexts have shown that we see what our frames expect us to see. Initial impressions bias the interpretations of later observations. Nickerson cites the work of Bruner:

Bruner and Potter (1964) showed people the same picture on a series of slides. The first slide was defocused so the picture was not recognizable. On successive slides the focus was made increasingly clear. After each presentation the participant was asked to identify what was shown. A hypothesis formed on the basis of a defocused picture persisted even after the picture was in sufficiently good focus that participants who had not looked at the poorly focused picture were able to identify it correctly.

---

[14] Ibid., p. 175.

James Reason argues that experts are more selective in their collection of information due to the strength of their mental models. This renders the expert more susceptible to confirmation bias.

> *The more entrenched a hypothesis, the more selective becomes the working definition of what is relevant. But those who enter the situation afresh at some later point are not so theory bound, at least initially. The nakedness of the emperor is readily seen by those who have not come to believe him clothed.[15]*

The 2-4-6 problem, developed by psychologist Peter Wason, is a simple illustration of confirmation bias. You are told that there is a rule called rule X that defines a type of three number sequence. The universe of all three-number sequences falls into two groups – those that obey rule X and those that do not. You are told that the number sequence 2-4-6 follows rule X. Your job is to figure out rule X. You can ask about other three-number sequences to test your ideas about what rule X might be. Wason concluded that people typically ask about sequences that would confirm their hypotheses. For example, they would ask about 7-9-11 if they thought that rule X specified any three numbers increasing by two; or 10-12-14 if they thought the rule was any three even numbers increasing by two; or even 20-25-30 if they thought that the rule required that the middle number be the average of the first and last. None of the above hypotheses is rule X, yet all of the test sequences passed the rule X test. It was uncommon for people to test sequences that would disprove their hypotheses. For example, to disprove any of the hypotheses above, one might ask about the sequence 1-2-5. Since this sequence does pass rule X, it would disprove all of the above hypotheses.

Rule X: any three numbers increasing from the first to the last.

---

[15] James Reason, *Human Error* (Cambridge: Cambridge University Press, 1990) p. 169.

Klayman and Ha criticized the Wason test as valid only when the rule to be discovered is very general.[16] But research has confirmed that in many contexts, we test out theories by looking for evidence that will confirm them rather than disconfirm them.[17]

Intuitive Versus Reasoned Judgment

Daniel Kahneman won the Nobel Prize for his work in the psychology of how people make decisions. His work with Shane Frederick explores the balance between intuitive judgment and deliberative thinking. They suggest that two cognitive systems carry out the formation of hypotheses.[18] System 1 is intuitive and fast. System 2 is deliberative and slow. For example, employing System 1, I might recognize a person on the other side of the room as my friend Xavier. I would recognize him anywhere, even from the back. After a moment of consideration, System 2 might reason that it could not be Xavier because I know he is at a wedding in San Francisco.

Three types of errors are common in the hypotheses formed by System 1. *Anchoring* occurs when we place too much importance on one aspect of a situation to the exclusion of others. Anchoring can cause us to fail to collect other information about a problem and proceed down one path of investigation. Such would have been the case with my recognition of Xavier had my System 2 not stepped in.

Availability errors occur when we are strongly influenced by an aspect of a situation that brings to mind cases that are readily available in memory. For example, we might worry more about dangers that are widely covered in the news media, such as child abduction,

---

[16] Joshua Klayman and Young-Won Ha, "Confirmation, Disconfirmation and Information in Hypothesis Testing," *Psychological Review*, 1987, Vol 94, No 2, pp. 211-228.

[17] Raymond S. Nickerson , "Confirmation Bias: A Ubiquitous Phenomenon in Many Guises" in *Review of General Psychology*, Vol 2, No 2, 175-220, 1998, Educational Publishing Foundation. p.180.

[18] Daniel Kahneman and Shane Frederick, "Representativeness Revisited: Attribute Substitution in Intuitive Judgment.." Pre-release of paper to appear in *Heuristics of Intuitive Judgment: Extensions and Applications* (New York, Cambridge University Press, 2002) p. 5.

rather than dangers that are far more likely but seldom mentioned, such as drowning in a bathtub.

Attribution errors occur in our hypotheses about the relationship between people and situations. We tend to blame people for the situations they find themselves in, rather than blame external circumstances. When we see someone trip over a rock, we blame the person. The one exception is when the person is our-self; then we blame the rock.

All of these errors occur in the hypotheses developed by System 1. Kahneman and Frederick argue that the quality control imposed by System 2 on System 1 is passive.

> *We suspect that the System 2 endorsements of intuitive judgments are granted quite casually under normal circumstances. Consider the puzzle, "A bat and a ball costs $1.10. The bat costs $1 more than the ball. How much does the ball cost?" Almost everyone we ask reports an initial tendency to answer "10 cents" because the sum $1.10 separates naturally into $1 and 10 cents. And 10 cents is about the right magnitude. Many people yield to immediate impulse. The surprisingly high rate of errors in this easy problem illustrates how lightly System 2 monitors the output of System 1; people are not accustomed to thinking hard, and are often content to trust a plausible judgment that quickly comes to mind.[19]*

Although these tests focus on judgment about facts, similar errors can occur whenever we call up frames to fit a problem situation. We rely on easily recognized characteristics of the problem to trigger a frame, although these characteristics may be superficial.

Rules of thumb are fast and intuitive, meeting Kahneman's definition of System 1. They latch on to readily available attributes. Given the human tendency to give inflated weight to initial hypotheses, it should not be surprising that conclusions reached by rules of thumb are not thoroughly vetted by a deliberative evaluation. System 1 often masquerades as common sense.

---

[19] Ibid., p. 7.

The Einstellung Effect

Problem situations trigger the recall of frames that have served us well in the past. When we are armed with a frame that has been successful, we tend to have a predisposition to that frame and minimize differences with the new situation. American psychologist Abraham Luchins dubbed this tendency the Einstellung Effect in the 1940s.

In a recent survey of prominent thinkers, Evgeny Morozov nominated awareness of the Einstellung Effect in response to the question: "What scientific concept would improve everybody's cognitive toolkit?"[20] Morozov is a prolific commentator on implications of the Internet and social media for democracy movements around the world. Rather than accepting widely held beliefs that the Internet is the ally of democratization, he sees a more complex mixture of costs and benefits. Morozov observed:

The Einstellung Effect is more ubiquitous than its name suggests. We constantly experience it when trying to solve a problem by pursuing solutions that have worked for us in the past - instead of evaluating and addressing it on its own terms. Thus, while we may eventually solve the problem, we may also be wasting an opportunity to do so in a more rapid, effective, and resourceful manner.

The irony here is that the more expansive our cognitive toolkit, the more likely we are to fall back on solutions and approaches that have worked in the past instead of asking whether the problem in front of us is fundamentally different from anything else we have dealt with in the past. A cognitive toolkit that has no built-in awareness of the Einstellung Effect seems somewhat defective to me.

As we apply our current frames to new situations, they guide our collection of information. It is during this process that we might notice a dissonance between the understanding embodied in the frame we have selected and the facts of the new situation. Failing to

---

[20] Steven Pinker, a cognitive psychologist at Harvard, posed this question to a cross section of leading scientists. One hundred sixty-four responses were published on the World Question Center of the Web site edge.org.

recognize a mismatch between frame and reality will not only lead to a distorted description of the situation but also will fail to modify the existing frame, perpetuating its misapplication. Self-awareness and self-criticism is the best antidote to the Einstellung Effect.

Overconfidence

Framing creates representations of problem situations. We treat these representations as if they are accurate depictions of the real world. To our mental processes, these representations *are* the real world. As we use a frame to build a representation, we collect information that will confirm the validity of the generalized model embodied by the frame and minimize evidence that might invalidate it. As a result, we can be overconfident in the representations that we create and the predictions that we derive from them.

The Dunning-Kruger Effect

Psychologists David Dunning and Justin Kruger of Cornell University have studied the relationship between competence and confidence. The have found clear evidence of an inverse relationship: the less we know about a subject, the more likely that we will overestimate our knowledge.[21] Dunning and Kruger have also found the reverse to be true. Highly competent people underestimate their ability relative to others.

They have determined that at least one cause of overconfidence in incompetent people is their preexisting self-views. In one study, they gave a test to two groups. They told the first group that the subject of the test was analytical thinking. They measured the students' views of their abstract reasoning ability before the test. Students who did poorly on the test were overconfident about their performance, consistent with prior studies. Dunning and Kruger gave the identical test to a second group but identified the subject matter as computer programming. The students' self-views of their comput-

---

[21] Justin Kruger & Davis Dunning, 'Unskilled and Unaware of It: How Difficulties in Recognizing One's Own Incompetence Lead to Inflated Self-Assessments." *Journal of Personality and Social Psychology*, 77 (6) pp. 1121-34. 1999.

er programming knowledge was low. After the test, students who did poorly made a far more realistic assessment of their performance.

Chapter 7 Mental Models are Not Reality

Problem solving depends on creating mental representations. As we become immersed in sorting through alternative courses of action, these mental models imbue us with a sense of confidence that we are dealing with an accurate representation of the real world. But mental models are fallible. They are shaped by previous experience. They are shaped to fit the mental tools with which we are comfortable. Awareness of these limitations will improve our effectiveness as problem solvers.

PROBLEM SOLVING PRINCIPLE #1:
MENTAL MODELS ARE NOT REALITY

Strategy #1: Be Aware of the Fallibility of Mental Models

Our best strategy for combating the inherent fallibility of mental models is awareness that they are, in fact, models, not reality. They are tools in our cognitive toolkit that we select, however intuitively, for their usefulness in a given situation. If we are aware of this, then we are open to self-criticism. We are open to assessing the usefulness of our current framing of a problem and the possibility of changing horses in midstream. Importantly, if we are aware that our current mental model guides us toward collecting information that supports its assumptions, we are more likely to be open to contrary evidence.

Strategy #2: Seek Disconfirming Evidence

As problem solvers, we must realize our tendency to seek out information that confirms the tightly held beliefs embodied in our mental models. How do we build representations that overcome this tendency?

44

Charles Munger, a partner of Warren Buffet at Berkshire Hathaway, made the following observation about the importance of debiasing:

> *... the great example of Charles Darwin is he avoided confirmation bias. Darwin probably changed my life because I'm a biography nut, and when I found out the way he always paid extra attention to the disconfirming evidence and all these little psychological tricks. I also found out that he wasn't very smart by the ordinary standards of human acuity, yet there he is buried in Westminster Abbey. That's not where I'm going, I'll tell you. And I said, "My God, here's a guy that, by all objective evidence, is not nearly as smart as I am and he's in Westminster Abbey? He must have tricks I should learn." And I started wearing little hair shirts like Darwin to try and train myself out of these subconscious psychological tendencies that cause so many errors. It didn't work perfectly, as you can tell from listening to this talk, but it would've been even worse if I hadn't done what I did. And you can know these psychological tendencies and avoid being the patsy of all the people that are trying to manipulate you to your disadvantage, like Sam Walton. Sam Walton won't let a purchasing agent take a handkerchief from a salesman. He knows how powerful the subconscious reciprocation tendency is. That is a profoundly correct way for Sam Walton to behave.[22]*

The example presented in *Appendix 6: Pascal's Triangle*, page 293, traces the process of disproving a series of hypotheses before finding one that works. I documented the steps that I went through, from problem discovery to failed efforts to solution without understanding to new tools and finally to understanding.

Strategy #3: Be Open to Criticism and Self-criticism

The German cognitive psychologist Dietrich Dörner reports on the problem solving capabilities of people cast in the role of mayor of

---

[22] Charles Munger, *The Psychology of Human Judgment*, A speech at Harvard Law School, 1995.

a small town.[23] The town is not real. A simulation presents the mayor with a series of decisions that determine the ongoing financial, educational, and social health of the community. The research team rated the performance of participants and tried to correlate their success with their problem solving style.

> *Both the good and the bad participants proposed with the same frequency hypotheses on what effects higher taxes, say, or an advertising campaign to promote tourism in Greenvale would have. The good participants differed from the bad ones, however, in how often they tested their hypotheses. The bad participants failed to do this. For them, to propose a hypothesis was to understand reality; testing that hypothesis was unnecessary. Instead of generating hypotheses, they generated truths.*

The unsuccessful participants failed to see the difference between their hypotheses and reality. Testing one's hypotheses is the essence of self-criticism.

Strategy #4: Strengthen Your System 2 Deliberative Muscle

Consider the distinction that Kahneman and Frederick have drawn between intuitive and deliberative thinking discussed in Chapter 6. They argue that System 2, the deliberative mechanism, is too passive in monitoring the conclusions drawn by System 1. We must work to strengthen our System 2 muscle. In some settings, it is productive to rehearse the role of System 2. I found this to be the case in coaching youth soccer. All manner of circumstances can arise during the course of a youth soccer game. In the heat of the moment, the supervisory role of System 2 can be altogether abandoned in favor of instinctive responses. We can substantially strengthen the deliberative role of System 2 by imagining situations that might occur and then rehearsing appropriate responses. The key test of a response is *How would I like to have handled the situation after all is said and done?*

---

[23] Dietrich Dörner, *The Logic of Failure* (Perseus Books, Cambridge, Massachusetts, 1989).

Strategy #5: Employ Miller's Law

George Miller, the cognitive psychologist, proposed the following strategy for understanding people with an apparently contrary view to our own:

> *MILLER'S LAW: To understand what another person is saying you must assume that it is true and try to imagine what it could be true of.*

Miller is saying that the statements that we make, our opinions, and our assertions as to what is true are actually about our own mental model of the world, not about the real world itself. Miller's Law asks us to try to understand how a person must be framing the world such that their statements make sense.

Architecture schools provide a fitting example. Design projects are subjected to a final review, often by visiting critics who have had little or no involvement in the student's work. Major projects, such as masters' thesis designs, can attract impressive judges who often play to the crowd with ripping criticisms. As much fun as this is for all but the student/victim, I concluded both as a student and as a faculty member that the final review scenario is fundamentally flawed. The question never asked of the student in such moments is "What is the problem that you are trying to solve?" Without knowing the answer to that question, how can we know if the critic is simply disagreeing with the definition of the problem, rather than criticizing the solution?

When we hear what appears to be total nonsense, we might want to ascertain what question the speaker is answering. In a sense, we must try to piece together the mental model that is the foundation for such statements.

Strategy #6: Recognize Your Level of Expertise

With regard to any particular system, there are many levels of understanding. Each level may be sufficient to serve the purpose of specific individuals. Mary Hegarty is a psychologist who studies spatial and mechanical reasoning. She proposes three levels of knowledge of mechanical systems:[24]

> **Intuitive knowledge**: Gained through observation of the way that objects move through our everyday environment. Intuitive knowledge can be described as rules of thumb. Often specific to situations with particular surface features - people can make different predictions about situations that are physically similar.

> **Practical knowledge**: Stems from active interaction with machines such as operating or repairing. Practical knowledge consists of causal models of specific machines or devices. Causal models differ in depth of understanding. Success in problem solving is a function of the quality of the causal model being used.

> **Theoretical knowledge**: Gained from studying physics and mechanical engineering. Theoretical concepts are based on particles and systems.

At each of these levels, a mental model of the mechanical system is maintained. We may intuitively feel that models grounded in theoretical knowledge are better than rules of thumb, but this would ignore the use of the model. Each of us maintains mental models across this spectrum. We are experts in some areas, and we get by with simple rules in others. When models are serving us well, they capture enough of the workings of real world systems to adequately guide our actions. The concern of problem solving Principle #1 is that we are not aware of the limited predictive power of our systems models at each of these levels.

The Dunning-Kruger effect discussed in the prior chapter asserts an inverse relationship between our level of expertise and our level of overconfidence. They have found no simple antidote for this problem. As with many of the principles discussed in this book, our best tool for avoiding this pitfall is awareness of it.

---

[24] Mary Hegarty, "Mechanical Problem Solving," Chapter 8 in *Complex Problem Solving*, Edited by Sternberg and Frensch (Hillsdale New Jersey, Lawrence Erlbaum Associates, 1991) pp. 262-5.

Strategy #7: Validate Mental Models

We should be ready to question the accuracy of information collected to fill out a representation. Ideally, we can test representations. That is, we can measure behaviors predicted by our mental representations against real world results. At minimum, the common sense and instincts of people who are immersed in the systems being modeled can be used to gauge the predictions that follow from representations. In our everyday experience, we form first impressions of people, places, or things only to find over time that the first impression must be modified or thrown out entirely. Only the most stubborn among us clings to a first impression under the weight of evidence that would invalidate it.

In some settings, the process of validation is formalized into a phase of problem solving. In the case of computer simulation, validation is an important step in the process of developing a model. A simulation predicts the behavior of a system. To validate a model, its behavior is compared to the behavior of the real world system that it models, under conditions where historical data is available. This comparison gives us a test of the validity of the original description, of the simulation results, or of both. For example, models of manufacturing require detailed descriptions of equipment and personnel productivity. Collecting these details often involves several organizational layers within the company and may be an imposition on personnel with no direct stake in the simulation effort. As a result, inaccuracies can creep in. When a set of production parameters results in model behavior that does not conform to real world experience, something has to give. Either there is a flaw in the logic of the model, or inaccurate data has been provided. Simulation provides a test of the validity of system description that is not available when we simply writing reports.

Although the development of valid system descriptions is a by-product of simulation projects, they can lead to a firmer foundation for future analysis and decision making beyond the specific goals of the simulation project.

Awareness that mental models are not reality is the foundation for all of the problem solving principles discussed in this book. We must train ourselves to think about thinking, to locate ourselves in the problem solving process, and to be aware of the fallibility inherent in the powerful mental tools that we so nimbly employ.

PART II   *Principle #2: Be Willing to Reframe the Problem*

Frames guide our efforts at problem solving. Once we have adopted a frame, it guides our collection of information and the steps we take to fabricate a solution. Frames have a powerful grip on our imagination. When they are not working, we tend to try harder within the same frame rather than looking at the problem in a new light. We fall victim to the trap of Principle #1, treating our mental model of the problem as if it were reality. In addition, our conception of the boundaries of a problem is shaped by the frame we have selected to solve it. We need to be aware of our progress in solving a problem and be willing to reframe it when our current frame is not moving us toward a solution.

Chapter 8 gives some examples of the power of frames to provide a pathway to solutions. After all, that is their one and only function. Chapter 9 looks at the sources of frames. If we are to develop the mental dexterity to reframe problems, it is important to understand where frames come from. Chapter 10 presents some cases where we are trapped by the wrong frame and identifies the obstacles to reframing. Chapter 11 lays out five reframing strategies.

Chapter 8   The Power of Frames

Frames are formidable tools. Once we have adopted an effective frame, problems that at first seem complex and ill structured can be understood and solved. The function of a frame is to organize a mental map of the problem that allows us to explore paths to a solution. This chapter presents several examples of the power of having a frame that comprehends for us the problem at hand.

The Game of Fifteen

The Game of Fifteen brings to light the value of having a frame. This is a simple game played between two people. Nine tokens lie on the table between the two players, as shown in Figure 4.

Figure 4: Game of Fifteen Tokens

Each token has a number between one and nine printed on it. Each player alternately takes a token. The goal of the game is to have any three tokens among the ones a player has selected adding up to exactly fifteen. The first player to achieve this wins. For example, a player with one, six, and eight would win. The rules of the game are easily understood, but how would one develop a strategy for winning? Let's say I'm playing you. I get the first move. I could approach my first move the way I play checkers, with no strategy at all. The only tactics I have ever used in checkers are those that I employ in a few situations where I see opportunities or looming disaster. Against a good player, this is usually too late.

So my first move is to take the five. Somehow, the middle seems like a good place to start. You take the three; I take the six. Again, no strategy. But now you can see that I have a total of eleven. The four will get me a group of three numbers adding up to fifteen, so you take the four to block me. At this point, we both recognize that the first order of business on each move is to block any number that will give the opponent a group of three numbers adding up to fifteen. So I look at your numbers. You have the three and the four. The eight will get you to fifteen, so I block with the eight, leaving the situation pictured in Figure 5.

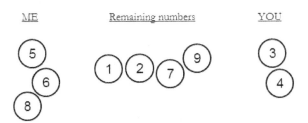

ME   Remaining numbers   YOU

Figure 5: Game Position After Five Moves

You now review my numbers to see if any remaining numbers will get me to fifteen. You have already blocked the five-six combination by picking the four on the last move. To block the five-eight combination you should pick the two. However, there is also the six-eight combination, where the one will get me to fifteen. Since you cannot pick both the two and the one, I will win on the next move.

So on the first playing of the game, we have learned how it can end. One player can win if he achieves a position like the one above where there are two ways to get to fifteen. There also seems to be a considerable advantage in going first. If I'm going first, I need to figure out how to get to a position with two ways to get to fifteen on my next move. If I'm going second, I need to figure out how to keep you from getting into that position.

But we already have a way of framing this problem, complete with rules for what moves to make and not make in every situation.

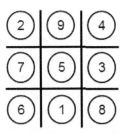

Figure 6: The Tic-Tac-Toe Frame

If we arrange the tokens tic-tac-toe fashion in the particular way shown in Figure 6, the rows columns, and diagonals add up to fifteen. The Game of Fifteen and the game of tic-tac-toe are essentially identical. In case you are rusty on tic-tac-toe strategy, every game should end in a tie. The first move must be the center or one of the four corners; otherwise, the player to move second has an easy path to victory. If the first move is a corner, the second player must take the center, or she will lose. If the first move is the center, the second player must take any corner or can lose. Assuming that the first player took the center and the second player took a corner, the first player can make the game interesting by taking the opposite corner. Every other move by the first player will force the second player to block a row, column or diagonal. All of these games play out to a tie, unless the second player simply fails to block a simple winning move by the first player.

There are three levels of understanding that we can bring to the Game of Fifteen. First, we can know the rules that determine the moves and what constitutes a win. Second, we can employ the tactic of looking one move ahead to try to prevent our opponent from getting to fifteen. Finally, we can have an overall strategy. In the case of the game of 15, the tic-tac-toe frame provides comprehensive understanding. There is nothing else to say or learn about the game.

Trainyard

Frames can pop out of thin air, as happened to me one day while pondering a problem in the game Trainyard. Trainyard is an App developed for the Apple iPhone and iPad.[25] The game provides a series of problems challenging the player to route individual train cars from points of origin to points of destination on a seven by seven grid. The player lays down track to create routes for the train cars. I had been playing the game for a couple of weeks, working my way from beginner's problems to layouts that are quite challenging. I bring this up as the context for one particular aspect of the puzzle. There are situations where one must route two train cars so that they reside on the same square at the same time. Each car moves at the same rate. It became clear to me early on that it is sometimes difficult to achieve this goal of two cars on the same square at the same time.

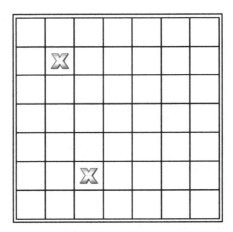

Figure 7: Trainyard Grid

In a recent layout of the game, I needed to get two train cars to the same square as part of a broader plan. The initial position of the cars is set by their point of origin. They enter the grid at the same time and then follow the path determined by the tracks that the

_____

[25] Trainyard is developed by Matt Rix. Details available on the Web at www.trainyard.ca.

player has put in place. Figure 7 shows such a situation. Only the two train cars in question are shown, leaving out the other elements of the game, such as points of origin and destinations. Can we get these two train cars to the same square, given that each car moves at the same time, one square vertically or horizontally? Diagonal moves are not allowed. It doesn't matter which square; we just need to get them to occupy the same square at the same time. I concluded that it could not be done.

Later I was idly contemplating how I could prove that it could not be done. Then the *aha* moment occurred. What if we looked at the grid as a seven by seven checker-board, as shown in Figure 8? Any move by the car on a colored square will take it to a white square (again, no diagonal moves). Any move by a car on a white square will take it to a colored square. This makes it clear, at least to my satisfaction, that these two cars can never occupy the same square. In each unit of time, each car moves one square. No matter which way either car moves or how many moves they make, they will always be on squares of different colors.

This bit of framing captures a rule about the interrelationship among the elements of a system. That is what frames do. The checkerboard is not framing the whole problem. It crystallizes a rule regarding one behavior, one relationship among elements. It provides the player a handy way of sorting out potential strategies for solving a subproblem. The checkerboard frame must be used in combination with other insights about the system to sort through alternatives and generate solutions.

This example illustrates one process by which we stumble onto frames. When we work on problems, we are not typically looking for general principles. We are trying to solve this one problem. Nonetheless, general principles can emerge if we let them. At the time the checkerboard occurred to me, I wondered why it took so long. I wondered whether the hundreds of thousands of other geeks in Trainyard nation had jumped on this little secret right away.

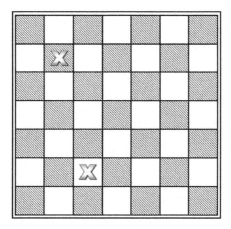

Figure 8: Trainyard Checkerboard Frame

The two simple examples in this chapter show the power of frames to provide understanding of problem situations. When we find a frame that suits a problem, the fog of confusion parts to reveal clarity of understanding. In these cases, understanding is expressed in terms of rules that guide us toward a solution.

Chapter 9   The Origin of Frames

Humans have an inventory of frames for dealing with the spectrum of problems that they have faced. Frames are generalized models of problem situations that guide us in building specific problem representations. The representation, in turn, is a launch pad for problem solving. These notions lead us to a twofold question: first, how do we conjure up the appropriate frame for each problem that we face? Second, where do frames come from?

Our inventory of frames is much like a collection of tools that accumulates in a workroom. When a problem arises, we are much inclined to use the tools we have, occasionally buying a new wrench or saw when needed. Over time, the history of problems we have confronted drives the accumulation of tools. We acquire new tools and refine our skills at applying the ones we have.

Frame Selection

Many problems come to our attention because we recognize that the world is not as we expect it to be. We are constantly predicting what is going to happen next. These predictions are the product of frames that guide us in the collection of local information. Predictions allow us to recognize problems that need our attention. These predictive frames, and their offspring representations, contain scripts for action when we recognize problems. Newell and Simon, in their seminal study *Human Problem Solving*,[26] formulate frames as sets of *if*

---

[26] Allen Newell and Herbert Simon, *Human Problem Solving* (Englewood Cliffs, New Jersey, Prentiss-Hall, 1972).

... *then* rules.[27] The *if* component of each rule guides our attention to look for conditions that match the rule's premise. A policeman on patrol is scanning her environment to recognize the symptoms of a problem. The *then* component tells us what to do when the *if* condition has been recognized.

Implicit in the phrase *frame selection* is the notion that the problem comes before we select the frame. Under this assumption, our frame inventory is like the tools in our workshop. I have a problem in the house, say a squeaky door. I go to the workbench to find a tool to fix it. I get a heavy screwdriver to tighten the hinge screws. Now, armed with the tool, I wander the house looking for other applications. The tool is urging my attention to look for problems that it can solve. I am transformed into a prospector.

In some scenarios, problems are brought to experts: doctors, lawyers, plumbers, computer types. The expert has a diagnostic frame that guides his collection of information about the specific case. The process of building a representation of the specific case may lead to related specialized frames, or even referral to more specialized experts. We should be aware that the "expert" we go to may drive the type of solution - and that in choosing an expert, we have already made some assumptions about the solution.

Occasionally we are confronted with problems where we do not know what to do or even how to think about what to do. In such cases, we can seek help of an expert or scan our inventory of frames for a metaphor, asking, *What is this situation like?*

Frame Building

The seeds of frames may be planted in school. However, these embryonic frames will only blossom as they are applied to real world situations. With each application, frames grow in strength and versatility. Frames evolve from rudimentary to complex. For example, consider the game of chess. First, we learn the rules of the game. The

---

[27] Newell and Simon, *Human Problem Solving*, p. 33. *Production* is a term used by Newell and Simon to define the basic building block of *production systems*. They used the term *production system* to refer to computer programs that solve problems using a set of *productions* or *if ... then* statements.

rules specify how the pieces can move and the objective of the game. As we play, we learn to look ahead a move or two for danger and opportunity. We learn to see patterns. As we become more serious about the game, we study chess books that talk of strategies and the great games of Capablanca and Fisher. Eventually, we can remember whole games. Experts can play many games simultaneously, seamlessly moving from one to the next. Expert chess players are able to remember the positions of all of the pieces on a chessboard far better than novices. This is unsurprising, except there is a condition. The pieces must reflect the positions in an actual chess game. If the pieces are placed randomly on the board, experts are no better than novices at remembering their positions.[28] This startling fact reflects that the expert frames a board position in the context of the flow of a game.

Frames evolve from fragmented to integrated. When we learn the geography of a city, we start with a mental map of well-traveled routes and neighborhoods. Gradually, these local maps expand and become interconnected through different routes. Fragments expand and become integrated with other fragments.

We create more generalized frames from multiple experiences of similar problems. When we are successful at solving a problem that is new to us, we create a model of what we did and file it away as a winning formula. We look for opportunities to apply this model to another problem. It is common to learn that we have overgeneralized. Sometimes it is difficult to know why a problem solving effort was successful. Perhaps we give ourselves too much credit. We may be able to reproduce only those aspects of the first effort that we controlled. We credit those aspects for success. We ignore other factors, those hidden from our view, at our peril. If we are lucky, the limited applicability of the first experience to the second will become apparent to us early on. We then take a step back, recognizing that the new problem calls for a revision of the old frame or for finding a new one. Whether the second effort succeeds or fails, we are in a position to integrate the two experiences and build a more robust

---

[28] Robert J. Sternberg and Peter A. Frensch, "Skill Related Differences in Game Playing," Chapter 11 in *Complex Problem Solving*, edited by Sternberg and Frensch (Hillsdale New Jersey, Lawrence Erlbaum Associates, 1991) p. 351.

generalized model. Hegerty captures the evolution of frames (what she calls *concepts*) in mechanical problem solving.

> *One dimension on which concepts change is their level of specificity. Mechanical intuitions, causal models, and problem schemata are induced from problem solving and observation in specific situations such that they initially retain some of the specificity of these situations. With development, they become more general and indexed by underlying mechanical principles operation in a situation, rather than the surface features of the situation.*[29]

Some frames are straightforward. Such was the case with Critical Path Method, a scheduling technique that I learned early in my career. We could take a few minutes, and I could teach it to you. But now we can create these schedules with Microsoft Project. It will frame scheduling projects for you. It turns out that the real art of scheduling is in extracting critical information from the people who know the activities being scheduled. In the case of the Alodex scheduling project (see Chapter 4), there were a half dozen people with overlapping knowledge of different parts of the development process. These different perspectives were not self-integrating. Different people have different ideas of what tasks must be completed before other tasks can be started. Sometimes, a task can be started before an upstream task is completed. However, studies have shown that people responsible for downstream tasks are overly optimistic about the usefulness of partially completed upstream tasks.[30]

Consider my experience building a schedule for Alodex. If this had been the second time that I had put a schedule together for a development project, my frame might have been quite different. Rather than building the schedule from basic task and relationship building blocks, I might have had a mental model of the schedule as a

---

[29] Mary Hegarty, "Mechanical Problem Solving," Chapter 8 *in Complex Problem Solving*, edited by Sternberg and Frensch (Hillsdale New Jersey, Lawrence Erlbaum Associates, 1991) p. 278

[30] David N. Ford and John D. Sternman, *Expert Knowledge Elicitation to Improve Mental and Formal Models*, System Dynamics Review, Vol 14 No 4, Winter 1998.

whole. I might have attempted to cast the Alodex process into a prototypical frame based on a single prior experience. We may be overoptimistic in applying limited experience to new situations that appear to be similar, as suggested by the Einstellung Effect discussed in Chapter 6. With luck and a bit of insight, I might survive a second project and form a more general mental model based on the commonalities between the two experiences.

Minsky puts frame development at the center of problem solving. He equates frame building to developing understanding.

> *The primary purpose of problem solving should be to better understand the problem space, to find representations within which the problems are easier to solve. The purpose of search is to get information for this reformulation, not - - as is usually assumed - - to find solutions; once the space is adequately understood, solutions to problems will be more easily found.*[31]

Minsky's use of the term *problem space* is appealing in that it conjures an image of exploration.

Furnace Replacement Program

Frame building is well illustrated by a program that I ran for the Wisconsin Gas Company (WGC) in 1982. The WGC wanted to encourage residential customers to replace old furnaces with new high efficiency units. The idea was to make homeowners an offer that they could not refuse. The homeowner would get a new high efficiency furnace at no cost, installed by the WGC. The new furnace would make a substantial reduction of gas consumption. The WGC would pay for the furnace by sharing in the savings over a five to seven year period with the homeowner. This project provides us a well-documented case of frame development at several levels.

In order to justify the installation of a new furnace, it was critical for us to measure the efficiency of the existing unit. Since the new high efficiency furnaces had a rated efficiency, savings could be

---

[31] Marvin Minsky, *A Framework for Representing Knowledge, Artificial Intelligence Memo No 306*, (Massachusetts Institute of Technology, Artificial Intelligence Laboratory, 1974) p. 56.

calculated if there was a believable test of the current furnace effi-ciency. For the homeowners to accept the program, they had to believe that the WGC portion of the savings charged to their gas bill was accurate.

The design of the program involved the intersection of three sys-tems: the existing furnace, the conduct of the field test, and the financing of the new furnace. We tested nearly three hundred furnac-es and replaced over one hundred. Since this was a pilot program, emphasis was placed on validating the accuracy of the tests, both through retesting of a sampling of the existing furnaces, and compar-ing actual savings to our projections.

This program provides us a sharply defined example of frame development. First, we created a generalized model of furnace behav-ior. This model specified what data must be collected to generate the representation of each existing furnace. Second, we designed the procedures for home visits and furnace testing. Standard operating procedures of this sort capture the essence of framing. They are generalized procedural models that must accommodate a wide range of particular situations. Third, we developed rules for projecting furnace performance and dollar savings once we had collected the data for an individual furnace. The entire point of this exercise was to predict the savings that would result from furnace replacement. Because this was a pilot project, we documented all of these models and procedures in detail.

Incremental Frame Improvement Through Testing

All home heating furnaces have an efficiency rating. Conven-tional furnaces are in the 80 percent range and high efficiency units are at 90 percent. These ratings are based on a standardized test that we could easily reproduce. This efficiency rating tells us the percent of the fuel converted to heat that goes into the home *while the furnace is running continuously*. However, furnaces do not run continuously. Furnaces are turned on and off by thermostats. When the room temperature at the thermostat gets down to the temperature set by the homeowner, the furnace is turned on. The furnace will run for a set period, usually two to six minutes, and then the thermostat will turn it off. The furnace will now remain off until the temperature goes back down to the thermostat set point. On colder days, the furnace *off period* will be shorter. On warmer days, the furnace off period will be longer. The furnace *on period* remains about the same, except under extremely cold conditions.[32]

Residential furnaces store significant heat within their steel components. When the furnace turns off, much of this heat is lost up the flue, degrading overall performance.[33] We developed a model that predicted efficiency during the full operating cycle of a furnace rather than just when it was running continuously. In order to do this, we had to measure the flow and temperature of the gasses going up the flue during the off-cycle.

A frame is not only a generalized model of a system but also a guide for how to collect the information needed to generate a specific representation. We used the first several furnace tests to try out different testing methods. We were mindful that the procedures that we developed had to be sufficiently flexible to work in a wide variety of residential furnace settings. Our testing teams were resourceful but not trained engineers. The testing methods had to be sufficiently robust that each situation would not require engineering knowledge. During the early stages of the pilot project, we modified the testing procedure numerous times to reflect the realities of collecting information in the field. These procedures constituted the frame that guided our teams as they evaluated each new house. The evolution of the test procedure is documented in *Appendix 4: Furnace Test* Proce-

---

[32] In many homes, there is a lag between when the furnace is turned off and when the temperature at the thermostat reaches its maximum. When the furnace receives its off signal, the burners turn off, but the fan continues to run to capture the heat that has built up in the furnace. There is also heat built up in the ductwork. This heat is brought into the rooms of the house after the thermostat signals the furnace to turn off. For this reason, if the thermostat waited for the room temperature to reach its off temperature (usually two or three degrees above the set temperature) the heat delivered to the house after the off signal is sent would overshoot the desired maximum temperature. The solution: the thermostat *anticipator*. Even the simplest thermostats have a feature that turns the furnace off after a fixed period of time, independent of the temperature in the room.

[33] Overall efficiency of the furnaces tested ranged from 50 percent to 70 percent with an average of about 64 percent.

dure – Wisconsin Gas Company, page 275. The information that we were able to reliably collect shaped the generalized models that we were able to build.

To recap, frames are tools that we maintain in our mental workshop. Although we usually elect the tool to use for a particular task rapidly and intuitively, we need to keep in mind that choosing the best tool for the job is under our control. We also need to be open to the possibility that we do not have the right tool.

Chapter 10   Trapped by the Wrong Frame

When we encounter new problems, we select from our toolkit of frames the one that best matches the characteristics presented by the situation. Each frame has key identifiers that qualify it for use. The new situation may match the selected frame superficially, but differ in details that the frame does not capture. Frames are subject to over-generalization. Their predictive power may be valid under only limited circumstances. Once we have committed to the wrong frame, it may be self-validating, and we may seek out characteristics in the new situation that are consistent with the frame's expectations.

In cases of simple descriptive overgeneralization, we may discover our error and be able to reframe the situation. In other cases, the faulty frame fails to capture an appropriate depth of understanding of the system's behavior. These frames can harm our problem solving efforts in two ways. First, errors may persist into the representations we create and be reflected in the actions that they were intended to support. When our actions fail to produce the desired results, we realize that we have made an error. The consequences may be dire for the problem at hand, but we are likely to learn from our mistake. Second, faulty frames may cause us to exclude opportunities for superior solutions. In these cases, the consequences of our error may not be apparent to us, and we may repeat the misapplication of the frame indefinitely. We have not learned from our mistake.

As I have argued in Chapter 2, we are prediction machines. At any given time, we want to know what will happen next. We use cues in our environment to call up predictive frames that best fit the situation. If we have only encountered one dog in our lives, that experience will supply our dog frame for future encounters. The second dog will certainly teach us that all dogs are not the same. Yet, if the first experience was strongly positive or negative, it will color the second experience. Overgeneralization is not a conscious act; it is the consequence of using what experience we have to shape our expectations of future events. The cases that follow present a wide spectrum of framing failures.

Case 1: Surprise

The phenomenon of surprise occurs when a thing happens that we did not expect. For example, our navigation through the physical world is guided by generalized models of streets, buildings, rooms, cars, busses, and airplanes. These frames guide our expectations of what we will encounter as we move from place to place. People are surprised when they walk through the front door of a courtyard house, finding themselves in an exterior courtyard. The reality that they encounter is at odds with their frame for entering a house, calling for an immediate reframing. In this case, the encounter is pleasurable, much like that evoked by the punch line of a good joke or the culmination of a magic trick. Surprises require an instant reframing of the situation. To say that we are surprised is to say that we recognize that our frame for the situation incorrectly predicted what would happen. Unless we are mentally impaired, recognition leads to learning. We will modify our mental model to reflect the surprising reality that we have encountered.

Case 2: First Impressions

We humans are facile at forming first impressions of people, places, and things. We use the slightest of clues to draw immediate conclusions. For example, in the last year that I coached youth soccer, I kept a diary to record what happened at each practice. After the first practice that year, I made an entry regarding three new players that had joined the team. One was a complainer, the second was not even remotely listening, and the third practiced with his tongue rather than his feet. These were thirteen-year-old boys, so I already expected that a firm hand would be required. I formulated a plan. I was going to come down hard on these guys – give them very little rope, maybe send one of them home from practice with little justification, just to send a message. At the next practice, I was ready for the worst. What I got was a complete turnaround. Nathan turned out not to be such a hard head at all and certainly had enthusiasm for

67

the game. Ian, for all his complaints, threw himself into practice, getting tired but bouncing back. Drew actually turned out to be somewhat funny, an attribute I could appreciate.

I took great pleasure in having been wrong, in having been surprised. I felt a bit embarrassed that I had formed such negative impressions with so little evidence. Fortunately, this situation corrected itself with no harm done.

A frame explains the behavior of a class of systems. It guides us in capturing only those characteristics of a new situation that are required to explain and predict system behavior. We identify a new situation as falling within the purview of a frame by certain identifying attributes. These attributes may cast a far broader net than the actual explanatory power of the frame. In the cases below, the situation at hand is superficially similar to those explained by the frame they evoke. However, the example situations differ from the selected frame in ways that render the predictive power of the frame ineffective. Since frames guide us in collecting information about new situations, often we do not notice the characteristics of the new situation that make the frame ineffective.

Case 3: Culture Shock

We become quite aware of the power of frames when they lead us astray. This happens regularly in foreign cultures where things are done a little differently. In January of 1973, my wife and I traveled to Switzerland to visit her aunt and uncle. We had skied in a variety of places in the US but not in Europe. We certainly had an idea of what to expect when we arrived at a ski slope, so much so that we did not give it a lot of thought. In Switzerland, we stayed in the shadow of the Piz Corvatsch, the highest peak in the Engadine Valley; so this is where we went for our first European skiing experience. As we drove up the hill toward the ski lift, we began to realize that this was not going to conform to our expectations – there was no extensive parking lot. Cars were shoehorned along the access road. We had to struggle to find a spot. We walked up the hill toward the lift. We could see massive cables ascending the mountain and then a large cable car entering the building as we approached. We looked for the usual charming chalet where we could warm up, change into our ski boots, and buy lift tickets. There was no such building. People were climbing up metal stairs into a drab gray facility that housed the lift itself. We followed. The interior was like a compact train station. People were standing in line to buy tickets and then moving directly to a line for the cable car. There was no seating, no lockers, and no heat. We trundled back to the car to change into our ski boots there.

The price we paid for using our *American ski lodge* frame was the sense of disorientation and the inconvenience of fumbling with our equipment at our car. No warm fire, no hot chocolate. Why did we use our American ski lodge frame rather than our *foreign place* frame? A foreign place frame would have warned us that things would be different. It would be wise not to assume anything before investigating. However, the *ski lodge* frame was more accessible, more easily imagined. Once we were operating under the guidance of the ski lodge frame, we disregarded mounting evidence of its inappropriateness, such as the grim, utilitarian edifice of the ski lift building. We were very much the jury that disregarded the judge's admonition to hold our judgment until all of the evidence is in.

Case 4: The Household Thermostat

It is commonly believed that if we want a house to heat up quickly, we can run the furnace harder by setting the thermostat to a higher temperature than we really want. Unfortunately, home heating systems have only two heating modes: on and off. Either the thermostat is happy with the current temperature it is sensing, or it is not. If it is happy, it will turn the heating system off. If it is not happy, it will turn the heating system on. We may think that we can dial up the temperature of a furnace as we do with the burners on a kitchen range, but we cannot.[34]

In this case, we may never learn that our mental model of the thermostat is defective. If we return from a trip and the house is at sixty degrees, we set the thermostat at eighty to heat the house up as

---

[34] The simple explanation for this is that a major design concern for furnaces is the percent of the heat that goes up the stack while the furnace is running. Running a furnace at a lower rate than it is designed for results in larger energy losses up the stack.

fast as possible. We may forget that we did this until the house feels overly warm. We then reset the thermostat at seventy-two and feel the satisfaction of a job well done. This result would have reinforced our mental model of running the furnace at maximum rate. We have no way to discover that the house would have heated just as fast if we had set the thermostat at seventy-two. In this way, flawed frames not only persist, but are strengthened by their application.

Case 5: Two-by-Fours on Edge

Many years ago, I designed a house in rural Wisconsin. There was a bedroom above the two-car garage. To avoid needing a post in the center of the garage, a beam was required to span about twenty-four feet. I designed what is called a box beam, made of two-by-fours and plywood. Box beams have a tall rectangular shape with plywood on the sides and two-by-fours at the top and bottom. The two-by-fours are oriented with the four-inch dimension running horizontally, as shown in Figure 9.

The carpenter on the job had never heard of a box beam. He took one look at the design and proclaimed that he would not build it. He was deeply concerned about the horizontal orientation of the two-by-fours. He *knew* that wood structural members used to hold up floors are always oriented vertically rather than horizontally. He knew this from years of building houses. Considering this a teachable moment, I asked him why wood joists are oriented vertically. "Because they are stronger that way." I asked him why they are stronger that way. "Just are!"

This rule of thumb, along with many others, had held this carpenter in good stead over the years. However, it did not enable him to consider the box beam as a whole. He focused on the parts of the beam as if they would act independently. Since the components of the beam were to be glued together, it would function as a unit. The box beam as a whole was oriented vertically, following the carpenter's rule of thumb. The orientation of its component parts was irrelevant.

However, this brings us back to the essence of the Einstellung Effect, discussed in Chapter 6. How does the carpenter know the range of problems for which his rule of thumb is applicable? Without knowing why the rule of thumb is valid, it is hard to know the limits of its application. To productively apply a rule of thumb, or any frame for that matter, we must understand the limits of its use.

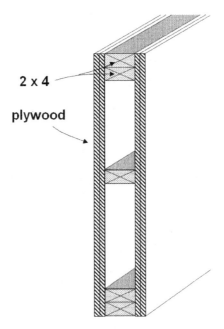

Figure 9: Cross section of Plywood Box Beam

This experience did not change the carpenter's understanding of the behavior of floor joists. We built the beam as I had designed it, and the world as we know it did not end. He considered the fact that the beam supported the required load an inadequate test of the beam design. It might have been strong enough, he reasoned, but it would have been stronger if the two-by-fours had been oriented in the *right* direction.

In this case, the carpenter had a valid frame for a limited range of situations. He understood that structural elements are stronger when they are oriented vertically. He did not know why. You might argue that he didn't really understand beams because he didn't know why they are stronger when oriented vertically. We need to be careful here. My test of the usefulness of a frame, and the representations that it generates, is that it provides a sound basis for predicting the behavior of the system that it models. His rule of thumb understanding failed this test in the case of the box beam. The rule of thumb frame did not capture sufficient understanding to predict the behavior of this beam, although it had served him well with more common construction methods over the years. The test for the usefulness of a frame is that it predicts relevant system behavior, not that it answers the question *why*. If frames had to answer the question why, we would not know where to stop asking why. Each explanation of why would lead to another question of why. Turtles all the way down.[35]

Case 6: The Yo-Yo problem

Andrea deSessa[36] is a physicist who has studied our intuitive notions of how the physical world behaves. He presents the scenario shown in Figure 10 in order to illustrate how we instinctively grasp the motion of spinning objects. A yo-yo is resting on a table. The string is pulled slowly so that the yo-yo does not slide across the table. Which way does the yo-yo move?

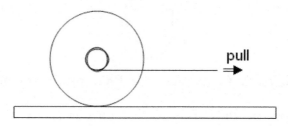

Figure 10: The Yo-Yo problem

Many people can readily imagine a yo-yo spinning counterclockwise on its axis as it descends from a string attached to its axle. When

---

[35] "Turtles all the way down" is an expression meant to convey an infinite regression. The expression comes from the answer to a question posed to a person who believed that the earth is flat and is supported on the back of a giant turtle. When asked what the turtle was standing on, she answered "Turtles all the way down."

[36] Andrea A. deSessa, "Phenomenology and the Evolution of Intuition," p.. 15 in *Mental Models*, edited by Dedre Gentner and Albert L. Stevens (Hillsdale, New Jersey, Lawrence Erlbaum Associates, 1983).

I first saw the problem, this is the frame that came to my mind to make sense of this scenario. I imagined a yo-yo descending from my hand. The resulting behavior would be a counterclockwise rotation, and the yo-yo would roll to the left. However, how could pulling one way cause motion in the opposite direction? No problem, I reasoned. When we are removing a screw from a piece of wood, we push with the screwdriver as we turn it. The screw moves toward us as we push in the opposite direction. This reinforced my mis-framing of the yo-yo scenario with the misapplication of the *screwdriver* frame. The yo-yo would rotate counterclockwise if there were no forces at its perimeter, but that is not the case. The only thing holding the yo-yo in place is the table. The yo-yo will move in the direction of the pull, winding the string up onto its axle.

deSessa's scenario is another example of a readily accessible frame failing to capture an important detail. We can visualize a yo-yo rolling off the string, movement to the left. There may be some discomfort with the notion of a pull to the right causing motion to the left. Being adept at confirmation bias, I was able to conjure an analogy to pulling a screw by pushing a screwdriver. People unfamiliar with the yo-yo system and its behavior might have less difficulty with this problem since the faulty frame would not come to mind. They might simply use the *when I pull something it comes toward me* frame.

Case 7: The Moon and the Earth

Most of my life, I have been satisfied with my understanding of the relationship between the moon and the earth. I have not really pushed to understand how the moon came to be in orbit around the earth, although recent theories are interesting. The tides have always been a bit of a mystery to me, particularly the question of why some ocean-fronts have larger tides than others. One day, several years ago, I was playing with an upgraded computer simulation program. Previously, simulation objects, such as machines or factories, were symbolized by icons placed on a computer worksheet. We would build a diagram of the process being simulated using these icons. We would describe the behavior of these objects by writing computer programs associated with them.

This new version of the software had the cool feature of allowing us to move the objects around on the worksheet using computer programs. To get familiar with how this worked, I created objects to represent celestial bodies – earth, moon, etc. Each object could be endowed with a mass and an initial velocity. I then wrote a program to simulate the gravitational pull of each object on all of the other objects on the worksheet. To test the program, I looked up the mass of the earth and the moon as well as the velocity of the moon in its orbit around the earth. I put the earth in the middle of the worksheet and put the moon the proper distance from the earth. If I had gotten all of these numbers right, and if I had the right formula for gravitational attraction, the moon should move around the earth in about twenty-seven simulated days.

The diagram of the earth/moon system shown in Figure 11 represents the way I visualized the system behaving. The moon rotates in a circular (or perhaps slightly elliptical) orbit with the center of the orbit being at the center of the earth.

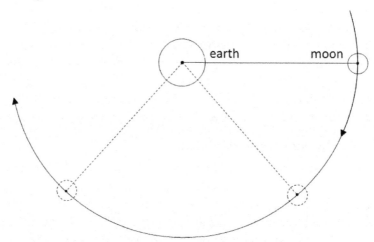

Figure 11: Earth-Moon System (not to scale)

After a bit of debugging, my little moon, about the size of a pencil eraser, moved slowly around my dime-sized Earth. As I stared at the screen admiring my work, I thought I detected a slight wobble in the Earth icon. I zoomed the screen, and the wobble was quite clear. The Earth was wobbling one revolution for each revolution of the moon around the Earth. Was this real or was it an anomaly of my model?

Think of the hammer-throw event in the Olympics. A three hundred pound man throws a sixteen-pound ball at the end of a four-foot cable. He does this by spinning three or four times with the hammer whizzing around him. If you can picture this, the man is leaning backward with his heels braced into the ground. We can look at the man and the hammer as a system that is rotating around a point in front of the man's chest. The man and the ball are circling this point. Think of the Moon as the hammer and the earth as the man.

Join me in one more analogy. If you think of a cheerleader's baton tossed in the air, it rotates around its center. The two weights on the ends of the baton are equal. If you made a baton where one weight was ten times the weight of the other, the baton would rotate around a point close to the end with the larger weight. The earth has about eighty times the mass of the Moon. The earth-moon *baton* rotates around a point that is about one-eightieth of the distance between the center of the earth and the center of the moon. Since the two bodies are about 235,000 miles apart, this point is about 2,900 miles from the earth end of the baton, or about 1,100 miles below the surface of the earth. Bottom line, every twenty-seven days or so the earth wobbles around a point about 2,900 miles from its center.

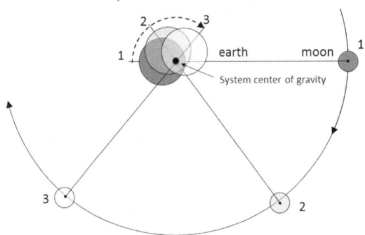

Figure 12: Earth-Moon System Rotates Around its Center of Gravity

In Figure 12, the earth and moon rotate around the point indicated as the *system center of gravity*. As the moon moves from position one to position two to position three, the earth also moves through positions one, two, and three. Every twenty-seven days, the earth wobbles around the system center of gravity.

Systems are typically dynamic. Our framing of them is often static. My previously simplified model of the earth-moon system has cost me little, except perhaps a too-shallow appreciation of the behavior of the tides. Yet, how often does the failure to recognize the dynamic relationship among the elements of a situation lead us astray?

A second lesson is available in this example. Our frames often capture primary system behaviors but neglect secondary effects. Newton postulated that for every action there is an equal and opposite reaction. We often imagine the primary action, in this example, the movement of the moon, while neglecting the secondary reaction, the wobble of the earth. In problem solving, we neglect how the world will react to our actions at our own risk, much like a chess player preoccupied with her clever offensive strategy while neglecting the potential reaction of her opponent.

Case 8: The Monty Hall Problem

Another area where our frames often fail us is decision making involving probability and risk. This is elegantly illustrated by the Monty Hall Problem.

Monty Hall was the host of the game show *Let's Make a Deal*. At the end of each show, he would offer one contestant the opportunity to give up their winnings in exchange for a chance to win *the big prize*. The big prize would be located behind one of three doors, named Door A, Door B, and Door C. At the outset, the probability of the prize being behind any one of the three doors is the same, and the contestant knows that. After the contestant selects one of the three doors, Monty intervenes by opening one of the other two doors. He always does this, and the door he opens never has the big prize. Say that the contestant had picked Door A, and the prize is behind Door B. Monty will open Door C. Of course, if the prize is behind Door A, Monty could open either of the other doors.

Monty now offers the contestant the opportunity to change from the door originally selected to the other door that remains closed. If Monty has opened Door C, the contestant can switch from Door A to Door B.

The question is: Should the contestant switch? Put in mathematical terms, what is the probability of the prize being behind the originally selected door, in our example, Door A, and what is the probability of it being behind the remaining closed door, in our example, Door B?[37]

The vast majority of people think that the probability is 50 percent for either of the two remaining doors, so switching would have no value, positive or negative. These people are wrong. It is important that they understand that Monty did not open Door C at random. He knows where the prize is and always avoids that door.

The correct answer is … the probability of the originally selected door remains one-third; it is not affected by the fact that one of the other two doors, the one Monty opened, does not have the prize. After all, the contestant knew that one of the other two doors did not have the prize before Monty opened it.

The probability that the prize is behind the remaining door not selected by the contestant, in our example, Door B, is two-thirds. One way to compute this is that the probability for the two remaining doors must add up to one. If the originally selected door is one-third then the other door must be two-thirds. This, or course, is not a satisfying explanation.

There are many approaches to explaining the answer. I will present my favorite. What if there were one hundred doors. The

---

[37] History of the Monty Hall Problem from Wikipedia: A restated version of Selvin's problem appeared in Marilyn vos Savant's "Ask Marilyn" question-and-answer column of *Parade* in September 1990 (vos Savant 1990). Though vos Savant gave the correct answer that switching would win two-thirds of the time, she estimates the magazine received ten thousand letters including close to one thousand signed by PhDs, many on letterheads of mathematics and science departments, declaring that her solution was wrong (Tierney 1991). Due to the overwhelming response, Parade published an unprecedented four columns on the problem (vos Savant 1996:xv).

contestant picks one of the doors. Monty opens ninety-eight of the other doors; none has the prize. Again, Monty knows where the prize is. Say the contestant originally picked Door 1. Why not - it has a one percent chance just like the others. Monty opens Doors 2 through 24, and Doors 26 through 100. What is the probability that the prize is behind Door 25? The contestant is now looking at two unopened doors, Door 1, the door he chose, and Door 25. He should reason that one of two things has happened. The first possibility is that he was very lucky and chose the door with the prize. Or, the prize was behind one of the other doors. If the first case is true, Monty randomly chose Door 25 to leave closed. If the second case is true, Monty left Door 25 closed because it is the door with the prize. Ninety-nine out of one hundred times, the prize will be behind the door that Monty did not open.

Experience has taught me that you may still not be satisfied. Consider one more pass through the above scenario. You pick Door 1 out of one hundred. Monty says that he will be opening all but one of the other doors. Before he does that, he will give you the option to switch from Door 1 to the entire set of doors from 2 through 100. Surely you would switch. You would rather have ninety-nine doors than one door. You would then have a 99 percent chance of winning the prize. You know that he will open ninety-eight of your doors, leaving one closed. You know that none of the doors that he will open will have the prize. You will then be back to one door, the one he did not open. But it will have a 99 percent chance of having the prize.

This problem is a testament to the strength of our frame for handling probabilities. The notion that two equal things have equal probabilities is well engrained. A coin has two sides. The chance of tails is fifty-fifty. The probability of a prize being behind one of three doors is one chance in three. When there are two doors, the chances are fifty-fifty. It seems simple to say, but this calculus leaves out important information that we might have about the two doors. What if you had watched *Let's Make a Deal* for years and knew that Monty liked to have the prize behind Door A? We still have three closed doors at the start, but you feel that they do not have equal probability. This is easy to see. However, the information that Monty is providing us by opening one of the doors that we did not choose is more subtle. Our probability frame does not easily grasp it. Why does the opening of Door C increase the probability of the prize being behind Door B but does not increase the probability of the prize being behind Door A?

What have we learned from these examples? Most broadly: frames are fallible. We are dazzling in our ability to call up models of the situations we encounter, but we should be more than casual in monitoring their quality. The presence of factors that we have not previously encountered may undermine the explanatory power of our frames. Generally, we would hope to learn from new experiences where existing frames have failed us, but this is not always the case, as illustrated by the thermostat and box beam examples. The earth-moon scenario suggests that we should be on guard for secondary effects. If there were need for evidence that we are imperfect framers of risk, Monty Hall should provide it.

Each of these examples suggests that we need, in Kahneman's terms, a stronger deliberative System 2 to monitor our intuitive framing of problems.

Chapter 11   Reframing

Frames have a powerful grip on our imagination. They are the prisms through which we see the world. To ask that we be aware of the role that frames play in problem solving may seem akin to asking fish to be aware of the water they swim in. However, unlike fish, we have conscious minds that can erect signposts to warn ourselves of potential hazards.

PROBLEM SOLVING PRINCIPLE #2:
BE WILLING TO REFRAME THE PROBLEM

As our attention is drawn from one set of sensory inputs to the next, we automatically invoke frames to organize our understanding of each situation and guide us in collecting additional information. The strategies presented here call for us to be aware of the water we swim in.

Strategy #1: Hunt for Helpful Ideas

Frames organize our perception of problem situations. The result is a representation of the situation that guides our path to alternative solutions and action. But what do we do when we recognize that our current frame is not working?

The Hungarian mathematician György Pólya wrote extensively on how problem solving should be taught and learned. In his classic work *How to Solve It*, he gives practical advice on how to proceed when your current way of looking at a problem is not working or, as he says, you are *hunting for helpful ideas.*

Consider your problem from various sides. Emphasize different parts, examine different details, examine the same details repeatedly, but in different ways, combine the details differently, approach them from dif-

*ferent sides. Try to see some new meaning in each detail, some new in-
terpretation of the whole.*[38]

Searching for a frame is, in essence, a search for understanding
of the systems that define the problem. We may have a rudimentary
understanding of the rules that govern a system without having a clue
as to how it actually behaves. The examples below illustrate tough
situations that call for reframing.

I was waiting for a train at Penn Station in New York. I left the
Acela waiting area to find a men's room. The one nearby was closed,
so I was directed to another area of the station. I wended my way
under some stairs and down a long arcade into a section of the
station handling commuter trains to Long Island. I asked again where
the bathrooms were and was directed a bit further, then to take a left
and another left. The bathroom was vast, with several entrances. I
thought that I left the same entrance that I entered and retraced my
path in full confidence that I would pass back through the arcade and
under the stairs that had been a landmark on my way to the bathroom. I walked for a while, but there were no stairs forthcoming. The
surroundings seemed a bit unfamiliar as if I had not been there
before. I retraced my path back to the bathroom. I looked in all
directions for familiar landmarks. Nothing registered. Not only did I
not know which way to go, but also I had lost my confidence in my
sense of direction. A mild panic set in. I was lost. The fact that my
train was boarding in ten minutes amplified the sense of disorientation. As I scanned the wide walkway for someone to ask for
directions, I saw a sign for Acela in the opposite direction from
which I thought I had come. The signs took me through an unfamiliar route back to the Amtrak section of the train station. It had been
hard to believe in signs that seemed to take me away from the direction I *knew* I came from. Nonetheless, problem solved.

My spatial frame had failed me. I had to find another way to organize my understanding of the problem. I normally eschew the *ask*

---

[38] G. Pólya, *How to Solve It; A new Aspect of Mathematical Method* (Princeton,
New Jersey, Princeton University Press, 1945) p. 34.

for directions frame, but I was ready to make that move. The *follow the signs* frame presented itself and saved the day.

The key to reframing is recognizing that the frame we are using is not working. We have to know that we are lost.

One day, I heard the dulcet tones of my dear wife's voice saying: *David, there is a snake in the courtyard!* I rushed out to find the snake. I am neither a snake person, nor do I have methods on board for dealing with snakes, but clearly, this was a problem that must be solved now. First, is it really a snake, or just a piece of palm bark? It was really a snake. Game on, and I was frameless. Sometimes we are confronted with problems for which we have no frame. It could be said that we have no understanding of the situation. Where to turn?

I went for the wasp spray, I guess because the snake, like a wasp, was a critter that I wanted to get rid of. Solution by analogy. What is the closest thing to a snake that I have tried to get rid of? I returned to where the snake was, and it was gone. I realized how bad this could be. Several doors from the house to the courtyard were open. What if the snake had found its way into the house? How would I ever find it? But there it was behind a large planter. I hit it directly in the nose with a blast of wasp spray to no apparent effect. I stood there and pondered. I decided to try to coax it toward a door from the courtyard to the outside of the house. I went and opened the door, keeping my eyes on the snake. I went back to the snake and tried to intimidate it into moving toward the open door. Absolutely no impact. I pondered - the hose. Why not spray the snake with water> This might move it along. I put the nozzle on the hose, turned the water on full blast, and drilled the snake's head. It reluctantly slithered in the right direction, across the back wall of the courtyard and toward the door. Finally, it moved past an open drain hole, which I subsequently took to be its means of ingress, and slithered out the door.

It may be that our most creative moments come when we have no ready courses of action or even ways of thinking about courses of action. My *it's like a wasp* analogy didn't work so I moved quickly to framing the problem *as moving things without touching them*. I've moved dirt around on the pool deck many times with the hose. It's the *snake is like dirt* analogy.

Strategy #2: Be Aware of Your Progress

When we have no clue how to attack a problem, we are at least in touch with our ignorance. Knowing what we do not know is preferable to the more common case where we think we know how to frame a problem but the approach is ineffective. Once we have adopted a frame, we have a hard time letting it go. The more highly developed a frame is, the harder it is to let it go when it's not really working.

Effective problem solvers monitor their progress toward a solution. They question whether the way they have framed the problem is actually moving them in the right direction. Is it adequately exposing the landscape of possible solutions? Are the rules and procedures associated with the frame getting results?

Alan Schoenfeld has studied the role of metacognitive monitoring in solving mathematical problems. He reports that college level math students tend too quickly to adopt an approach to problems and do not consider other approaches even when there is no progress.

The students read the problem, quickly chose an approach to it, and pursued that approach. They kept working on it, despite clear evidence that they were not making progress, for the full twenty minutes allocated for the problem session. At the end of the twenty minutes, they were asked how that approach would have helped them to solve the original problem. They couldn't say … Such behavior does not generally appear when students work routine exercises, since the problem context in that case tells the students which techniques to use. (In a unit test on quadratic equations, for example, students know that they'll be using the quadratic formula.) But when students are doing real problem solving, working on unfamiliar problems out of context, such behavior more reflects the norm than not. In Schoenfeld's collection of (more than a hundred) videotapes of college and high school students working unfamiliar problems, roughly sixty percent of the solution attempts are of the "read, make a decision quickly, and pursue that direction come hell or high water" variety. And that first, quick, wrong decision, if not reconsidered and reversed, guarantees failure.[39]

Schoenfeld contrasts this behavior with that of professional mathematicians:

> *... the mathematician spent more than half of his allotted time trying to make sense of the problem. Rather than committing himself to any one particular direction, he did a significant amount of analyzing and (structured) exploring -- not spending time in unstructured exploration or moving into implementation until he was sure he was working in the right direction ... as he worked through the problem the mathematician generated enough potential wild goose chases to keep an army of problem solvers busy. But he didn't get deflected by them. By monitoring his solution with care -- pursuing interesting leads, and abandoning paths that didn't seem to bear fruit -- he managed to solve the problem, while the vast majority of students did not.*

Self-awareness and self-criticism require that we step back from our problem representations and assess their effectiveness. We must recognize that our current way of framing a problem is an artifact of our own making. It is a tool that may be right for the job - or not.

Strategy #3: Be Curious - Seek Real Understanding

Sometimes we can muddle through a situation with a superficial understanding. Curious people look at problems as opportunities to deepen their understanding. They are unsettled when their framing of a problems falls short of clear understanding. The cases of the yo-yo and the Monty Hall problem presented in the previous chapter require dissatisfaction with one's initial instincts. In the case of the yo-yo, one can so easily visualize it moving to the left. However, we must be able to set aside our mental image of a yo-yo rolling off its string. We must regroup and look at the forces at play. The Monty

---

[39] Alan H. Schoenfeld, "Learning to Think Mathematically: Problem Solving, Metacognition and Sense-Making in Mathematics," in *Handbook for Research on Mathematics Teaching and Learning*, pp. 334-370. (New York: MacMillan, 1992).

Hall Problem challenges our ability to frame probabilities. We are anchored in the notion that two doors that initially have the same probability of housing the big prize must still have equal probability even after we have been given new information. Reducing the problem to the absurd, such as imagining the case of one hundred doors, is a productive way to get past a well anchored but incorrect understanding. Two cases are discussed briefly below and more extensively in the appendices. In each case, I was inspired to document my thought process while working on a problem. You might consider that being both the observer and the observed might have distorted the process and my description of it. I can only reflect that my need to understand the underlying structure of these two problems was a familiar feeling.

I was given the *Pyramid of Oranges* problem one morning by a friend.

Given a pyramid of oranges with a square base that has N oranges along one side, how many oranges are in the pyramid? This calls for an equation for total oranges as a function of N.

In this case, I arrived at a frame for the problem that led to a solution, but the frame gave me no sense that I understood the problem. This initial solution came as a result of more or less random thrashing about, as recommended by Pólya (See page 80).

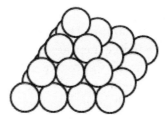

Figure 13: Pyramid of Oranges With Base of Four

The answer came in the form of an equation as a function of N, the number of oranges on one side of the square base of a pyramid.

Total number of oranges = $[\ 2N^3 + 3N^2 + N\ ] / 6$

As you will see from the discussion in *Appendix 5: A Pyramid of Oranges*, page 281, I had no clue why this equation worked. After arriving at this initial solution, I explored different ways of looking at the problem, searching for an approach that provided a more transparent solution. This came in the form of a rather elaborate visual exercise. I'll leave the details for you to discover in the appendix.

I have this need to understand why things work in the realm of numbers. I have learned over the years that not everyone shares this compulsion. I am convinced, however, that we all have systems in one realm or another that we are driven to understand. Perhaps this is just a hopeful thought about human nature.

Appendix 6: Pascal's Triangle, page 293, gives one further example of my curiosity run amok. Mathematical problems force themselves on me in the course of everyday life. I have long done sit-ups in the morning. Over the years, I gravitated to doing five sets of twenty-five. In an attempt to make this exercise interesting, I count off each set of twenty-five in groups of varying length. For example, I count from one to seven, then from one to six, then from one to five, and finally from one to four. The next time through, I might count from one to twelve twice, then just *one* to round out the twenty-five. After playing this game for many years, it occurred to me to wonder how many different ways I could do this. How many ways could I divide twenty-five sit-ups into a variable number of segments? One of these ways would be one segment of twenty-five. At the other extreme, I could count twenty-five segments with one sit-up in each. And everything in between. You will see in *Appendix 6: Pascal's Triangle* that I explored a number of frames for looking at the problem, again as suggested by Pólya. At some juncture of frustration, a friend led me to *Pascal's triangle*. How this was not a part of my mathematical ammunition, I cannot say. It led me to marvelous parallels between this problem and several others, equally frivolous.

Strategy #4: Be Skeptical of Expert Opinion – Even Your Own

When we are confronted by a situation that is beyond our depth, we naturally seek the help of experts. We are desperate to get a handle on the problem and are eager to attach ourselves to the first plausible explanation. Be aware of this tendency. Although an expert may have a higher level of knowledge, he may also have a predisposition to see the problem from a perspective counter to your own objectives. Such was the case in the following example.

The screaming coming from the front yard was clearly the voice of our daughter. I dashed out to see her and her bike sprawled on the strip of grass between the sidewalk and the street. She was holding her side and clearly in agony. In five minutes, we were at the emergency room at the nearby hospital. An emergency room doctor quickly saw her. We then waited an hour for a surgeon to arrive to offer his opinion: mostly likely a ruptured spleen. He gave me a quick lesson on the nonessential nature of the human spleen. He recommended that we *go inside* to determine the extent of the damage, and remove the spleen if necessary.

I called our pediatrician. He took a cautious stance. Recent studies had shown that the spleen may play an important role in fighting certain kinds of infection. He suggested that there would be little risk in waiting a while. It might be best to take her to Children's Hospital in Milwaukee. The implication for me was that this would get her away from the surgeon. I called my neighbor, an orthopedic surgeon. Given a description of the circumstances, ruptured spleen sounded right to him. Usually, ruptured spleens have to be removed. I talked to an oncologist friend in Boston. He was a bit hazy on spleens but thought he had seen something about their newly discovered usefulness.

The crux of this case is my state of mind when I received conflicting opinions from experts. The surgeon on call at the hospital wanted to *go inside* to determine whether the spleen should be removed. The pediatrician on the phone wanted to take it slow and easy. My orthopedic surgeon friend in Milwaukee felt it was a ruptured spleen from the start and figured it might have to be removed. My oncologist friend in Boston counseled caution but did not have much else to add. Ultimately, the pediatrician strongly suggested that we move her to Children's Hospital, where the staff was more used to looking at little spleens. Pressure was added by the overt negative body language I was getting from the nursing staff in the emergency room. *What was my problem?* I asked the pediatrician to come to the hospital to help me decide what to do. We took her to Children's Hospital. We found out during a long night of evaluations that there was no spleen problem at all.

On reflection, I think that the key factor was that the perspective of the pediatrician was closer to my own. The surgeon and his staff seemed to have a vested interest in solving the problem with the knife. They also seemed to be in too much of a hurry.

It is difficult in the face of an assured professional to ask for a second opinion. But what if the assured professional is myself? At what point do I question a strongly held first framing of a problem, seeking another perspective? To do this, I need to embrace doubt rather than defend against it. I need to keep my mind open to disconfirming evidence.

Strategy #5: Think Metaphorically

We can think of many scenarios as models of problems solving. For example, we can cast problem solving as a marketplace. When we go to the market, we have an idea of what we want, be it a single item or a shopping list. We also arrive with the means to pay for it, cash, credit, or barter. The state of our world when we enter the market, like the balance sheet of a corporation, has certain assets and liabilities. Our shopping task is to exchange assets that we have for assets that we want. When it comes down to a buyer and a seller, we have what economists call a non-zero sum game. When I trade my cash for your turnip, we are both better off. How can that be? Well, the turnip is worth more to me than the cash, and the cash is worth more to you than the turnip.

So it is with all problem solving. We are looking for opportunities to rearrange the assets of the world so that it is a better place. Of course, many problems require more than a simple trade. The value of the market model of problem solving is that it keeps in focus the notion of conversion. We are *changing* the world, not creating solutions out of thin air. This model invokes the laws of conservation of mass and energy. In the introduction, I referred to human activity as a pandemonium of problem solving. By this, I am trying to convey a marketplace along the lines of the floor of the New York Stock Exchange. People are buying and selling. The world on both sides of each transaction is becoming a better place.

Sometimes it helps me to think of problem solving as a trip from point A to point B. Point A is the world as it is. Point B is the world as we would like it to be. As simple as this metaphor seems, the problem of a trip can take many forms.

- We are planning a vacation. We must decide where we want to go and how we are going to get there.

- We are lost. We need to find out where we are in order to get to where we want to go.

- We want to explore. The trip itself is the goal.

Problems can present very different challenges not just in content but also in form. Is the core of the problem clarifying where we really want to go, or is it trying to find out where we are? Thinking of a problem as a trip may help answer these questions.

At the heart of all of these reframing strategies is our awareness of the mental battles we are fighting. Mental models are not reality. Our current way of looking at things is one of many. We must be able to periodically rise above the battlefield, look down to assess our progress, and change strategies when what we are doing is not working.

PART III   *Principle #3: Seek Understanding Through Exploration*

Even problems that are apparently simple may conceal challenges and opportunities beneath the surface. Effective problem solvers start the problem solving process by exploring the nooks and crannies of a problem, seeking an understanding of its possibilities.

Problem exploration requires discipline and imagination. The goal of problem exploration is to discover a wide range of possible solutions. The problem explorer does this by investigating potential solutions to each aspect of the problem independent of the constraints presented by other aspects. Through this process, we will discover both the hard parts of the problem and the opportunities for innovative solutions. Discipline is required to move quickly from one part of the problem to the next without becoming bogged down in any one area. Imagination is required to consider the full range of possibilities, throwing off preconceptions or limitations that early conceptual commitments might impose.

Effective problem solving calls for a period of rapid-fire problem exploration. We should explore all aspects of the problem with an open mind before we firm up decisions in any one area. Chapter 12 reviews paths for developing alternative solutions. The cases presented in Chapter 13 suggest that the framing of problems can prematurely lock us into solutions before we fully understand the problem. Chapter 14 presents strategies for seeking understanding of problems through a disciplined search for challenges and opportunities.

Chapter 12   Generating and Evaluating Alternative Solutions

To lay the groundwork for discussing the role of problem exploration, this chapter looks at the process of getting from the statement of a problem to a solution.

To solve a problem, we generate and evaluate alternative solutions. To generate alternatives, we must have a grasp of the landscape of potential solutions. To evaluate alternatives, we must cast the goals of the problem as measurement tools. To determine which alternative to select, we must determine a common denominator among goals. Not only do we have to be able to score an alternative against each goal, but we also must be able to compare the total value of one solution to the total value of another. Of course, in most problem solving, such calculations are hidden in the secret chambers of intuitive thought.

The process of generating and evaluating alternatives can take many forms. These are shaped by the mechanisms of generating and evaluating. Generating an alternative solution to a problem may be a deliberative process designed to converge on a good solution. Such is the case with many maintenance and repair problems where a checklist of possible causes leads inexorably to a proscribed solution. In such cases, evaluation of the solution is reduced to a confirmatory test. On the other hand, alternative solutions may be generated at random, as is the case with the evolution example below. Many problems call for imagination, use of metaphor, thinking outside of the box - what Edward de Bono called *lateral thinking*.[40] Any time we preface an idea with *what if*, the burden falls on evaluation.

Evaluation of alternatives may take the form of instant recognition, the *aha* moment. On the other hand, determining the value of a solution may require exhaustive modeling or even the testing of real world prototypes. The few examples below illustrate a broad spectrum of the balance between generation and evaluation.

Incremental Problem Solving

Some problems lend themselves to linear step-by-step solutions, for example, the jigsaw puzzle. After preliminary work sorting pieces into categories, edge pieces, barn pieces, flower pieces, etc., each piece becomes a problem of its own. Each successful fitted piece brings us closer to a successful solution.

Let's say we are moving into a new city and want to buy a house. We might start by considering what part of the city we want to live in. We develop and evaluate alternatives. The need to make this decision causes us to consider our goals with regard to neighborhoods: schools, traffic, microclimates, shopping, and so on, although these considerations may not have been part of the goals that led us to move here. We cruise around the city and evaluate our alternatives. Based on this process, we select several areas that seem to fit. Having made this decision, even tentatively, has brought us closer to a solution to our problem.

Now we look at houses that are on the market in the selected neighborhoods. Eventually we find one we like, make an offer, and complete the deal. Problem solved! Well, that depends on how you define the problem. We have not moved in. We have not considered in detail what new furniture we have to buy. However, we have substantially narrowed the range of possible outcomes.

This is one way that problem solving unfolds. We make a series of milestone decisions, cycling through the generation and evaluation of alternative courses of action. This is like finding one's way through a maze, as shown in Figure 14. This maze is segmented into three

---

[40] Edward de Bono, *The Mechanism of Mind*. (New York, Penguin Books, 1969).

stages. We have to find our way from point A to point B to point C then to point D. At each milestone, we know we are headed in the right direction. Of course, sometimes in life we are wrong. What if there is no suitable house in the neighborhoods we have picked? We have to go back to the beginning and evaluate new neighborhoods.

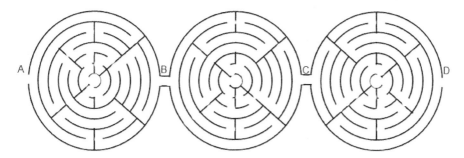

Figure 14: Sequential Problem Solving

Evolution

Evolution gives us a very different model for how problem solving unfolds. Forms in nature evolve through a series of incremental changes. The goal is reproduction. Each form is tested by how well it reproduces itself. The changes that result in survival of the species are retained. Those that do not are lost. Certain problems lend themselves to design by natural selection. The evolution of solutions can be carried out in a computer world, where solutions are randomly altered and scored against a set of goals. If a change makes an improvement, it is retained.

Imagine a blind man trying to find high ground in a natural terrain. He can take a step in any direction. If he senses a rise, he keeps his new position. If he does not sense a rise, he steps back to where he was. The landscape that he is in defines all possible solutions to his problem. Each landscape of solutions has a character to it. If there is a single high point, then his method is bound to succeed. But what if there are foothills, local minor high points? Would he not get stuck with a less than ideal solution? In applying this technique to the design of computer components, methods have been developed to characterize the nature of the landscape. This has led to techniques for backing down from local high points to search for better solutions.[41]

In design by natural selection, alternatives are generated by making simple random changes in the overall solution. There must be a simple way of scoring the quality of each alternative in order for many cycles of change to be completed.

Newell and Simon's *Problem Space*

In the early 1970s, Newell and Simon developed a rule-based computer model, *General Problem Solver* (GPS). The underlying logic of the model grew out of research on the way people solve actual problems. They asked subjects to record in detail the steps they took in solving sample problems. James Reason summarizes the results as follows:

> *Newell and Simon began with the notion of a problem space. This consists of a set of possible states of knowledge about the problem, and a set of operators that are applied to these states to produce new knowledge. A problem is posed by giving an initial state of knowledge and then asking the subject to find a path to the final state of knowledge that includes the answer to the problem. The path to the problem solution is characterized by a problem behavior graph that tracks the sequence of states of knowledge through which the subject passes on his or her way from the initial state to the final state and by the operators applied to move along this path.[42]*

As esoteric as this work by Newell and Simon may seem, I cite it as a vision of how problem solving, under some circumstances, may work. Their goal was to develop computer logic that would mimic human problem solving. In order to do this, they had to describe problem solving in a formal manner. However, behind the formality,

---

[41] This approach was described in a lecture series by Bradford Dunham of IBM at the Harvard math department, 1965. *Appendix 1: Design by Natural Selection* describes application of Dunham's technique to a simple space-planning problem.

[42] James Reason, *Human Error* (Cambridge: Cambridge University Press, 1990) p. 42.

there is a notion of problem solving as finding a path through a terrain of connected ideas.

Computer Simulation

Computer simulation tilts the balance between the generating and evaluating of alternative solutions heavily toward evaluation. Simulation is a method of evaluating the behavior of complex systems. In order for a simulation to be run, one or more specific solutions must be proposed.

Computer simulation has grown in popularity as computer power has matured. Simulation is an evaluation tool. The behavior of complex systems is often beyond the capability of mathematical analysis, particularly where random disturbances are involved. Models of manufacturing systems, for example, can predict performance improvement that will result from greater reliability of individual components.

In the design of computer simulation models, a set of factors defines a solution space. For example, in a factory production operation, the number of machines and the reliability of the machines might be two factors. If there were five alternative values for each of these factors, they would define a solution space of twenty-five scenarios covering all combinations of the two factors. The performance of the operation would then be simulated for all twenty-five alternatives. The simulation results would be evaluated against goals such as total throughput, wasted material, and operating and maintenance costs. When there are many potential factors, we use sensitivity analysis to determine the factors that have the greatest impact on performance.

Construction of Functioning Alternatives

In the design of complex systems, the most difficult step is often evaluating the performance of a proposed solution. In extreme cases, such as the design of fighter aircraft, competing contractors produce fully functioning prototypes that are performance-tested in use. In contrast to design by natural selection, there is only one cycle of generating and evaluating alternatives.

The examples presented in this chapter stake out a wide range of approaches to generating and evaluating alternative solutions. Each of these approaches provides a context for problem exploration.

Chapter 13   Frames Can Impede Exploration

Frames guide us along the path of developing alternative solutions, but they can limit our perspective on problems in several ways. First, they can cause us to focus overly on the immediate situation, the problem at hand. It may be critical to bring longer-term considerations into our calculations early in the problem solving process. Second, frames based on past successes may preordain pursuit of certain alternatives, preventing us from considering courses of action with higher potential value.

First Things First Syndrome

Many problems have short-term and long-term considerations. Action on part of the problem is required now, while further action is required later. There are three factors that auger for focus on the current problem with minimal consideration of longer-term issues. First is the pressure of time. We see traffic on the interstate slowing ahead. We are coming to an exit. We know the next exit is miles ahead. Should we take the exit or stay with the interstate hoping that the slowdown in short-lived? Of course, our knowledge of the alternative route offered by the exit is critical. In the few moments that we have available, our focus is on assessing the traffic ahead. Boom! The exit has passed. We are committed.

Second, we are able to collect more information about the current situation than we can foresee about future situations. We adopt the *we'll cross that bridge when we get to it* frame.

Third, decisions that we make now will provide a context for later decisions. The implication here is that having fewer alternatives to consider later on will lead to better solutions. This is the *jigsaw puzzle* process frame. Each piece that we put in place makes finding the remaining pieces easier. But with a Rubik's Cube, solving each face of the cube makes the remaining faces harder.

First things first syndrome leads to a kind of confirmation bias. We prefer to concentrate on the aspects of the problem that are in clear focus. Successfully framing the problem at hand gives us confidence that we will cope with future factors that are currently obscured by time, distance, and uncertainty.

Case 1: The Stadium Caper

It was six in the morning on a cold November day in Boston. My college roommate and I were walking along North Harvard Street adjacent to the Harvard stadium. Our work was done. We had successfully installed a four hundred foot piano wire from the top of one side of the stadium to the other. At the upcoming football game, an apparatus on rollers would roll down this wire and unfurl a sign suspended over the fifty-yard line. All of the details had been considered. We had already forged a ticket that would get me to the concealed cable that would launch the sign down the wire. All that remained was returning to our dorm and well-deserved sleep. Then we noticed the campus police car rolling up behind us. The two cops got out and approached. They asked what we were up to. Dick was carrying a coffee can with some wire and a few tools. We looked at each other. Neither of us had a story. "Just walking back to the dorm" was the best we could do.

This had been a plan three months in the making. Materials and devices had been tested and retested. We had reconnoitered the stadium, planning every step of the operation. Yet, we had not anticipated the need for a cover story for this moment. Since we were unable to provide any convincing reason for our being there, the cops took us back to the dorm, threatening to wake up the professor who ruled it from his penthouse apartment. Perhaps he could be more persuasive. We relented and told the cops what we had done.

The police accommodated our plea to return to the stadium and launch the sign following the procedures planned for the game. We gained the small satisfaction of seeing all systems function as designed.

Our focus for months had been on getting the job done. Our mental model of the caper ended when we left the stadium compound undetected. We had failed to follow the story to its conclusion.

Case 2: Ski Area Display

Apparently, I learned nothing from the ending of the stadium project. Four years later, I was living in Cambridge and was contacted for an emergency construction project. A local planning firm had put together an exhibit for a new ski area that included a large aerial view rendering of the ski valley. They needed me to build a rustic display case to house the four by six foot plastic sheet on which the rendering was painted. This would include lighting from behind. It was Friday afternoon, and they wanted to truck the display to New York on Sunday.

I was largely done with the work by Saturday night. The head of the planning firm had lent me his office as a construction site. I came in early on Sunday morning for some finishing touches. There was a note attached to the front of the case that instructed me to play the tape recorder on the office desk. I pushed the play button to hear John dictating a letter. After a moment, there was a pause. "Oh God, Parsons, it won't fit out the door." It took only an instant to verify his observation.[43]

At times, I think the more focused and intense the problem solving effort, the more blind we are to contextual considerations. We become captives of a particular way of framing the problem. A video called *The Awareness Test*[44] is a marvelous example of the power of focus to exclude extraneous information. Two teams of basketball players weave in and out while each team passes a ball among its members. The narrator asks you to count the passes of one of the teams. At the end, you are delighted to find that you counted correct-

---

[43] There was no time for clever solutions. I sawed horizontally through the entire display case one foot from the bottom, took the two sections outside into an adjoining courtyard, and reassembled the pieces. The horizontal scar added to its rustic charm.

[44] *The Awareness Test* is on YouTube at
http://www.youtube.com/watch?v=Ahg6qcgoay4.

ly. Then the narrator says "... but did you see the moonwalking bear?" How do we really know what information is extraneous?

Case 3: Frames Take Root

Consider the way we develop preferred routes through a city. Initially when we need to plan a route somewhere, we consult a map and choose what looks to be a reasonable route. If the route proves acceptable, the next time we go to that destination, or another destination in the same area, we take the route previously chosen. Over time, these routes become ingrained. The tributary area of a route may grow quite large, like the reaching branches of an oak tree. Any destination even remotely close to the route will evoke that route without consideration of alternatives. I have had situations where the tributary areas of two of my favorite routes have grown to touch each other. I suddenly realize that certain destinations for which I have been taking route A would be more accessible from route B.

De Bono[45] provides several evocative physical analogies for the process by which patterns of thought become engrained. He argues that the more that a pathway on the memory surface of the brain gets used, the stronger it becomes, much like rainwater etching gullies in a barren landscape. These pathways define what de Bono terms *vertical thinking*.

It is in the nature of these frames with ingrained solutions that we never consider alternatives. Therefore, we are satisfied with the results we get. Combine this with the power of confirmation bias and our fate is sealed – mediocrity.

Case 4: Overdevelopment of Simulation Software

For years, our firm, SDI, built computer models of manufacturing processes. We built them from component parts that represented manufacturing steps. Each new plant seemed to present a unique configuration of process interrelationships, linking stages of production, intermediate inventories, and product runs. Product/process compatibilities dictated the routes that products could take through the maze of processes and holding areas. Each production system

---

[45] Edward de Bono, *The Mechanism of Mind*. (New York, Penguin Books, 1969).

moved through a production cycle of starting up, operating, emptying out the system, and cleaning for the next run. Periodic failures would interrupt manufacturing operations. Upstream and downstream systems were logically linked together to ensure that no product was stranded in systems or intermediate inventories.

After many such models, we decided to invest in development of a higher-level kit of parts called *Plant Builder*. Plant Builder captured all of the logic of production systems and the operations that make them up. Once Plant Builder was developed, it became the eyes through which we framed the representation of plants on new projects. This is the essence of framing. The value of using Plant Builder was immense. Models could be built faster and capture greater operating detail than before. Our main challenge became selling customers on a new way of describing their operations. Once we created a Plant Builder representation of a plant for a new customer, we could run it under a wide range of capacity scenarios.

On each new project, we would be confronted with important operating details that were not anticipated by the Plant Builder frame. We had three ways of dealing with these anomalies. Ignore them; cleverly reinterpret them so that they could be described in Plant Builder; or develop add-on software features. Over time, Plant Builder developed layers of features added from project to project. The urgency of meeting project schedules did not allow for well-structured management of these features. This was particularly true of production scheduling logic, where variation from plant to plant is extreme. Eventually, application of Plant Builder to new projects required burdensome reinterpretation of the realities of the plants we were modeling. Ultimately, we put Plant Builder on the shelf and returned to the finer grain modeling elements from which it was built.

The beauty of Plant Builder for our current discussion is that it is a documented example of the transition of a frame from its roots in multiple experiences through a period of useful application into later stages of overdevelopment. Frames can be overly comforting. They are imbued with the certainty of *knowing*. The whole process of framing a scenario is self-fulfilling in that we describe only those aspects of the real world scenario that the frame is equipped to process. Aspects of the problem not captured by the frame are considered anomalies, and so they are, as seen through the eyes of a well-developed frame.

Case 5: Cannot See the Trees for the Forest

Some problems are begging to be taken apart, but frames may get in the way. Once we have conceived a project as a whole, it can be difficult to consider that doing part of the project might be better than doing the whole project. We may, in fact, have a stake in seeing the project as a whole, as illustrated by the following example.

An engineering firm in Green Bay, Wisconsin, invested considerable effort in developing plans for a project to convert waste from a cheese plant into methane. The project was justified financially when viewed as a whole in combination with a process to convert cheese whey into a protein product. Our firm was brought in to supply financing. We looked at each part of the project to see if it was justified individually. The protein process would pay for itself in less than one year. The methane part had a payback of over three years, outside of the feasibility threshold of our financing model. Viewed together, the two-year payback looked attractive. The engineering firm specialized in waste treatment plant design and construction. They were motivated to assess the viability of the project as a whole rather than to look at the viability of each part. We chose to finance only the protein part of the project. As a result, the engineering firm had no role to play.

Case 6: Paradigm Shifts in Science

Thomas Kuhn paints a fascinating picture of the business of science. In Kuhn's model of the conduct of science, scientists commit to a scientific paradigm, gradually expanding its explanatory power. Eventually, a parallel, competing paradigm emerges that views the world in a different light. Suddenly, behaviors not explained by the existing paradigm can be studied and explained. Some adherents are drawn away from the prevailing paradigm; others doggedly remain. Kuhn characterizes these paradigm shifts as revolutions. He characterizes the revolutionaries as follows:

> *Their achievement was sufficiently unprecedented to attract an enduring group of adherents away from competing modes of scientific activity.*

Simultaneously, it was sufficiently open-ended to leave all sorts of problems for the redefined group of practitioners to resolve.[46]

Kuhn's insight captures the power and resilience of highly developed frames to shape the way we sort through evidence to build our understanding of the world. The more highly developed the frame, the harder it is to change.

Steven Wolfram is a paragon of Kuhn's scientific revolutionary. An indicator of Wolfram's trajectory in science and mathematics is that he received his PhD in particle physics from the California Institute of Technology at age twenty. In 1986, he founded the Center for Complex Systems Research at the University of Illinois. Soon after, he founded Wolfram Research, developing the computer application *Mathematica,* a widely accepted tool for mathematical analysis.

In the 1990s, Wolfram became convinced that the sciences have historically avoided the study of complex systems, since mathematics is limited in its ability to describe them. He dedicated himself to the development of a new approach to scientific modeling. In 2002, he published *A New Kind of Science*, where he proclaimed that he had developed a paradigm that would open the door to the study of complex systems in a wide range of fields.

When mathematics was introduced into science it provided for the first time an abstract framework in which scientific conclusions could be drawn without direct reference to physical reality. Yet despite all its development over the past few thousand years mathematics itself has continued to concentrate only on rather specific types of abstract systems—most often ones somehow derived from arithmetic or geometry. But the new kind of science that I describe in this book introduces what are in a sense much more general abstract systems, based on rules of essentially any type whatsoever.[47]

---

[46] Thomas S. Kuhn, *The Structure of Scientific Revolutions* (Chicago: The University of Chicago Press, 1962) p. 10.

[47] Stephen Wolfram, *A New Kind of Science* (Champaign Illinois, Wolfram Media Inc, 2002) p. 4.

Wolfram argues that the tools available to us when we frame problems with mathematics are unable to provide understanding of the behavior that arises in complex systems, such as economics, weather, thermodynamics, and evolution. He has proposed that *cellular automata* can fill this void. Cellular automata are patterns that occur in grids of squares where the properties of each square are governed by the state of its neighboring squares. Wolfram discovered that the patterns generated by even the simplest cellular automation rules are rich and complex. They have the potential to model complex system behavior in many fields.

The common thread in all of these cases is the yin and yang of frames. We have evolved the capacity to rapidly and instinctively trigger frames based on first impressions. This ability allows us to navigate effortlessly through rapidly shifting landscapes. But we pay a price. We need readily available frames to guide our path to solutions, yet they can prevent us from fully understanding a problem's challenges and opportunities.

Chapter 14 Seek Understanding Through Problem Exploration

PROBLEM SOLVING PRINCIPLE #3:
  SEEK UNDERSTANDING THROUGH EXPLORATION

Through a process of problem exploration, the problem solver comes to understand the challenges and possibilities that lie below the surface. Explorers must set aside preconceived organizing concepts. They must have the discipline to reserve judgment until evidence has been collected. They must have the curiosity to study the parts of a problem with fresh eyes, unclouded by what they have already seen. They must be open to unexpected opportunities. The strategies set forth below grow out of a wide range of experiences in design, project management, manufacturing, modeling, coaching, and miscellany.

Strategy #1: Relax Constraints

Initially, we should consider each part of a problem independent of the other parts. Consider the possibilities for each part unconstrained by solutions to parts previously investigated. Most problems are not like jigsaw puzzles where solving the easy parts first makes the remainder of the puzzle easier to solve. Real world problems are more like Rubik's Cubes, where solving each face makes the remainder of the puzzle more difficult. Robert Axelrod has studied complexity and is widely cited for his work on the evolution of cooperation. Axelrod and Cohen call this *constraint relaxation*.[48]

Constraint relaxation ... seeks solutions to a hard problem by generating variants that violate one or more of the situation's constraints. It

---

[48] Robert Axelrod and Michael Cohen, *Harnessing Complexity*, (New York: The Free Press, 1999) p. 42.

105

introduces new variants by starting with materials of established feasibility and modifying them. A nice example is the one-opening kettle, which was achieved by relaxing the constraint that kettles needed a wide hole for filling and a narrow one for pouring.

Sometimes constraints that can be overcome in this manner are not external to the problem but, rather, result from decisions in some realm of the problem that have been made before other affected realms have been explored.

Edward de Bono warns that vertical thinking, where one thought follows logically from another, is a double-edged sword.[49] The power of vertical thinking, such as logic and mathematics, distinguishes us from other animals. It enables us to manipulate ideas and plan complex courses of action. But it also channels our thinking along wellworn paths. In a sense, de Bono warns that vertical thinking is anticreative. As an antidote, de Bono proposes *lateral thinking*. When we think laterally, we leap out of the well-worn paths of logic. We think outside the lines. De Bono even proposed a new word, *po*. *Po* would be used to introduce ideas into conversation that might otherwise be considered illogical, much like using the expression "what if …". De Bono asks us to set aside the current constraints of a problem to allow freedom of exploration. Lateral thinking removes the logical limitations of vertical thinking, opening up new directions.

De Bono's call for lateral thinking is an invitation to problem exploration. He wants us to consider the problem unconstrained by our current vertical thinking frame.

Strategy #2: Think Outside the Box

Exploration must challenge both the internal and external assumptions of a problem. There are classic puzzles that imply certain restrictions on the puzzle's playing field. Going beyond these restrictions results from disciplined exploration, not simply acts of imagination. For example, the Connect the Dots Problem in Figure

---

[49] Edward de Bono, *The Mechanism of Mind*. (New York, Penguin Books, 1969) p. 236.

15 suggests by its form that one must play within the square defined by the dots.[50]

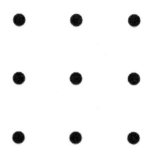

Figure 15: Draw Four Straight Lines Connecting All Nine Dots Without Lifting Your Pencil

A more elaborate example is the Candle Problem, a test of problem solving developed by Karl Duncker. Duncker was a Gestalt psychologist who created this problem as an example of *functional fixedness* – using things only for their intended purpose. Subjects were given a box of thumbtacks (popular in the 1930s), a candle, and a box of matches. The problem is to attach the candle to a corkboard wall. The ironic thing about this is that the solution is to think *inside* the box.[51]

Pushing the presumed limits of a problem should be a routine aspect of problem exploration. In the above two examples, framing is the box that traps us. We frame the problem in a certain way and work within the limits defined by that frame. Framing not only guides how we create a representation of a problem, it also provides the

---

[50] One solution is to start at the lower left dot and draw a line that extends to the right beyond the lower right dot. The next line can then move diagonally up and to the left through the two dots adjacent to the upper right dot. The third line drops vertically back to the lower left dot, and the last line goes diagonally through the middle and upper right dots. All other solutions are variations on this approach.

[51] Solution: Tack the box to the corkboard and set the candle in the box.

rules, procedures, skills, and tricks we use to explore the possibilities and generate solutions.

Strategy #3: Do Not Fall in Love With Your First Idea

When we start to explore a problem, we have to start somewhere; we cannot have the entire breadth and depth of the problem in mind at one time. When we start exploring a problem, we select one part to work on first. At this point, we are ignorant of the constraints and possibilities that will be presented in other problem sectors. Problem exploration investigates potential solutions to subproblems as if they were free-standing, so this initial ignorance of other aspects is beneficial. For example, if we are designing a hall of fame for the National Football League, we might start by considering the need for a symbolic statement. Why not make the form of the building suggest a football? We might also consider it looking like a football player or goal posts or a stadium. This is what exploration is all about. With luck, we might consider other, less literal, symbolic statements.

As we move to other sectors of the problem, we must put aside these first ideas. We must not let them limit our exploration. As discussed in Chapter 6 under the topic of confirmation bias, once we have latched onto an initial idea about a problem, it will frame our consideration of the additional evidence that we gather. We must step back and exercise discipline. We cannot fall in love with our first idea. Remember, the first idea was unconstrained by real knowledge of the other parts of the problem. If allowed to frame further exploration, the first idea may block consideration of great ideas in other problem sectors. We must move through all of the areas of the problem with an open mind, exploring both the potential for great solutions to these parts and the constraints they may ultimately impose on other parts.

When we first define the goals and scope of a problem, personal experience limits our ability to imagine solutions. We may not realize what opportunities await. These must be discovered. In order to find them, we must explore the problem space without being constrained by preconceived limitations.

The problem with the *big idea first* approach is that the big ideas that jump out at us are often the easy ideas, the superficial ideas. These ideas may lead us away from solving the challenging parts of the problem. They may deaden our creativity.

Strategy #4: Be Able to Relinquish Good Solutions

The idea of problem exploration is to look at subproblems independently of one another. This allows consideration of a wide range of possibilities that would never been considered if we kept in mind constraints dictated by previously considered problem parts. The difficulty here is that we may fall in love with some of these creative solutions, but we may not be able to keep them all. We must make hard choices as we try to integrate incompatible sub-solutions.

The clearest proponent of patience in problem solving in my life was Jerzy Soltan, professor of Architecture and Urban Planning at the Harvard Graduate School of Design from 1959 to 1979. He was a larger than life figure with a studied Polish accent, bright sense of humor, and a keen intellect. As my design thesis advisor, he taught me to explore problems - to look at the big picture, the small picture, and everything in between before committing to organizing concepts. He taught me that exploration of a problem means to look at its parts in isolation from one another, thereby allowing the freedom to explore the possibilities within each part, unconstrained by the others. This process requires discipline, but the results can be rewarding. It allows us to discover possibilities that would be hidden by the constraints we create when we commit too early to partial solutions.

In the worst case, we solve the easy parts of a problem first. This gives us a sense of progress, of moving closer to an overall solution. But these early decisions often preclude solutions to the more difficult parts that are yet unexplored.

Strategy #5: Look at Multiple Solutions to Each Part of the Problem

What makes one part of a problem easy and another part hard? Hard parts are inflexible. They are highly interrelated with other elements of the problem and require that other parts of the problem provide a proper context. Easy parts can be solved independently; they are not sensitive to the solution to other elements. The diagram in Figure 16 depicts this relationship. The ability to solve easy parts is less likely to be impaired by commitments to solutions of hard parts because the easy parts are either independent of the hard parts or their flexibility allows them to adapt.

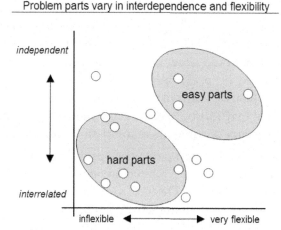

Figure 16: Hard Parts vs. Easy Parts of a Problem

Flexibility has two dimensions. First, a problem part may have many alternative solutions. For example, there may be many ways to arrange a building on a site to take advantage of views, environmental orientation, and the use of outdoor space. Second, the goals that the problem part must meet may be satisfied over a range of values. The size of a space to meet a particular function may have marginal benefits over a wide range. Inflexible requirements, such as those dictated by building codes, may have rigid requirements with no benefits gained by exceeding the minimum.

Strategy #6: Seek Out the Hard Parts of a Problem and Explore Solutions to Them

Our goal as problem solvers should be to seek out the hard parts and explore the opportunities for great solutions to them, independently of other parts of the problem that would potentially constrain them. Once we know these possibilities, we will put solutions to the easy parts in a new light. Making decisions on parts of a problem before we have fully explored the problem can easily result in precluding opportunities to solve the hard parts well.

The key to reaping the benefits of problem exploration is discipline. As we move from one part of the problem to another, we must be willing to set aside the opportunities that we have already discovered and be open to independent exploration of other parts. Different aspects of problems often require different frames. The problem explorer must be able to move nimbly from one part of the problem to another, without leaving a trail of premature decisions behind him.

Strategy #7: Move Quickly Through All Parts of the Problem. Then Do It Again. And Again.

My thesis project in graduate school was the design of the Bunker Hill Community College in Boston. My thesis advisor, Professor Soltan, had one overriding message for me:

> *David, move from the general to the particular, and from the particular to the general. Move quickly. You must understand the problem before you can solve it.*

As it turned out, much of the form of my overall design of the community college grew out of the design of student lockers with integrated seating. This was a commuter college, where the only homes students had on campus were their lockers. I created modules of faculty offices and student lockers with integrated seating. The opportunity to consider this approach arose only because I considered locker design before I had fixed other aspects of the design in place.

In 1979, our firm, Syncon, designed a new bookstore in a tight corner of a new Milwaukee downtown mall developed by the Rouse Company. The goals of the bookstore presented several challenges.

- The configuration of the store space was the severe test. It had one diagonal wall with several zigzags in the opposite wall.

- Conventional book display cases slope to the front, giving the customer a decent view of the books on the lower shelves. Since the face of the bookshelf slopes outward, they could not form the right angle turns needed to form an alcove.

- It was conventional wisdom to have the cash register at or near the store entrance for security and customer convenience reasons.

- A major metric of design was to maximize the number of books on display.

- A clear view of all areas of the store from staff workstations was desirable for security reasons.

We explored the store layout without considering the constraint presented by conventional trapezoidal bookcases that slope forward from top to bottom. This led to a design with alcoves that defined subject-area zones. The designers and the store owner were intrigued by this concept. To make the approach possible, we developed a new bookshelf design. In this new design, the face of the display case was vertical. View of the books on lower shelves was improved by allowing the lower shelves to tilt upward. The store was sufficiently small that the existence of cul-de-sacs was not considered a security problem, even though some areas were not visible from the cash register.

The next bookstore that we designed for the company was about three times the size of the first store. We continued with the use of cul-de-sacs to define special areas within the store, again enabled by the use of our custom bookshelf design. Checkout areas were not immediately adjacent to the two store exits. We convinced the owner that security concerns were not a problem, since there were many sight lines from the two checkout stations and the help desk. In addition, there was sufficient staff moving around in the store to keep an eye on the hidden areas.

In this case, the hard part of the problem was the conflict between the cul-de-sac design and two factors, store security and book visibility on lower shelves. We did not allow assumptions about bookshelf design and store security to sidetrack exploration of store layout. The cul-de-sac design concept came through design exploration; it was not a part of the initial statement or understanding of the design problem.

Strategy #8: Conduct Experiments

Experimentation is commonly thought to be the province of scientists working in their labs. With the advent of computer simulation, engineers in many industries are using their computers as virtual labs to study new approaches to manufacturing and logistics. A simulation experiment is a set of simulation scenarios designed to reveal relationships between system capabilities and the forces to which they are subjected.

For example, a simple component of an industrial simulation is a tank with a pattern of supply and demand, as shown in Figure 17. The rates of flow in and out may have random variation. We may want to know how big the tank has to be in order to not overflow, or its average contents, or how often the tank runs dry. Even as simple a problem as this is difficult to solve without simulation if the flows have random variation.

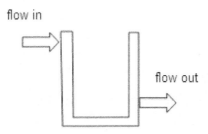

Figure 17: Industrial Tank

The scenarios in an experiment may vary the size of the tank while keeping the flow patterns the same. For each scenario we would want to know if the tank overflowed (or blocked upstream flow if the tank is capable of doing that) and if the tank ran dry. Conversely, we might want to know how a given tank would behave when subjected to a range of flow patterns. We might design an experiment with four input flow patterns and four demand patterns, resulting in sixteen flow scenarios.

Beyond the technical world of science and engineering, Roger Shank argues that experimentation is a tool we use in everyday life. Shank was a pioneer in artificial intelligence and learning theory. Most recently, he has focused on developing innovative approaches to on-line education.

> *While it is difficult if not impossible to conduct controlled experiments in most aspects of our own lives, it is possible to come to understand that we are indeed conducting an experiment when we take a new job, or try a new tactic in a game we are playing, or when we pick a school to attend, or when we try and figure out how someone is feeling, or when we wonder why we ourselves feel the way we do.*
>
> *Every aspect of life is an experiment that can be better understood if it is perceived in that way. But because we don't recognize this we fail to understand that we need to reason logically from evidence we gather, and that we need to carefully consider the conditions under which our experiments have been conducted, and that we need to decide when and how we might run the experiment again with better results.*[52]

Shank is arguing for a meta problem solving perspective on experimentation. If we consciously recognize that we are doing experiments in the course of solving everyday problems, we are more likely to rationally assess the evidence that experiments produce.

Strategy #9: Be Flexible as to the Granularity of Your Mental Models

At what level of detail should frames be developed? Consciously or not, the frames that house our knowledge are at a certain level of granularity. At one extreme, sweeping generalizations give us quick answers that are often superficial or wrong. At the other extreme, unintegrated detailed understanding may require too much effort to rebuild representations for each new problem. Development of simulation software has been a good teacher on this subject.

---

[52] Roger Shank, *Experimentation*. Response to the question: *What scientific concept would improve everybody's cognitive toolkit?* World Question Center of the Web site edge.org.

Computer programs that model the behavior of complex systems involve thousands of lines of computer code. People in the business of developing simulation models face a recurring question: Where should we start when we build a model? If we start each time with a blank sheet, we will have maximum flexibility, but the cost and time to develop a model will be high. If we start with a canned program, that is, one developed on another project, development time will be short, but many compromises will be required to fit the model to the new project. The chart in Figure 18 asserts that more highly developed modeling tools require less development to get to a finished model but are less flexible in that we can apply them to a narrower set of real world situations.

The shape of this curve does not mean that there is a preordained threshold of performance that cannot be exceeded. We are continually trying to push tools toward both greater flexibility and reduced model building time and effort.

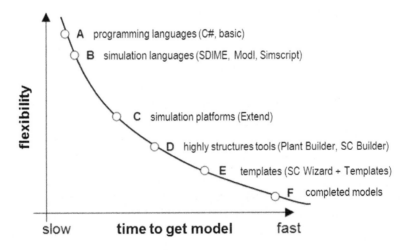

Figure 18: Degrees of Software Development

At the granular end of the curve, on the upper left, programming languages give us maximum flexibility but requires the greatest time to develop an individual model. It is in the nature of computer languages, particularly the current generation of object-oriented languages, that programs are developed in modular parts. A simulation language is a programming language where certain reusable building blocks are the foundation for model building. It is more efficient to build a model in a simulation language than in a general programming language.

Simulation platforms take development one step further, with component parts that represent elements of the system being simulated. These elements are quite generic, so they can be used in a wide range of applications. Highly structured tools capture rules that govern the interrelationships among system elements. These tools are applicable to a narrower range of systems, such as supply chains or manufacturing plants.

Model templates can sometimes be developed for repetitive application, such as plants at different locations that manufacture the same product. At the lower right end of the spectrum is the individual simulation model.

The property of granularity applies to frames that we use in everyday life. For example, when we move to a new city, every trip through the city has to be built from scratch, from small conceptual maps that get us from street to street to get to our destination. As we learn to navigate the city, integrated routes emerge that we can splice together far more quickly. Certain repeated routes become single frames in our memory. And so it is in any field where we develop expertise. Our mental models tend to follow an arc from highly granular to more integrated components. As our experience builds, we can throw together models of new situations from larger chunks of experience. More integrated frames allow us to solve problems more quickly but may miss important differences between the real world situation and the assumptions built into the frame.

During the late 1990s, our simulation firm, SDI, built several supply chain models for major corporations. My partner, Andy Siprelle, challenged me to design a highly structured tool from which we could build these models more quickly. The resulting software, Supply Chain Builder, was a fusion of the experience we had on a variety of supply chain and logistics projects. The basic building blocks of Supply Chain Builder remained at a granular level – inventories, resources, locations, and controls. We did not impose a higher-level structure as we had with some of my other efforts at higher-level modeling tools. The granular nature of the Supply Chain Builder frame enabled its application to a wide range of projects, going beyond the initially conceived definition of *supply chain*. For example, we used the tool to model production of pharmaceuticals and rehabilitation of nuclear weapons. On reflection, I view Supply Chain Builder as showing the power of modeling tools that capture system behavior at a granular level, without building in restrictive concepts at a global level.

Strategy #10: Allow Good Solutions to Emerge From Understanding of a Problem From Both the Top and the Bottom

In previous chapters, we have already seen several examples of emergence. The behavior of the earth and moon emerges from their gravitational attraction, not some broader law about things orbiting other things. Wolfram's *New Kind of Science*[53] is all about emergence. In essence, he grows complex forms by application of simple rules to patterns of cells. It is in the nature of emergent phenomena that their occurrence is not obvious from looking at the systems from which they emerge. Both good solutions and unintended consequences fall nicely within this paradigm.

The concept of emergence has been used to support both sides of the meta problem solving question: *Should we solve problems from the bottom up or top down?* Nicholas Christakis is a professor of medical sociology at Harvard Medical School and coauthor of *Connected: The Surprising Power of Our Social Networks*. Christakis argues that with systems, the whole is often greater than the sum of the parts:

> *I think that the scientific concept that would improve everyone's cognitive toolkit is holism: the abiding recognition that wholes have properties not present in the parts and not reducible to the study of the parts.*[54]

---

[53] Stephen Wolfram, *A New Kind of Science* (Champaign, Illinois, Wolfram Media Inc, 2002).

[54] Nicholas Christakis, *Holism*. Response to the question: *What scientific concept would improve everybody's cognitive toolkit?* World Question Center of the Web site edge.org.

117

Michael Shermer, publisher of *Skeptic Magazine,* is on the other side of the argument.

> *One of the most general shorthand abstractions that if adopted would improve the cognitive toolkit of humanity is to think bottom up, not top down. Almost everything important that happens in both nature and in society happens from the bottom up, not the top down. Water is a bottom up, self-organized emergent property of hydrogen and oxygen. Life is a bottom up, self-organized emergent property of organic molecules that coalesced into protein chains through nothing more than the input of energy into the system of Earth's early environment.*[55]

Both viewpoints, Christakis's *top down* and Shermer's *bottom up,* embrace the notion that the properties of systems emerge from the interaction of their parts. *Holism* argues that in our quest for understanding system behavior we *hit bottom.* That is, there is a level of detail where we do not understand the rules of interaction among the parts of a system sufficiently to predict how they will behave as an ensemble. However, the bottom of our knowledge is a moving target. For Socrates, all matter was composed of earth, fire, water, and air. Science has come a long way in discovering the rules by which the elements that make up matter govern its properties.

The *bottom up* position argues that we should seek understanding of systems by understanding how the interaction among their parts results in the properties of the whole. This seeking is what science does.

Problem solving Principle #3 asks us to seek understanding of the forces that make up a problem. To *allow* good solutions to emerge is to strip away preconceived notions of what a solution should be: to solve a problem from the bottom up.

---

[55] Michael Shermer, *Think Bottom Up, Not Top Down.* Response to the question: *What scientific concept would improve everybody's cognitive toolkit?* World Question Center of the Web site edge.org.

The study of enzyme pathways discussed below illustrates the emergence of orderly system behavior from simple rules of interaction among system elements.

An enzyme pathway is a series of one or more chemical reactions that converts molecules introduced into the body into a form that the body can either dispose of or use. Enzymes are complex protein molecules that act as catalysts for reactions at each step of a pathway. For example, *lactase* is an enzyme that locks onto lactose molecules and divides them into glucose and galactose.[56] After the reaction, the enzyme may remain unchanged, as is the case with lactase. Or the enzyme might change form slightly, enabling it to perform a catalytic function in another reaction. As with other chemical reactions, the rates of these reactions is a function of the concentration of the enzyme and the molecules it is operating on.

In 1992, I developed a computer simulation of chemical reactions that was suitable for modeling enzyme pathways. I was part of a team headed by chemist Frank Shaw[57] that was investigating the process by which the arthritis drug Auranofin is converted into useful form.[58]

Having worked in manufacturing, I came to admire how enzyme pathways organized themselves in the blood stream. In a factory, it is common to have a series of operations that convert a product from one form to the next. To function smoothly, a production line must be balanced. That is, each stage must have the same throughput. If one operation is inherently slower than others, several work stations will be put in parallel at that stage to balance the line. If the work is being done by hand, lines can be balanced by moving workers from faster operations to slower operations to equalize flows.

---

[56] People who are lactose intolerant are short on lactase molecules.

[57] Frank C. Shaw, professor of Inorganic Chemistry, Illinois State University; previously at the University of Wisconsin-Milwaukee.

[58] Jacqueline R. Roberts, Jun Xiao, Brian Schliesman, David J. Parsons, and C. Frank Shaw III, "The Kinetics and Mechanism of the Reaction Between Serum Albumin and Auranofin (and its Isopropyl Analogue)," in *In Vitro, Inorganic Chemistry*, 1996, 35 (2), pp. 424-433.

Enzyme pathways present a similar challenge. In the case of Auranofin, the enzyme mercaptalbumin transforms itself through three variations before returning to its original form. Each molecule does this independently of the others. At each stage, Auranofin is being transformed and combined with other molecules until the final product of the pathway is created, a compound combining gold and albumin. Each enzyme reaction has an inherent rate that is a function of the concentrations of the molecules involved. A rate constant characterizes the rate of each reaction. The rate constants of these three reactions are quite different. This is like saying that an individual worker at a workstation produces less product per hour than the same worker at other stages of the process. To balance the line, there need to be more workers at the slower work station, in inverse proportion to the rate. So it is with enzyme pathways. A slow process in the middle of the pathway will require more enzyme molecules than in the other steps in the process.

So here's the thing. The enzyme process is self-balancing. At first, the slow process in the middle gets behind. The number of molecules at this stage grows, since not as many are being converted to the next stage as are being produced upstream. As the number of molecules at the middle stage grows, that rate of conversion increases. This is like putting more workers at the middle stage. Eventually, the rate in the middle reaction grows to match the rate feeding it. At that point, the number of molecules waiting to be converted at the middle stage stops growing. When a dynamic equilibrium is reached, we have a little factory, with all of its workers and materials floating around at random in our bloodstream. Of course, they are sharing this happy sea with countless other factories going about the business of supplying needed materials to our bodies.

Enzyme pathways provide a powerful example of emergent phenomena. The balanced production line is not designed or managed, it just happens as its parts obey their rules of behavior.

In short, understanding the dynamics of a system's basic elements can allow us to predict emergent behavior.

Strategy #11: Let Creativity Happen Without Seeking It

Problems often call for creative solutions. However, we should not set creativity as a goal in its own right. Creativity will result from open-mindedness, persistence, and curiosity. We must give ourselves the time and freedom to allow creativity to emerge where it is called for.

Robert Fritz is a creativity consultant who advocates conscious striving for creative solutions in a wide range of organizational settings. In Fritz's view,[59] problem solving is inherently anticreative since it focuses on eliminating negative conditions. He views problem solving as trying to return the world to a previous state that was thought to be satisfactory. This excludes the creative acts of envisioning new and better states of the world. People, in the view of Fritz, are either circumstance-driven or vision-driven. Circumstance-driven people are responsive to their environment; these are the problem solvers. Vision-driven people are creative. They control their environment. According to Fritz, creators love their work. Responders do it out of obligation.

I take issue with Fritz on two fronts. First, problem solving is not only remedial. We may be pushed by the badness of the world as it is or pulled by the goodness of a future world that we imagine. In both cases, we are trying to change the world from the way it is to the way we would like it to be.

Second, what we are looking for is good solutions not creativity, per se. Solutions may be found in unexpected places, places not found by following the paths of logic and mathematics. But Fritz raises creativity to the level of a goal. This is self-indulgence rather than self-awareness. We can open the door to creative solutions by relaxing constraints, as argued by Axelrod (see page 105), and by exploring problems with an open mind, as recommended throughout this chapter.

There is often more than one way to frame a problem. The two examples in *Appendix 5* and *Appendix 6* are illustrations. At times, the first way that we look at a problem does not guide us to a happy

---

[59] Robert Fritz, *The Path of Least Resistance* (New York: Fawcett Columbine, 1984).

solution. It is an act of imagination to reframe the problem in order to open up new possibilities. Metaphorical thinking invokes frames from seemingly unrelated realms to reboot our thinking. A metaphor asserts that *this system* is in some regards just like *that system*. For example:

> *Memory is a crazy woman that hoards colored rags and throws away food.* ... Austin O'Malley

The representation of a problem defines, either explicitly or implicitly, the landscape of possible solutions. We narrow the range of possibilities with each decision that we make. We often miss opportunities for creative solutions because of constraints imposed by other aspects of the problem. The goal of problem exploration is to develop the possibilities in each subproblem free from potential conflicts with other subproblem areas. This freedom is an invitation to creativity.

Generally thought of as the analysis phase, early exploration of a problem can be extremely creative. We are not only breaking the problem up into parts, we are also exploring the opportunities for solutions unconstrained by the other parts. Discoveries made during the exploration phase can echo around the canyons of the problem, producing marvelous and unexpected effects. But we must be ready for disappointment. We can become enamored with a clever solution to a difficult aspect of a problem. Our perspective on the entire problem can be reframed by our yet untested solution to one problem part. Witness the work of architect Frank Gehry. In the 1990s, he discovered that curved building forms developed by playing with cardboard models had a certain cachet in the world of architectural critics. Application of these forms to the Guggenheim Museum in Bilbao, Spain, gained Gehry celebrity status. Ever since, Gehry's firm appears to have framed major projects as an opportunity to further experiment with these forms. As a result, he did not give himself the opportunity to discover in these later projects a character or a vitality that might have led to different fundamental forms.

Hawkins suggests that a key to creativity is persistence. This appears to run counter to the intuition that to have new ideas we need to step away from a problem, free up our minds to let new perspectives rise spontaneously. Hawkins combines these notions as follows:

I have found that there are ways to foster finding useful analogies when working on problems. First, you need to assume up front that there is an answer to what you are trying to solve. People give up too easily. You need confidence that a solution is waiting to be discovered and you must persist in thinking about the problem for an extended period of time.

Second, you need to let your mind wander. You need to give your brain the time and space to discover the solution. Finding a solution is literally finding a pattern in the world, or a stored pattern in your cortex that is analogous to the problem you are working on.[60]

In George Pólya's book, *How to Solve It*, he advises persistence:

Perhaps your next idea will lead you to a solution right away. Perhaps you will need a few more helpful ideas after the next. Perhaps you will be led astray by some of your ideas. Nevertheless you should be grateful for all new ideas, also for the lesser ones, also for the hazy ones, also for the supplementary ideas adding some precision to a hazy one, or attempting the correction of a less fortunate one. Even if you do not have any appreciable new ideas for a while you should be grateful if your conception of the problem becomes more complete or more coherent, more homogeneous or better balanced.[61]

When we are children, we are natural explorers. We are curious about how the world works. We need an educational philosophy that nurtures this curiosity in all children. Work in the twenty-first century will require a childlike openness to new approaches. The most productive people will be those who embrace exploration and experimentation.

---

[60] Jeff Hawkins, *On Intelligence* (New York: Times Books, 2004) p. 189.

[61] G. Pólya, *How to Solve It; A New Aspect of Mathematical Method* (Princeton, New Jersey, Princeton University Press, 1945) p. 35.

PART IV   *Principle #4: Create Maps of Complex Problems*

Some problems are mind numbingly complex. They require the integration of many interests, the coordination of many components of a solution, and may require the management of a problem solving process that takes many years. Problems are made up of interrelated parts. Even on the most complex projects, we can map the relationships among the parts in such a way that participants in the problem solving effort can find their way about. Just as with simpler problems, exploration of the challenges and possibilities of complex problems is essential before locking into any aspects of a solution. It is particularly tempting on more complex projects to try to simplify the problem by breaking it up into manageable subproblems to be pursued independently. If we do this before the problem has been fully investigated, some opportunities for great solutions may be foregone. If a problem is to be broken up into parts, it is essential that we explore the interrelationships among the parts before defining subproblems.

Chapter 15 discusses the structure of complex problems. Chapter 16 explores several examples of complex problems where mapping allowed a more coherent understanding of the process. Chapter 17 presents mapping strategies for each phase of solving complex problems.

Chapter 15   The Structure of Problems

Some problems are sufficiently complex that we cannot consider all aspects simultaneously. To work on complex problems, we must decompose them into parts, consider the parts separately, and then put the parts back together.

How do we go about breaking complex problems into parts? Christopher Alexander[62] addressed this question in his ground-breaking handbook on design methodology, *Notes on the Synthesis of Form.*[63] As both a PhD in mathematics and an architect, Alexander brought a uniquely analytical approach to understanding design. His principal insight was that problems have an inherent structure that should guide the way we decompose them into subproblems of highly interrelated elements. He argues that *concepts* are a poor guide for this purpose. Referring to designers, Alexander argues as follows:

> ...*he tries to break the problem down, and so invents concepts to help himself decide which subsets of the requirements to deal with independently. Now what are these concepts, in terms of the system variables? Each concept identifies a certain collection of the variables. "Economics" identifies some part of the system, "safety" another, "acoustics" another, and so on.*
>
> *My contention is this. These concepts will not help the designer in finding a well-adapted solution unless they happen to correspond to the*

---

[62] Alexander is an architect, mathematician, and pioneer in theories about design. He and his team in Berkeley, California, have authored a series of books on the theory and practice of pattern languages, which express principles of design ranging from the dwelling to the city. They have applied these principles to many projects in the US and abroad.

[63] Christopher Alexander, *Notes on the Synthesis of Form,* (Cambridge: Harvard University Press, 1964).

system's subsystems. But since the concepts are on the whole the result of arbitrary historical accidents, there is no reason to expect that they will in fact correspond to these subsystems.

Alexander argues that the problem solver must map out the interrelationships among the requirements of a problem and identify clusters of highly interrelated subsets.

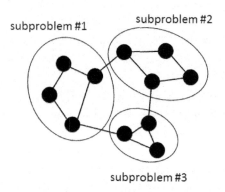

Figure 19: Defining Subproblems

Once these subproblems are defined, alternative solutions can be developed at the subproblem level, resolving the highly interrelated requirements where conflicts arise. These subproblem solutions can then be recombined, a task that Alexander asserts is relatively easy, since there are relatively few interactions that need resolution. The cases below illustrate the process of defining subproblems based on problem structure.

Case 1: Cereal Plant Scheduling

In my simulation work, I was confronted with a problem that perfectly demonstrated Alexander's insight. The problem required modeling of production schedules at dozens of cereal plants of a major US food company. This was part of a broader exercise to model the distribution system of the company. This company makes over two hundred brands, and it packages each in as many as a dozen different box sizes. There were over one hundred manufacturing systems making brands at several dozen plants. Many brands could be

126

made on more than one system, and most systems could make more than one brand. The company had sophisticated software to create production schedules. Our task was to create schedules within our simulation model that reasonably reflected what went on in their real world.

Put in Alexander's terms, our challenge was to identify the inter-relationships among requirements and break the problem down into subsets of highly interrelated elements. The requirements of the problem were clear: each brand had to be made on one or more specified systems and each system had to be scheduled to make one or more compatible brands. We created what we called *capacity groups* of compatible systems and brands. In an ideal world, each brand would belong to a capacity group that contained all of the systems that could make it. In addition, each system would belong to a capacity group that contained all of the brands that it could make. There were a few examples of systems that could only make one brand, and that brand could only be made on that one system. These would define capacity groups that contained only one brand and one system. These were the exception. We created a procedure that would sort through all of the brand-system relationships and create capacity groups. It turned out that there were about sixty completely independent groups. Some groups had as many as two dozen brands and a dozen systems. Within a group, it was seldom the case that all systems could make all brands, or that all brands could be made by all systems.

Capacity groups defined a map of the problem that dramatically simplified development of schedules. Each capacity group represented an independent scheduling problem. Writing rules for scheduling even the largest groups was far easier than trying to take on the full set of hundreds of systems and brands.

How Do We Identify the Components of Systems?

The real world has no seams. It is composed of a vast sea of sub-atomic particles interacting with one another. We may perceive that systems have certain *natural* physical components, but such perceptions do not necessarily serve us well in defining the elements of a system. The guiding principle in defining system elements is to cut across as few lines of interaction as possible. The credo of problem decomposition is to *cut the bird at the joints.*[64]

Case 2: Truss Design

To illustrate the process of defining the elements of a system, we will visit the world of structural engineering. In the structural analysis of trusses, the directive to cut the bird at the joints could be misleading. The diagram in Figure 20 shows a simple bridge truss with eleven structural members, labeled A through K, and seven joints.

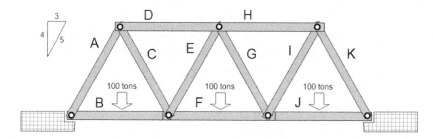

Figure 20: Loading on Simple Truss

If we were building the bridge, or taking it apart, decomposing the problem into the eleven structural members would make sense. However, to analyze the stresses in the members of the truss, we need to take an entirely different approach. Figure 21 shows a subproblem diagram that isolates the leftmost joint and one end of each member connected to it. The elements within the subproblem diagram are highly interconnected. We analyze each joint in this manner. There are seven joints defining seven subproblems. The subproblems are linked to each other through the structural members. As the forces in each joint are solved, information is provided that helps solve for the forces in adjacent joints.

---

[64] Usually attributed to Plato's dialog *Phaedrus*, where he has Socrates saying "The second principle is that of division into species according to the natural formation, where the joint is, not breaking any part as a bad carver might."

The lesson from this example is that problem decomposition does not necessarily fall along obvious conceptual lines. I have included a primer on truss analysis in *Appendix 3*, page 265.

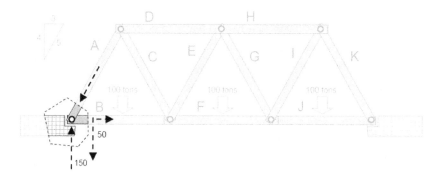

Figure 21: Isolation on One Joint as a Subproblem

Case 3: Bifurcation of Class Action Suits[65]

Our judiciary system provides another example of sorting out the structure of a problem: How can a collection of cases, with both common and distinct elements, be tried efficiently? A class action suit is a combination of the claims of many individuals. The commonalities of these claims give rise to the class action, but individual claims also may differ in important regards. It would be highly inefficient for these cases to be tried individually. Since cases have many factors in common, it makes sense to try large groups of cases with common complaints as one case. The challenge arises from the fact that the cases within a class may have many individual differences. The solution to this challenge is bifurcation of cases into the parts that have a common factual claim and into the parts that are unique.

Let's take as our starting point the class of all people complaining that they were damaged by the actions of cigarette manufacturers. This represents a complex set of interrelated causes of action. The

---

[65] Detailed discussion of this issue is given in "The reexamination clause: exploring bifurcation in mass tort litigation: analyzing the constitutional hurdle to bifurcated trials," *Defense Counsel Journal*. January 2006.

first level of decomposition is whether separate classes should be formed based, for example, on individual manufacturers. The second level of decomposition is identification of what the complaints of members of each class have in common. These common complaints would form the basis of the class action suit. For each member of the class, aspects of their cases not found to be in common with all other members of the class would be heard in a separate trial. Thus, their claims would be bifurcated.

The constitutional hurdle to this approach is found in the Reexamination Clause of the Seventh Amendment. This clause prohibits the retrying of facts tried by a jury. When a case is bifurcated into parts, the facts tried in the first part cannot be retried in the second part. This imposes a strict discipline on identification of what facts are to be heard in the class action. For example, the class could claim that a specific manufacturer knowingly made a product that would damage the health of the user and advertised falsely that it would not be harmful. An individual case could determine whether the claimant actually used the product and actually was exposed to the advertising.

Case 4: Level of Detail

How do we determine the level of detail of our system descriptions? I learned a valuable lesson on this score from one of my first simulation projects.

I built a computer simulation model of a large milk drying system at a cheese plant in Wisconsin. (Drying is the last stage in making powdered milk.) The dryer was a steel chamber the size of a house, with massive fans blowing hot air in and more massive fans sucking air out. One of the questions the client wanted to answer was to what extent capacity of the dryer would increase by increasing the size of one or more of the exhaust fans. The performance of industrial fans is measured as the amount of air, measured in cubic feet per minute (CFM), that moves through it. Fan performance is a function of the pressure the fan is pulling against. For example, a fan mounted in the wall of a warehouse blowing air from inside to outside has no resistance to flow. It will operate at maximum CFM performance. The same fan with fifty feet of ductwork upstream will be pulling against substantial resistance and therefore will move less air. Industrial performance is described by a *fan curve* that shows the CFM a fan will move as a function of the pressures upstream and downstream.

As I looked at the performance curves for the existing fan and the one we were considering substituting for it, estimating the effect of the change on the overall system performance seemed fairly straightforward. Wrong! Simulation with the new fan showed less improved performance than expected. I searched all aspects of the model to find any logical or programming errors that might be behind this surprise and found none.

The new fan was moving more air than the old fan but not as much as I had calculated. Ultimately, I realized that the shortfall resulted from the lowering of the pressure inside the large drying chamber caused by the new fan. This lower pressure resulted in a slightly lower point on the fan performance curve. However, this did not nearly explain the overall shortfall in performance indicated by the simulation model. Then, aha! The reduction of pressure in the drying chamber not only affected the performance of the replacement fan but also the performance of all of the other exhaust fans. They were all operating at a lower point on their performance curve as a result of the reduced pressure in the drying chamber.

If I had described the behavior of the fans as a fixed CFM performance level, the effect of changes in chamber pressure on their performance would never have been discovered. Although it had not occurred to me when I was building the model that changing the size of one fan would affect the performance of the other fans, I was fortunate that I described their performance as a function of the air pressure in the drying chamber.

System behaviors can emerge from surprising places. This case illustrates the value of digging deep into the dynamic elements of a system.

Connections Among Problem Parts

In the cases above, we have discussed several sorts of structural challenges. In scheduling cereal production, the task was to define subproblems in terms of highly interrelated parts, and minimal links between subproblems. As it happens, the facts of that situation made it possible to define clearly isolated subproblems called capacity groups.

In the structural analysis of trusses, we had to define a sequence of subproblems based on joints rather than structural members. Taking this approach, the solution to one subproblem provides information required to solve the next.

In class action suits, the challenge was to balance two opposing goals: maximize the benefits of collecting a large number of cases into one class versus maximize the commonality among the cases.

The fan problem offers an example of unexpected linkages. Sometimes it is only because of instinct that we describe a problem in sufficient detail that such interrelationships are exposed.

In each of these cases, the problem solver is assessing the nature and the extent of the interrelationships among the problem's parts. The parts of problems vary in the degree of their interdependence, as shown in Figure 22. Alternative solutions may vary in their structure. Some alternatives are functionally integrated; some are functionally segregated.

Degree of interdependence among problem parts		
Independent ↑ | | | | | ↓ **Integrated**	Independent	Parts can be considered separately
	Competing for resources	Coordination is required: timing is the issue
	Competing for budget	Prioritization is required: cost is the issue
	Interdependent	One part relies on the performance of another
	Functionally integrated	The parts perform together to produce a benefit

Figure 22: Degrees of Interdependence

Jigsaw puzzles illustrate a class of problems where solving any part makes the remainder of the problem easier to solve. When we take the thousand pieces of a jigsaw puzzle out of the box, we turn all of the pieces face up and spread them out so all pieces have their own place on the table. From this point, it is standard practice to separate the edge pieces, locating them on the table as best we can as guided by the patterns and colors of the picture. We begin to find pieces that fit together. There may be some distinctive colors or patterns in the middle of the picture that make non-edge pieces easy to match, but generally progress happens around the edge. The problem here is to put all of the pieces together, to finish the puzzle. To reach this goal, each piece must be fitted to one or more other pieces. *Every fit that we make makes the remaining fits easier.* The blue sky pieces will always be harder than the grill of the Edsel or the edge pieces, but once all of the other pieces are done, the blue sky pieces will be easier than they were before the other pieces were done. Why? First, there are fewer pieces to look through to find blue sky pieces. Second, there are fewer pieces that they match.

The Rubik's Cube puzzle has a rather different dynamic. The puzzle can be viewed as six interrelated puzzles, getting the colors on each of six faces of the cube to be the same. In this case, the more faces that are solved, the harder it is to solve the remaining faces without upsetting the faces that are in place.

Many problems are like the Rubik's Cube: solving the easy parts makes solving the harder parts harder, or even impossible. Or, solving some parts of the problem lowers the value of solving other parts. Or, a problem when viewed as a whole seems valuable or feasible to solve, but when viewed in parts, some of the parts do not make financial sense. The table below lists scenarios described in this book that illustrate this range of problem structures.

Examples of interdependence among problem parts			
Relationship among parts	Scenario	Description	Page
Problem part not feasible when viewed independently	Methane plant	Industrial project viewed as a whole was feasible. Methane plant component of the project viewed independently did not meet payback criteria. Separation of problem parts requires that they be functionally independent.	102
High performance of one problem part reduces the performance of others	Furnace program	Improving the weatherization of a house reduces the cost-effectiveness of installing a high efficiency furnace.	62
	Milk dryer fan	Increasing the size of one fan in a dryer system reduced the pressure in the main chamber, thereby reducing the performance of all other exhaust fans.	130
Solving easy part first makes hard part harder	Display case	Building a display case too large to exit doorway.	99
	Inland Steel Building Systems	Design of the systems themselves was the easy part. Getting the system to market was made difficult by the lack of a product specific sales force.	213

Chapter 16   The Structure of Problem Solving

Beyond the structure of problems, the problem solving process has a structure of its own. As problems become more complex, the contributions of multiple specialists must be integrated as a solution unfolds. The cases below illustrate the value of mapping the problem solving process in the context of engineering and construction projects.

Case 1: Design and Construction of Buildings

Building projects range widely in complexity and in the nature of the constraints that must be overcome. Nonetheless, the phases of the design-build process constitute a common thread that connects the perceived needs for the ultimate building to the actual construction process. These phases call on the participants in the process to frame the project in very different ways.

- The process begins with an assessment of the shortcomings of the current environment of the activities to be housed. This assessment leads to a building program – a statement of the problem that expresses a shared understanding of the goals of the project between the client and the designer.

- The designer then transforms this representation of the problem into a schematic design. The designer takes the client through this virtual building as a check to be sure they are traveling down the right road. Cost and schedule estimates are brought along to the extent that the schematics will support.

- The bulk of the architect's work is then in developing the schematics into detailed drawings and specifications sufficient for contractors to bid. At this stage, the design work is not yet completed, it has just shifted over to the people who actually make things.

135

- Many of the components of building projects require that subcontractors prepare *shop drawings* to spell out in detail how they are actually going to make the parts of the building. The general contractor prepares a detailed schedule to allow the architect and client to track the progress of the project.

The architectural firm of Caudill, Rowlett and Scott (CRS) pioneered programming as a formal architectural phase. They dubbed their programming phase *problem seeking*,[66] reflecting the practice of sending a team from their office in Houston to the site of the new building for an intensive analysis of the building problem. The analysis teams were known as *squatters*. In the CRS firm, the programming team was a separate group within the office that passed the building program on to one of several design teams.[67]

The project representation coming out of each phase serves both as a foundation for the following phase and as an evaluation tool for measuring the quality of subsequent representations and of the completed building. To be effective, these representations must be readily understood by the problem solvers of the next phase. Contract documents – working drawings and specifications – are a case in point. They are framed by traditional standards of organization and detail. Specifications, for example, are typically organized according to the standards of the Construction Specifications Institute (CSI).

These traditional phases of the building process, together with the standard practices that connect one phase to the next, constitute a procurement framework. This framework could be thought of as a *super-frame* that ties together a series of frames that together organize the problem solving process.

---

[66] William M. Peña and Steven A. Parshall, *Problem Seeking: An Architectural Programming Primer* (New York: John Wiley and Sons, 2001).

[67] I discussed this process with Mr. Peña in 1968 at their Houston office. The structure that they had established was rather impressive to me. I was taken aback, however, that once the programming team handed the project off to a design team, their involvement ended. There was no subsequent evaluation of the design or of the built project by the programming team. Mr. Peña offered that the programmers had a lot of confidence in the design teams.

Case 2: US Army Procurement Study

Several institutions with ongoing building programs have challenged the traditional framing of the building process. In 1981, the US Army Construction Engineering Research Laboratory (CERL) retained our firm, Syncon, to propose a way to think more flexibly about how to procure buildings. The impetus for the study was CERL's desire to open up military building construction to innovative procurement methods.

We developed a framework, shown in Figure 23, that put procurement planning in the context of other project decision making areas. The framework is described in the report as follows:

> *A model of project decision making is presented below which puts procurement planning in the context of four other project decision areas: ASSESSMENT OF OWNER OBJECTIVES, RESOURCE ANALYSIS, ACTIVITY ANALYSIS, and DESIGN. Once the model is presented, each of the five areas is discussed. Lastly, a variety of procurement responses is given to a series of problem areas.*

> *The principal conclusion of this report is that a procurement plan cannot be produced automatically as a function of project characteristics at the beginning of the project. The project characteristics including owner's goals and the construction environment can only influence procurement planning as it develops in parallel with project design, resource analysis, and activity analysis. These decision areas must be developed together through several phases, since the development of information and decisions in each area depends on information produced by the others.*[68]

---

[68] The entire report is reproduced in *Appendix 7: Procurement Planning*.

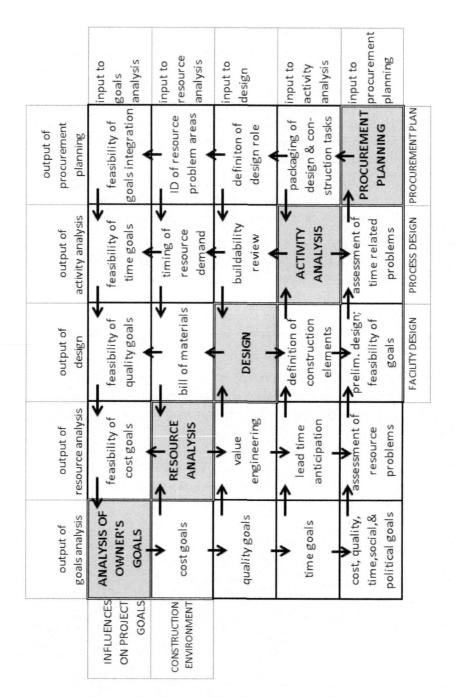

Figure 23: Model of Project Decision Making

Different Views of the Same System

Many circumstances call for us to view a system from several perspectives. For example, we enter a shopping mall looking for a shoe store. We approach a central axis with a three-story open space lit by extensive skylights. Since this is our first visit to this mall, we find a kiosk with a guide to the stores. It has a plan view of the mall's various levels. A classified listing specifies the location of several shoe stores. We now have to connect this plan view representation with the three dimensional representation that we are building of the actual mall as we stand there.

Architects represent the design of buildings in plan, elevation, cross section, and perspective views. Beyond manipulating these different views, designers transform an initial verbal statement of the requirements of a problem through the phases of design. Schematic design may employ diagrammatic representations that hardly look like a building at all. As the design develops, drawings take on a building-like hard edge. Eventually the focus is on the details of how materials come together. All of these are representations of the same building.

Corporate budgeting requires moving from profit and loss projections to balance sheets to cash flow projections, each providing a different perspective on the financial position of the corporation over time. Underlying budget projections are predictions of monthly financial and business activity. Each unit of projected activity is linked to each of these views of the behavior of the corporation.

Different representations of the same system allow us to focus on different aspects of system behavior. These system views are linked in the sense that elements of one view map onto the same elements in another view. In the case of the mall, we know that a store shown in the floor plan exists in the visual representation that we have constructed of the mall itself. Of course, it may not be visible from where we stand.

Nimbly managing this mapping from one frame to another is an acquired skill. Studies of the way humans represent spatial routes indicate that representational flexibility is affected by the sequence in which different forms of representation are learned. The work of Brunýe, Rapp, and Taylor looks at three forms of spatial learning:

text-based, map-based, and first person experience.[69] They tested for representational flexibility after exposing subjects to different forms of information in different sequences. Flexibility refers to the subject's ability to switch from one form of representation to another.

Case 3: Milwaukee Water Pollution Abatement Program

The Milwaukee Water Pollution Abatement Program (WPAP) provides us an excellent example of the need for a framework that integrates the perspectives of a diverse set of interests.

In the mid-1970s, the city of Chicago sued the Milwaukee Metropolitan Sewerage District for dumping raw sewage into Lake Michigan. Lake currents, Chicago claimed, were depositing this material on the pristine beaches of Chicago's lakefront. The federal courts agreed. The result was the WPAP, a massive program to reengineer the Milwaukee sewerage system.

In early 1978, I found myself in the office of Tom Gibbs in downtown Milwaukee. Mr. Gibbs was the chief engineer of the WPAP, at the time the most complex construction project in the US. My partner Joe White had arranged this meeting with the notion that we might do some sort of planning or scheduling work on the project. I found out later that there were already one hundred rather capable civil engineers on the WPAP staff. After he reviewed the many aspects of the project, Mr. Gibbs was saying "So what we need is a plan that ties this whole thing together." I explained that we didn't know the first thing about sewage treatment plants or deep tunnels or any other sewer stuff. He said, "Great. Then you will be able to give the problem a fresh look."

It turned out that the client required a specific piece of planning work called a program delivery analysis (PDA) –a roadmap for how the entire program would fit together.[70] The client was the Milwaukee Metropolitan Sewerage District. They were operating under federal

---

[69] Tad Brunýe, David Rapp, Holly Taylor, "Representational Flexibility and Specificity Following Spatial Descriptions of Real-World Environments," *Cognition* 108 (2008) pp. 418-443.

[70] Discussed *in Appendix 8 WPAP Process Model: Milwaukee Water Pollution Abatement Program.*

and state court orders to dramatically improve sewage treatment in Milwaukee.

Back to Mr. Gibbs. He explained that in spite of the overwhelming engineering talent that was on the project, they were not able to produce a PDA that satisfied his clients and the regulators, thus his call for a "fresh look." This was a clear example of preexisting frames getting in the way of developing a new course of action.

It took several weeks to get even the most general sense of the scope and complexity of the program. All aspects of a complex system of pipes and treatment plants were to be renovated or replaced. Of course, the system had to continue to function every day. Previous versions of the PDA written by in-house engineers were assemblages of individual projects rather than an integrated view of the program as a whole.

Several months into our project, Mr. Gibbs called Joe and me into a meeting with some big wigs from his firm, CH$_2$MHill.[71] There were several vice presidents and Frank Moolin, who had been retained as a consultant to the firm. Frank was the project manager on the incredibly complex Trans-Alaska Pipeline project.

The group sat in the rather tight quarters of Mr. Gibbs's conference room. The point of the meeting was for these senior engineers to share their insights on how the WPAP should be organized. They offered preliminary views on the unique nature of the project – a complex system of sewage transport and treatment that had to continue to function at full capacity while it was being replaced or renovated from end to end. Numerous general opinions were offered at a conceptual level. This reflected a top-down planning philosophy. According to this view, top people have the big ideas that divide the program into logical parts. They then assign these parts to senior engineers who further divide the project, and so on. At that very time, our team was engaged in analysis of the structure of the problem at a detailed level, including not just engineering issues, but also contractor relations, community relations, affirmative action, the potential for multi-use facilities, and more. All of these were stated

---

[71] CH$_2$MHill of Corvallis, Washington, was the principal engineering firm on the project.

objectives of the client but were not on the radar of the group in this room. The level of knowledge that these senior people had of the project would only support a high-level conceptual discussion. They were given no time to absorb the intricacies of the program, nor did they have the inclination to do so. This kind of *conceptual* problem decomposition is exactly what Christopher Alexander warned about (see page 125), since it bears no automatic relationship to the structure of the problem.[72]

These senior engineers represented vast experience in management of complex construction projects. Their concepts of how to organize giant projects were grounded in years of managing project efforts at many levels. But their observations did not grow out of their experience with integrating the details of projects but rather out of general concepts of project organization. They had little experience with reconstruction of systems so vital to the daily life of a city as its sewerage system. The kinds of issues that arise in keeping such a system operational throughout the process of rebuilding it are quite different from the issues that arise on an oil pipeline project or a suspension bridge. Yet they felt that general models of organization derived from these other project types could be applied to the WPAP, while explicitly recognizing how different and challenging this project would be.

A key concern expressed was that subprojects should be kept relatively small – fifty to one hundred million dollars – with complete autonomy given to project managers. This appeared to be the same kind of thinking that had led to the prior program delivery analyses that had not been accepted by the client.

Viewed through the lens suggested in this book, these experienced engineers were anxious to impose a *manageable projects* frame. This frame did not reflect an understanding of the degree of interaction among the thirty or more independent projects that would result. For example, the program as a whole was going to put considerable stress on certain categories of construction contractors in the Midwest. If this demand was not carefully coordinated, substantial delays

---

[72] Christopher Alexander. *Notes on the Synthesis of Form*. (Cambridge: Harvard University Press, 1964) p. 63.

and cost overruns could result as subprojects competed for limited resources.

Only through analysis of the interaction among elements of the program could we develop a sensible breakdown of the work. In the PDA that ultimately emerged from our work, a process was established for defining projects in the course of exploring and understanding the interactions among program elements.[73] The PDA Manual itself described its purpose as follows:

> *A program of the size and complexity of the Milwaukee Water Pollution Abatement Program requires careful and systematic planning. As the Program unfolds and moves through its various phases, from preliminary facilities planning to startup, the requirements for successful execution change since each phase is very different from the preceding phase and the phases which will follow. The personnel requirements, resource needs and activities performed in facilities planning differ markedly from those of construction, although facilities planning and construction are integral parts of the same Program. It is important to thoughtfully simulate the transition between phases so that Program needs can be identified and anticipated. This kind of program planning is program delivery analysis. It determines how the Program will be actualized - how the objectives of the Milwaukee Metropolitan Sewerage District with reference to this Program are converted into operating facilities.*

This statement was an explicit call for a clear headed integration of the multiple representations required to solve this massive and complex problem. The introduction to the PDA Manual goes on to say:

> *The Program is made up of several very different phases. It begins with abstract statements of objectives and ends with a physical facility. A structure is required to carry the objectives through to attainment. In order to develop the structure, the characteristics of each phase of the Program must be understood so that the transition between phases can*

---

[73] See *Appendix 8: WPAP Process Model: Milwaukee Water Pollution Abatement Program.*

be carefully converted. A process model, described in detail later, was developed to simulate the structure. Program delivery analysis follows this model in the development of the implementation plan.

We developed a process model to map the relationships among five representations of the program: influences, objectives, program elements, contract packages, and sources. Four matrices link these representations together. The matrices provided a framework for describing how the elements of each representation are decomposed and reintegrated into the next representation. The following is an overview description of the model from the PDA:

The process model is made up of four matrices. As time passes, the Program moves from one matrix to the next, from the Definition of Objectives, through Facilities Planning, on to Design, and finally Implementation. Each of these matrices can be thought of as an activity center, the function of which is to define the Program in a particular way - the decisions of each activity center build on the decisions of the previous one, and become the input into decisions of the following activity center ... However, information required to make informed decisions requires a reverse flow.

Different ways of framing the WPAP problem are suggested by each grid in the diagram in Figure 24. The diagram suggests a gradual shift of perspective as the program moves through phases of problem solving over a span of years. However, successful generation and evaluation of alternative solutions requires developing and testing ideas across all of these frames during each phase of the program. Examples of this are given in *Appendix 8: WPAP* Process Model: Milwaukee Water Pollution Abatement Program, page 349.

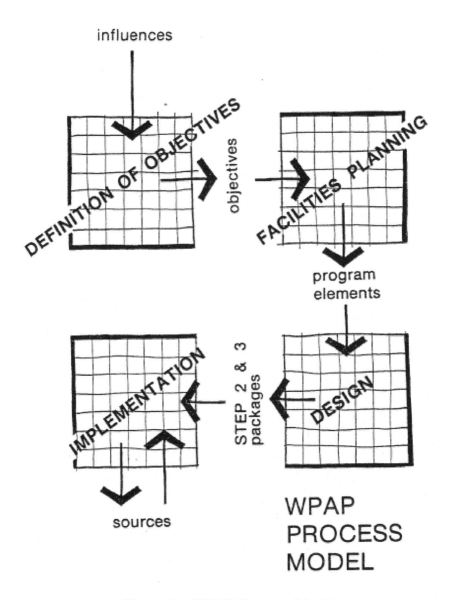

Figure 24: WPAP Process Model

Complex projects are challenging. Mapping in one form or another can enable us to explore the detailed structure of a complex problem without losing track of where we are in the scheme of things. Without such maps, the alternative is to latch onto available elements of a solution before we have determined their impact on parts of the problem yet unexplored.

Chapter 17   Mapping Complex Projects

In the course of solving complex problems, it is common that we call on multiple representations of different aspects of the problem and the several phases of the problem solving process. These may be different views of the same system or views of interrelated systems. It may take a series of representations to bridge from a problem to its solution. In order to manage our exploration of complex projects, we need to develop a map that integrates these multiple representations. Project maps can allow us to move from one representation of the problem to another without getting lost.

PROBLEM SOLVING PRINCIPLE #4:
CREATE MAPS OF COMPLEX PROJECTS

Complex problems can be viewed as moving through four stages:

- Integration of goals
- Integration of solutions
- Integration of actions
- Resolution of resource conflicts

Problems vary widely in the extent that conflicts arise at these four stages. As we invest increasing time and energy in solving a problem, our confidence in feasibility at all four of these stages must grow. We must explore and map these stages of problem solving to determine where the hard parts of the problem lie.

Geographic Maps

Mapping is a visual exercise. Geographic maps, such as road maps, are organized by two dimensions: north-south and east-west.

Each location on the map is defined by its vertical and horizontal position on the map. Some detailed maps are labeled along the bottom with letters and along the side with numbers so that each location in the map can be roughly identified by a reference like E3. When there is an alphabetical list of streets or cities, the associated code allows us to find the item on the map. Geographic maps can be said to have two *facets*, east-west and north-south. In a geographic map, the two location facets allow us to locate information about the elements represented on the map. There may be additional information about these elements, such as the size of cities, the type of road, land use, and topography. The two location facets organize the information in a systematic way.

Concept Maps

Project mapping is similar to geographic mapping in that it attempts to organize project information in a way that allows one to navigate among related elements. A rudimentary form of mapping is the *concept map* developed by Joseph Novak at Cornell University in the 1970s.[74] The example below is one of many readily found by searching "concept map" on Google.

Concept maps attempt to capture all relevant concepts at a manageable level of detail and identify their relationships. The arrangement of concepts on the map reflects an effort to group highly interrelated concepts together. Generally, the map is organized with broad concepts at the top and narrow concepts at the bottom. On complex projects, such maps can become unmanageable. We can bring organization to a concept map by giving specific meaning to the horizontal and vertical axes. We can do this by defining *project facets*.

---

[74] Joseph D. Novak, A.J. Cañas, and Fermin M. González, *Concept Maps: Theory, Methodology, Technology*, Proceedings of the First International Conference on Concept Mapping, Pamplona, Spain (September 14–17, 2004).

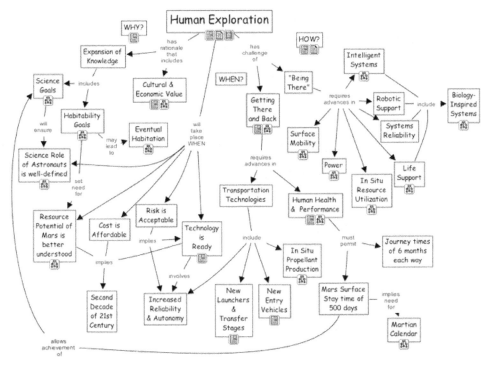

Figure 25: Example of Concept Map

Five Project Facets

Projects consist of a set of activities that convert resources into a solution to a problem. Problems are defined by the goals of one or more people we will call stakeholders. In these two sentences, we have defined five project facets: stakeholders, goals, solutions, activities, and resources.

- Stakeholders: All people and organizations with an interest in the project.

- Goals: The goals of stakeholders with regard to the project outcome, including the changes that will result, costs, time, and resources that will be utilized.

- Solutions: The changes that will be made in response to the goals of stakeholders.

149

- Activities: The actions required to create a solution, including schedules and side effects, such as disruptions of ongoing activities.

- Resources: Types of resources are a function of the type of project. They may include people, facilities, equipment, energy, land, materials, information, and cash.

As a project proceeds, the elements that make up each facet are defined. The goal of project mapping is to provide a structure that manages the definition of facets and their relationships.

Facet Interactions

The diagram in Figure 26 indicates direct and indirect interactions among project facets. Pairs of facets where no interaction is shown are connected through other facets. For example, stakeholders relate to solutions and activities through shareholder goals.

Direct Interactions

- Stakeholders/goals: Goals are properties of stakeholders.

- Goals/solutions: Goals measure the value of solutions.

- Solutions/activities: Activities produce solutions.

- Activities/resources: Resources are the inputs to activities.

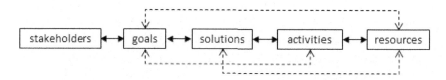

Figure 26: Interaction Among Project Facets

Indirect Interactions

- Goals/activities: Stakeholders may have goals regarding project activities, the most obvious being completion time. There may also be ongoing operations, where disruption must be minimized.

- Goals/resources: Stakeholders may have goals regarding resource utilization, for example, use of resources currently under the control of a stakeholder.

- Solutions/resources: The design of solutions may be affected by resource availability, for example, in health programs in underdeveloped countries, scarcity of medical personnel.

Integration Grids

Each pair of interacting facets can be mapped by creating a grid that represents the interaction between the two facets. Figure 27 shows an interaction grid between the goals and solutions facets.

System elements		Goals → GENERAL (a)	PHYSICAL SUPPORT (b)	DURABILITY/ MAINTENANCE (c)	CONTROLLED ENVIRONMENT (d)	ACOUSTICAL ENVIRONMENT (e)	ILLUMINATION (f)	FIRE SAFETY (g)	HEALTH SAFETY	APPEARANCE (h)
STRUCTURE	S-1	●	●	●		●		●		●
HEATING VENTILATING COOLING	S-2	●	●	●	●	●		●	●	●
EXTERIOR WALLS GROUND FLOOR & ROOF	S-3	●	●	●	●	●	●	●	●	●
WINDOWS & EXTERIOR DOORS	S-4	●	●	●	●	●	●	●	●	●
PARTITIONS & INTERMEDIATE FLOORS	S-5	●	●	●		●		●		●
INTERIOR DOORS	S-6	●	●			●		●		●
TOILET PARTITIONS	S-7	●	●	●		●				●
PLUMBING	S-8	●	●	●	●				●	●
LIGHTING & ELECTRICAL SERVICE	S-9	●	●	●			●	●	●	●
FINISHES	S-10	●		●				●		●
FURNISHINGS	S-11	●								

Figure 27: Navy Barracks Specification Table of Contents

The grid shows the table of contents for construction specifications for a Navy barracks at the Memphis Naval Air Station.[75] The eleven system categories define the design solution on the left side of the chart. Across the top, eight categories of goals are defined, plus a general category. Each black dot indicates that there is a section within the specification defined by the solution and goal facets. For example, S-4/E defines the section on the lighting requirements of windows and exterior doors. This document was used to determine compliance of building systems with project requirements.

Facet Interdependence

The density of dots on the grid in Figure 27 indicates a highly interdependent relationship between goals and solutions in this example. The degree of interdependence between facets of a problem is a significant property in guiding problem exploration. An important benefit of mapping project elements in this way is that it visually reveals the degree of interdependence in each project sector. Figure 28 shows four extremes of interdependence between the goal and solution facets. In the lower left corner of the diagram, goals and solution components are independent. They could be pursued as separate projects unless their relationship to other project facets binds them together. In the upper left, goals link to multiple components and therefore call for integration of component design. In the lower right, components link to multiple goals, requiring that each component perform several functions. And in the upper right of the diagram, both facets require integration. The chart in Figure 27 illustrates a common situation where elements in both facets vary in the degree of integration they require.

---

[75] See *Appendix 8*, page 352, for description of the project.

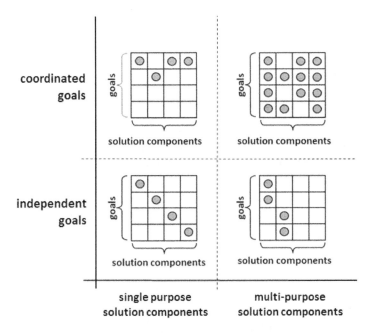

coordinated goals

independent goals

solution components

single purpose solution components

multi-purpose solution components

Figure 28: Degrees of Interdependence Between Two Facets

To illustrate strategies for project mapping, this chapter uses work done for the Milwaukee Water Pollution Abatement Program (WPAP), described in Chapter 16. The project combines the influences of a diverse group of stakeholders with technical, legal, business, and social challenges that evolved during the course of the program. The program mapping presented in this chapter was part of an overall strategic plan for the program called the Program Delivery Analysis or PDA. The PDA was required by Milwaukee Metropolitan Sewerage District to coordinate all aspects of the WPAP. The core of the PDA was a series of facet maps that built a bridge from stakeholders to resources.

Although this example is fundamentally an engineering problem, the interests of federal state and local authorities, the contractor, business and minority communities, as well as environmental advocacy groups had to be balanced. Many problems appear to have a technical core but ultimately require the management of legal, political, social, and economic factors. Such is the case with health care

153

initiatives, education reform, protection of the environment, and banking regulation, to name a few. Your challenge is to superimpose these mapping concepts onto the complex problems in your life, should you happen to have any.

Strategy #1: Map Project Goals

A grid that relates goals to stakeholders maps the process of goal setting. The WPAP had many stakeholders, including agencies at all levels of government, federal and state courts, and a broad spectrum of local advocacy groups. Identification and clarification of the goals of these groups was an ongoing effort throughout the project. In some cases, major engineering decisions determined whether a group had a significant interest in the project.

The following four-step process describes the development of a stakeholder/goals grid.

1. **Identify stakeholders:** With each stakeholder, it was essential to establish a clear point of communication so that the interests of the stakeholder could be consistently represented. In some cases, a stakeholder group had to be created by the program to represent a particular stakeholder interest.

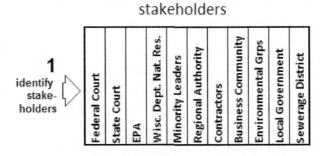

Figure 29: Identify Stakeholders

2. **Identify goals of stakeholders**: In order to develop a coherent set of goals for a project, the goals of individual stakeholders must be identified and, if possible, quantified.

154

It is important that goals be expressed in terms of the impact that a change in the world might have on the stakeholder, not in terms of solutions. If a goal can only be expressed in terms of a solution, it must be clearly identified as such. There may be ways to meet a stakeholder's goals that cannot be imagined at the outset. For example, some stakeholders on the WPAP felt that it was mandatory that the sanitary and storm sewers be separated. They had not considered the possibility that large storage tunnels could achieve their goal of avoiding treatment plant bypasses.

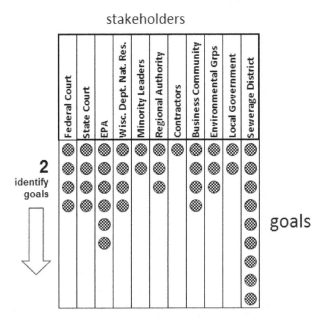

Figure 30: Identify Stakeholder Goals

3. **Integrate goals**: In order for goals to be useful in evaluating alternative solutions, we must resolve the differences among stakeholders with regard to individual goals. The grid in Figure 31 shows alignment of stakeholder goals and, on the right side of the grid, program goals that reflect resolution of stakeholder conflicts. At the detailed level, coordination and integration of WPAP goals requires iden-

tifying specific physical locations where engineering, business, and social interests intersect.

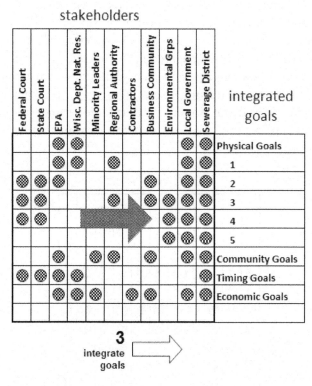

Figure 31: Integrate Stakeholder Goals

4. **Prioritize goals**: Finally, we need to sort out priorities among goals, such as the value to the community of using local contractors versus solutions that require technologies only available from out of state or even overseas. These opposing goals were major factors in at least one crucial engineering decision. Separating sewer lines in the streets would create many local construction jobs. Solving the storm water surge problem by digging deep tunnels for storage would require use of international contractors from Japan or Germany.

On any complex project, the test of a functional goals statement is whether it provides a yardstick for evaluating alternative solutions. We can then embark on a feasibility study to generate and assess alternative solutions and alternative ways of paying for them.

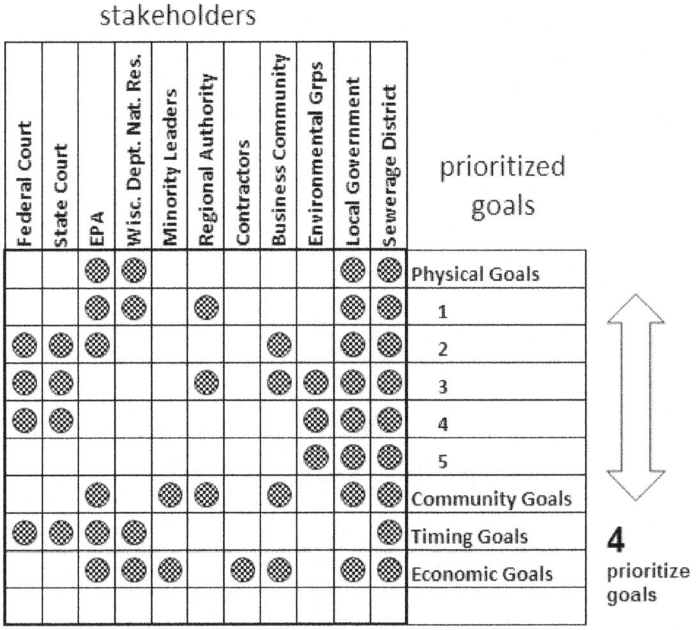

stakeholders

Federal Court	State Court	EPA	Wisc. Dept. Nat. Res.	Minority Leaders	Regional Authority	Contractors	Business Community	Environmental Grps	Local Government	Sewerage District	prioritized goals
		●	●						●	●	Physical Goals
		●	●		●				●	●	1
●	●	●					●		●	●	2
●	●				●		●	●	●	●	3
●	●						●	●	●		4
							●	●	●		5
		●		●	●		●		●	●	Community Goals
●	●	●	●							●	Timing Goals
		●	●	●		●	●		●	●	Economic Goals

prioritized goals

4 prioritize goals

Figure 32: Prioritize Project Goals

One factor determining the character of a problem is the degree of integration required when we are sorting out its goals. In some spheres, reconciliation of goals is at the heart of the problem. When there are multiple stakeholders with conflicting interests, a process must be established to reconcile these interests before a consistent statement of the problem can be developed. The value of mapping project goals is that it encourages consideration of the impact of each goal on each stakeholder.

At the outset of a project, the lists of goals and stakeholders will be incomplete. In some cases, new stakeholders will be brought into the project as a solution takes shape. For example, in the case of the WPAP, the option to install separate storm water pipes in city streets would result in considerable disruption of traffic and would require extensive coordination with existing utility rights-of-way.

Strategy #2: Create Planning/Evaluation Maps

It is typical in problems with multiple goals that we cannot solve the goals independently. Each goal will be addressed by multiple elements of the solution, and each element will address more than one goal. The example in Figure 27 is an evaluation map.

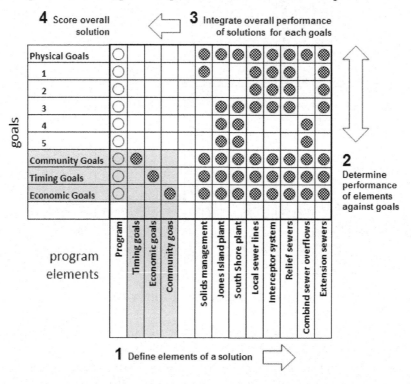

Figure 33: Program Planning and Evaluation

The map in Figure 33 shows the interaction of the goals and solutions facets of the WPAP. The following four-step process presents an idealized picture of the interaction between goals and solutions.

1. **Define elements of a solution**: At the early stages of the program, the WPAP was divided into eight major program

elements. These were defined by the two treatment plants, sewage collection lines and the problem of handling storm water overflows. Community timing and economic goals were directly affected by program elements. In addition, the shaded area of the map shows a shorthand method of linking the goals facet of the program to the activities and resources facets that are discussed below.

During the course of a complex project, definition of project elements is dynamic. The objective is to define project elements that bring together highly interacting parts of the problem so that the elements can be managed with relative independence. The elements shown Figure 33 were vast in scope with budgets in the $100 million to $500 million range. Managers of the WPAP felt that separate construction projects in the range of $25 million to $50 million should be defined. Our program mapping approach helped us to understand that the major program elements shown in this map were too highly interrelated to break up into smaller pieces that could be managed independently.

2. **Determine performance of elements against goals**: The feasibility of each program element is initially assessed against each program goal. Goals that prove to be unrealistic must be reevaluated. In some cases, new goals might be added. For example, installation of new sewer lines in streets might provide opportunities for improvement of neighborhood infrastructure – roads, power lines, and other utilities.

3. **Integrate overall performance of solutions for each goal**: For goals that are met by more than one program element, an integrated picture of program performance must be developed.

4. **Score overall solution**: An overall score for each alternative program solution is developed in order to select the best approach.

This map is an attempt to describe what we actually do as we evaluate alternative solutions to problems. It is idealized in the sense that there is seldom such a simple step-by-step evaluation process. Evaluation occurs continuously as we piece together alternative solutions. However, in the end, we either explicitly or implicitly execute these steps in order to draw conclusions about the best course of action.

Strategy #3: Map the Relationship Between Elements of a Solution and Program Activities

Definition of the WPAP activity facet moved through a progression from broad activity categories, as shown in Figure 34, to detailed project action plans as the program progressed. Initially, the primary concern is assessment of the feasibility of timing goals. As the design of program elements firmed up, the focus shifted to coordination among the activities of the several program areas.

program elements	Program	Timing goals	Economic goals	Community goas		Solids management	Jones Island plant	South Shore plant	Local sewer lines	Interceptor system	Relief sewers	Combind sewer overfl	Extension sewers
Conceptual design	◯	●	●	●		●	●	●	●	●	●	●	●
Design	◯	●	●	●		●	●	●	●	●	●	●	●
Specs/contracts	◯	●	●			●	●	●	●	●	●	●	●
EPA/DNR review	◯	●	●			●	●	●	●	●	●	●	●
Funding requests	◯	●	●			●	●	●	●	●	●	●	●
Contrator selection	◯	●	●			●	●	●	●	●	●	●	●
Contr. Mobiliztion	◯	●	●	●		●	●	●	●	●	●	●	●
Shop drawings	◯	●	●			●	●	●	●	●	●	●	●
Fabrication	◯	●	●			●	●	●	●	●	●	●	●
On-site construction	◯	●	●	●		●	●	●	●	●	●	●	●

activities   activity analysis

Figure 34: Interdependence of Actions

Throughout the program, the main challenge faced in the management of program activities was the need to maintain full operation of the Milwaukee sewage collection and treatment systems while they were undergoing renovation and replacement. The inertia of existing systems is a major challenge in many complex projects. This is true for physical infrastructure projects, such as the WPAP, major highway projects, and airports. It is also true in healthcare, education, and political systems that must maintain their operations while undergoing dramatic change.

Strategy #4: Map Resources

Even in the early stages of a complex project, resource constraints must be considered. The map in Figure 35 shows resource demands of program activities at an early stage of analysis.

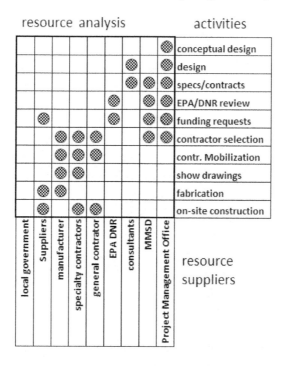

Figure 35: Interdependence of Resources

A fundamental question of resource feasibility regards the availability of resources at the time and in the quantity that the project demanded. In the case of the MMSD, both high-tech and low-tech solutions had their own resource issues. Use of deep tunnel drilling resources required coordination with other tunneling projects world-wide, since they were competing for limited tunneling equipment. Installation of new storm lines would require construction contractors beyond those available in the region, unless the work could be carefully scheduled across a period of years. Resource considerations impact preliminary activity analysis, design of program elements, and the feasibility of program goals.

Strategy #5: Recognize the Need to Shift Among Representations of the Problem

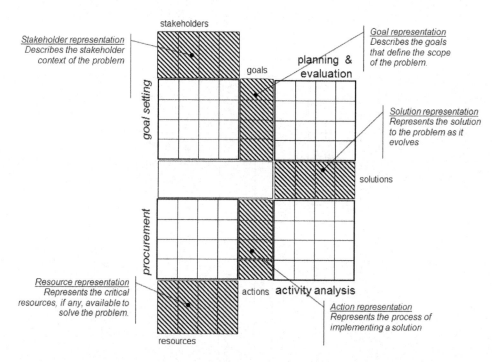

Figure 36: Multiple Representations of a Problem

As problems move through the several phases that connect the goals of stakeholders to the resources available to solve the problem, different systems interact. Figure 36 looks at the relationship among the five facets that map the terrain of complex projects. The grids in this diagram reflect the interactions among these representations discussed above.

Beyond the internal structure of problems, the process of solving them has its own interconnected elements. Just as we must explore the nooks and crannies of a problem's structure, we must also investigate the different phases of problem solving in search of challenges. Each stage calls on us to take on a different perspective, to frame the problem with different considerations in the foreground.

Integration of the four stages of solving complex problems requires looking forward from goals to solutions to actions and to resources in order to discover where hard parts of the problem are lurking. These discoveries can then feedback to test and inform the prior steps in the process.

Problems have a structure much like the turkey that we must learn to carve at the joints. Ignorance of the interconnections among the elements of a problem will dull your knife. Likewise, the process of problem solving has its own array of elements that vary widely in their degrees of interconnectedness.

PART V   *Principle #5: The Perfect is the Enemy of the Good*

When we are given problems in school, we seek the correct or perfect answers. Our performance is measured by test scores. But in life, the perfect is the enemy of the good. Chasing after the perfect solutions to life's problems can be a fool's errand. Problem solving in the real world is rife with compromise. Often we must integrate goals of several people into a single purpose. We must weigh the trade-off between risk and potential benefits. We must decide when continued investment of time and other resources in refining the solution to a problem is no longer worth the cost. We may learn, as we pursue a solution, that our goals are unrealistic or that we must stretch the boundaries of the problem to expand the realm of possibilities. Seeking perfect answers to life's questions can blind us to the possibilities for simple, even elegant, solutions. Chapter 18 makes the point that the boundaries of a problem are fluid, subject to redefinition as our understanding of the problem unfolds. Chapter 19 explores the nature and structure of goals. Chapter 20 presents strategies for seeking good rather than perfect solutions.

Chapter 18   The Scope of Problems

The problems we have traditionally been given in school have perfect answers because they are perfectly defined. Problems of the real world are fluid. We are responsible for drawing the boundaries around them, but these boundaries are not rigid. As we go about solving a problem, we decide how much of the world to change and how widely to search for alternative solutions. Problems may emerge as symptoms of deeper problems. What may initially seem like an isolated problem may be so interconnected with other problems that we must solve them in aggregate. On the other hand, problems may be so complex that we must divide them into parts to be solved separately.

Once we have decided to attack a problem, we form an initial notion of its boundaries. This initial definition of scope may evolve as we explore the problem. For example, the purchase of shoes may be the final step in solving a problem that started with a sore heel. The initial scope of the problem was defined by the symptom, the heel pain. The ultimate scope of a problem is affected by the path taken toward a solution. Do I view the sore heel as a medical problem or an equipment problem? Should I buy a shoe stretcher to make my current shoes longer? Should I take my current shoes to a shoemaker to have them modified?

Problem Versus Context

The scope of a problem defines the boundary between the problem and its context. The more narrowly defined the context, the fewer moving parts are within the problem, but the narrower the range of solutions. Consider a person's job search. The search may be restricted to those possibilities that would not require a move to a new house or a new city. This individual is a passionate shark surgeon and is not happy in her current position at a dog shelter in Cleveland. If the search is narrowly confined to jobs in the Cleveland area, it is less complex than a nationwide search. The problem of finding a new house, a job for the spouse, and schools for the kids would not be part of the problem. We could say that the local search is relatively simple. However, simple does not mean easy. There may be few opportunities for a shark surgeon in the greater Cleveland area.

Broadening the scope of the problem to include Miami and San Diego will open up many more job opportunities but will now bring housing, spousal employment, and lifestyle into the problem. The problem is now more complex, but the number of potential solutions has increased.

This example suggests a process where we start with a narrowly defined scope, searching for solutions within a small landscape. If we fail to find solutions for the problem as narrowly defined, we broaden the scope, giving access to more solutions but also giving rise to related problems. Sometimes the definition of problem scope is treated as a *phase* of problem solving, as if, once completed, one can move on to the next phase without turning back. This example suggests that the problem solver must always be open to reconsideration of scope.

Redefining the Problem

The context of a problem defines a fixed structure within which a range of solutions is possible. Sometimes, however, in the course of generating and evaluating alternative solutions, we think of sensible avenues for redefinition of the context, moving toward a happier ensemble of context and solution.

In 1966, Buckminster Fuller was commissioned to design a tower in Japan taller than Mount Fuji. The top of Mount Fuji is at 12,388 feet above sea level. The base of the mountain is at sea level. Fuller designed a tripod structure 4,000 meters high – 200 meters higher than the summit of Mount Fuji – for the Yomiuri Corporation, which was to have featured a pressurized observation capsule 30 stories tall providing a 360-degree view of all the Japanese Islands. Apartment *complexes built around each leg of the tripod would have been taller than the Eiffel Tower. Costed at US $1.5 billion in 1966, the project technically remains on hold to this day but has in effect been abandoned.*[76]

Fuller asked for engineering help on this project from the firm of Geometrics, Inc. in Cambridge, Massachusetts. At the time, I was in design school and had developed a liking for the offbeat thrust of this firm's design practice. The story, as told to me at the time by Bill Wainwright of that firm, was that their feasibility analysis had indicated that it would be more cost-effective to build a tower 2,500 meters high and remove the top 1,500 meters of Mount Fuji.

A more down to earth example was discussed in Chapter 13. The problem of building a plant to process cheese whey was defined as having two major components: a plant to extract protein from the whey and a plant to convert the waste stream from the first plant into methane. During the course of analyzing the project as an investment, our firm looked at building only the first component, the protein plant. This redefinition of scope reduced the cost by 50 percent while retaining 80 percent of the income.

Disaggregation

The world, taken as a whole, is a complex place. We humans are blessed with the capacity to focus on relatively small parts of the whole. George Miller, founder of the Center for Cognitive Development at Harvard, pointed out in the 1950s that we are able to handle only seven, plus or minus two, things in our short-term memory at one time.[77] We use concepts such as bicycle and building to separate out and process parts of the world. Pattern recognition is our

---

[76] Martin Pawley, *Terminal Architecture* (London, Reaktion Books Ltd, 1998) p. 213.

[77] George Miller, "The Magical Number Seven, Plus or Minus Two: Some Limits on Our Capacity for Processing Information." Originally published in *The Psychological Review*, 1956, Vol 63, pp. 81-97.

strength. However, the problems that we face often entail interconnections among several or many of the entities that we perceive.

Simpler problems are typically easier to solve than more complex ones. When we consider the universe of problems, we can arrange them along a complexity scale that measures the number of issues being confronted and the number of interrelationships among the issues. When we contemplate a set of issues as a problem, they probably have some form of cohesion; otherwise, we would already be considering it as independent problems to be solved individually.

There are several reasons to break problems into parts:

- The problem is actually a set of independent problems that can be attacked one at a time.

- A problem can have cost-effective solutions when considered as a whole, but when subdivided into parts, some parts are cost-effective and others are not. The parts that work should not carry the parts that do not.

- Parts of a problem can be solved on paper independently, but implementation requires a high degree of coordination.

- The requirements of a problem are too complex to be contemplated all at once by the human mind. The problem must be decomposed into parts, solved piecemeal, and reintegrated.

Innovative Problem Solving Under Fixed Price Contracts

The scope of a problem should be subject to redefinition as information develops during problem solving. This can be a particular challenge when innovative projects are being carried out under fixed price contracts. It was common in our simulation business to work under fixed price contracts. This required defining the scope of the work to be carried out under the contract before the problem had been fully explored. There were two strategies for dealing with this conundrum. First, at our own expense, we would invest considerable time in exploring a problem before the contract was written. Second, during the course of the project, informal scope redefinition would occur as a form of horse-trading between our team and the customer. Both of these strategies required trust on both sides of the contract.

This trust was built up as we worked with clients over a period of years.

The boundaries of a problem are fluid. They should be subject to refinement as our understanding of the problem, its constraints, and the range of possible solutions unfolds.

Chapter 19   Goals

Goals are the yardsticks that we use to measure the value of alternative solutions. In essence, goals define the problem. Yet as we explore problems, we must be open to reevaluating our goals in light of what we learn or even incorporating new goals as opportunities are discovered.

If we accept initially stated goals as sacrosanct, as definers of the perfect, we give up the possibility of learning what the real problem is all about. This was well captured by Dewey in his treatise, *Education and Democracy*.

> *We have spoken as if aims could be completely formed prior to the attempt to realize them. This impression must now be qualified. The aim as it first emerges is a mere tentative sketch. The act of striving to realize it tests its worth. If it suffices to direct activity successfully, nothing more is required, since its whole function is to set a mark in advance; and at times a mere hint may suffice. But usually—at least in complicated situations—acting upon it brings to light conditions which had been overlooked. This calls for revision of the original aim; it has to be added to and subtracted from. An aim must, then, be flexible; it must be capable of alteration to meet circumstances.*[78]

Problem solving often addresses the interests of more than one stakeholder. In order to evaluate alternative solutions, the problem

---

[78] John Dewey, *Democracy and Education, an Introduction to the Philosophy of Education*, Macmillan Company, 1916. Republished as an e-document by the Penn State Electronic Classics Series. p. 109.

solver must integrate the goals of different parties into a coherent evaluation tool.

Goals must not only measure the change that we want in the world, but also what we are willing to give up for it. Furthermore, we must consider the urgency of the problem. If a tidal wave is crashing into our seaside community - no time for planning. The pope will be visiting San Marino on June 19 of next year. Street repairs had best be completed by that date. The cost and timing of the changes we make create a triangle of goals with the sought after changes themselves.

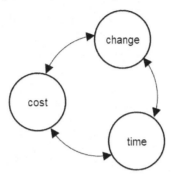

Figure 37: Interaction Among Goals

Last is the consideration of risk. As we consider alternative solutions to a problem, not only should we evaluate the predicted results, their costs, and the schedule of their implementation, but also the reliability of these predictions. One course of action may score very high on its expected results but carry significant risk in one area or another. In order to choose among alternatives, we must be able to weigh our tolerance for risk.

Maslow

All goals start with the personal drives of individuals. The goals of groups are synthesized out of these individual goals. One of the first psychologists to study normal human behavior was Abraham Maslow. Until Maslow, psychologists focused largely on the behavior of animals or the abnormal behavior of humans. Maslow sought to understand the motivation of humans. In the conclusion of his seminal work on motivation, Maslow summarizes his theory as follows:[79]

There are at least five sets of goals, which we may call basic needs. These are briefly physiological, safety, love, self-esteem, and self-actualization. In addition, we are motivated by the desire to achieve or maintain the various conditions upon which these basic satisfactions rest and by certain more intellectual desires.

These basic goals are related to each other, being arranged in a hierarchy of prepotency. This means that the most prepotent goal will monopolize consciousness and will tend of itself to organize the recruitment of the various capacities of the organism. The less prepotent needs are minimized, even forgotten or denied. But when a need is fairly well satisfied, the next prepotent ('higher') need emerges, in turn to dominate the conscious life and to serve as the center of organization of behavior, since gratified needs are not active motivators.

Thus man is a perpetually wanting animal. Ordinarily the satisfaction of these wants is not altogether mutually exclusive, but only tends to be. The average member of our society is most often partially satisfied and partially unsatisfied in all of his wants. The hierarchy principle is usually empirically observed in terms of increasing percentages of non-satisfaction as we go up the hierarchy.

Note that Maslow uses the concepts of goals, needs, wants, and motivation more or less interchangeably. I will be using the term goals to capture all of the factors that we use to evaluate alternative solutions.

Risk and Uncertainty Thwart Perfection

In the real world, risk and uncertainty abound. The weather alone is enough to undo well-laid plans. Prediction, the linchpin of our ability to solve problems, is subject to imperfection.

As problem solvers, we must be aware of our natural tendency toward risk aversion. When we perceive a situation as risky, research

---

[79] A.H. Maslow, "A Theory of Human Motivation," originally published in *Psychological Review*, 50, pp. 370-396, 1943.

has shown that we undervalue its outcome. For example, the St. Petersburg Paradox[80] asks what you would pay up front for the following deal: a coin is tossed multiple times until it comes up heads. If it is heads on the first toss, you get one dollar and the game ends. If it comes up tails, it is tossed again. If it comes up heads the second time, you get two dollars, and the game ends. If not, it is tossed again. A heads on the third toss pays out four dollars. On the fourth toss, a heads pays out eight dollars. And so on. With each additional toss required to get to a heads, the payoff doubles.

In assessing how much this deal is worth, we have to multiply the probability of each potential outcome times the payoff that would result. The probability of the game ending after one toss is one-half. With a payoff of one dollar, the value of this outcome is fifty cents. The sum of all of the possible outcomes is $\frac{1}{2}$ x \$1.00 + $\frac{1}{4}$ x \$2.00 + $1/8$ x \$4.00 + $1/16$ x \$8.00 and so on to infinity. By rational calculation, the objective value of this proposition is infinite. However, when people are asked what they would pay for this deal, they commonly say five to ten dollars. We are risk averse.

There can be no objectively best solution to problems that entail substantial risk, since assessment of alternative courses of action is clouded by the subjectivity of risk aversion. This brings us to a discussion of rationality itself.

Rationality

Much of the history of the discussion of goals has presumed that humans are rational in their decision making. Recent work has cast doubt over this presumption. (I have often thought that the function of the rational mind is to conjure up reasons for what we *feel like doing* - to rationalize our instincts.) Kahneman and Tversky have pioneered work on the relationship between how we frame a choice and the decisions that we make.[81] They have shown that the value we place

---

[80] The St. Petersburg Paradox was published by Daniel Bernoulli in *Commentaries of the Imperial Academy of Science of Saint Petersburg* in 1738.

[81] Amos Tversky and Daniel Kahneman, "Rational Choice and the Framing of Decisions," in *Choices, Values and Frames*, edited by Kahneman and Tversky (Cambridge, UK; Cambridge University Press, 2000).

on certain alternative courses of action can be manipulated by how the problem is *framed*.

They give the following example to illustrate.[82]

> Problem 1: Imagine that the US is preparing for the outbreak of an unusual disease, which is predicted to kill six hundred people. Two alternative programs to combat the disease have been proposed. The scientific estimates of the consequences of the programs are as follows:
>
> If Program A is adopted, two hundred people will be saved. If Program B is adopted, there is one-third probability that six hundred people will be saved, and two-thirds probability that no people will be saved.
>
> Which of the two programs would you favor?

In Problem 1, 72 percent of 152 test subjects chose Program A. Twenty-eight percent chose Program B. The majority choice in this problem is risk averse: the prospect of certainly saving 200 lives is more attractive than a risky prospect of equal expected value, that is, a one-in-three chance of saving six hundred lives.

A second group of respondents was given the cover story of Problem 1 with a different formulation of the alternative programs, as follows:

> Problem 2: If Program C is adopted, four hundred people will die. If Program D is adopted there is one-third probability that nobody will die, and two-thirds probability that six hundred people will die.
>
> Which of the two programs would you favor?

---

[82]Amos Tversky and Daniel Kahneman, "The Framing of Decisions and the Psychology of Choice," *Science*, Vol 211, January 1981, pp. 453-458.

In Problem 2, 22 percent of subjects chose Program C and 78 percent chose Program D.

The majority choice in Problem 2 is risk taking: the certain death of four hundred people is less acceptable than the two-in-three chance that six hundred will die. The preferences in Problems 1 and 2 illustrate a common pattern: choices involving gains are often risk averse and choices involving losses are often risk taking. However, the two problems are identical. The only difference between them is that the outcomes are described in Problem 1 by the number of lives saved and in Problem 2 by the number of lives lost.

Secondary Goals

Hippocrates is often quoted as imploring doctors to *do no harm*. Problems have a set of primary goals, the ways in which we would like the world to be better. However, we must be concerned that in the course of solving a problem, there might be harmful side effects that detract from our achievement. We seek to minimize collateral damage, to the extent that we can foresee it. On the positive side, problem solving may also offer opportunities for collateral benefits.

Redefinition of Goals

During the course of problem solving, we will encounter opportunities and roadblocks that should trigger reconsideration of goals. The problem solver should be open to this. It happens, particularly with quantitative goals, that a specific level of performance becomes rigidly specified. Once a quantitative goal is set, its correctness may take root unjustifiably. When we select from among alternatives to meet a particular goal, we tend to cast aside the negative attributes of the selected alternative, while remembering *only* the negatives of the rejected alternatives.[83] The vitality of a problem solving effort may rely on a dynamic reconsideration of goals, as possibilities and roadblocks are uncovered during exploration of the problem.

---

[83] See discussion of confirmation bias on page 36.

In order to be effective problem solvers, we must recognize the fluid nature of goals. We must be able to state goals as clearly as we can at the outset while retaining the flexibility to reshape them as we explore the problem, discovering new possibilities.

Chapter 20   The Perfect is the Enemy of the Good

In school, we are led to believe that problems have objectively correct or perfect answers, but this is seldom the case in the real world. Problems require a balancing act that contends with competing goals, the weighing of costs and benefits, and recognizing when a solution is good enough. Simon coined the term *satisficing*[84] to capture the notion that problem solving efforts may reach a point of diminishing returns. As is said in politics, the perfect can be the enemy of the good.

PROBLEM SOLVING PRINCIPLE #5:
   SEEK GOOD ANSWERS NOT PERFECT ANSWERS

Strategy #1: Develop a Clear Statement of Goals

When problem solving efforts involve multiple participants, a clear and agreed upon statement of goals is essential. Alternative solutions should be evaluated against a known set of goals not the private objectives of each participant. Disagreements about goals should be resolved through goals integration not by generating solutions that pursue private agendas.[85]

Often the goals of more than one person or organization must be resolved into a single course of action. This is certainly the case with legislative bodies that represent many interests. Goals may conflict directly, where the change desired by one party is not desired by another. For example, one group wants to erect a monument to a

---

[84]Herbert A. Simon, "Rational Choice and the Structure of the Environment," *Psychological Review*, March 1956; Vol 63 No 2, pp. 129-138.

[85]See discussion of *Problem Seeking* on page 142.

religious leader in the town square. Another group objects to the use of public property for religious purposes.

A model for the process of goal setting is given in Chapter 17. It lays out four steps in developing a set of integrated goals:

- Identify stakeholders
- Analyze stakeholder goals
- Integrate goals across stakeholders
- Prioritize goals

Goals may conflict indirectly in that the meeting of the goal of one party has side effects that bother another party. Such has been the case with the erection of wind farms off the coast of Cape Cod. The wind energy company is not putting the wind machines up to enjoy looking at them. The wind farm seascape is a side effect of meeting the goal of producing energy from the winds off the Cape. Residents of the coastline may value their uncluttered view of the seascape more highly than the development of alternative energy sources.

A more subtle form of goal integration is required when parties agree on certain goals but not on their importance. For example, when they must make decisions on the allocation of limited resources, compromises are required. Goals must be prioritized.

We can certainly imagine problems with one stakeholder and one goal. The grid collapses to a single cell, and the prioritized goals reduce to a single goal. Furthermore, there are problems that have many stakeholders, each with a rich set of goals that bear on the problem, where no cohesive statement of goals occurs or is appropriate. Consider for a moment the election process. The direct stakeholders are the electorate. There may be many others affected by the election who may try to influence the electorate. For the stakeholders to evaluate the alternative candidates, they explicitly or implicitly determine what is important to them individually. They use their individual goals to evaluate alternative candidates. There is no need for a cohesive statement of goals for the electorate as a whole because candidates are not being evaluated by the electorate as a whole. They are being evaluated by individual voters. In political elections, it is common to hear of single issue voters, who only consider one goal. Others may have several important goals that they must weigh in order to evaluate candidates. The collective prioritization of the goals of all stakeholders happens through the election mechanism.

We can imagine this process in the development of a community park. There could be two or three schematic designs put before the community for a vote. In this way, there is no need to express a single coherent set of goals at the outset. This approach has the appeal of achieving integration of community goals in the context of actual proposed solutions rather than as an abstract calculus of values.

Strategy #2: Understand the Nature of Goals and Be Ready to Compromise

Goals vary in their degree of elasticity. An elastic goal can be partially satisfied. If our goal is to be on time for a dinner appointment, being a little late largely meets the goal. The goal of being on time for departure of a flight is inelastic. Being a little late is of no value.

Acoustical separation between hotel rooms is an elastic goal. As hotel clients, we might claim to require complete isolation from noises coming from the next room. Acoustical separation is measured in decibel drop between spaces and is *never* absolute. In a more reflective moment, we might agree that hearing an actual gun shot from the next room would be acceptable, but hearing it from a television in the next room would not be, if the TV is operated at a reasonable volume. The cost of achieving incremental increases in acoustical separation is a curve of ever-increasing slope. These increases, on the other hand, have diminishing returns.

Many of our goals have this property of elasticity. That is, the level of quality that makes sense will depend on the cost curve. As achieving higher levels of quality becomes less expensive, we move in the direction of higher quality. Other goals are inelastic. Such is the case with building facilities for the Olympics. There is some value in early completion, in that it gives the planners peace of mind. The value of late completion, at least as far as the Olympics is concerned, is nil.

Figure 38 illustrates elasticity on the left, where incremental improvements in performance result in incremental increases in benefit. On the right, inelasticity reflects that performance below a certain level is of no value, and above that level is of no increased value.

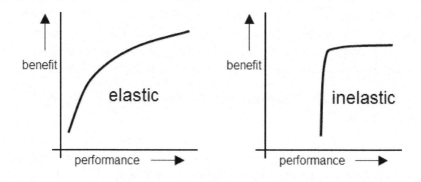

Figure 38: Elastic v. Inelastic Goals

Problems inevitably entail multiple goals. They may be initiated by one driving goal, for example, getting a better job. But other goals, such as the quality of local schools, are brought into the picture as alternatives are considered.

Few goals are completely inelastic, although they may be expressed as such. For example, building codes regulate construction to achieve fire safety. Having safe buildings would seem to be an absolute. Fire codes express elaborate rules that dictate how one can and cannot build buildings. From the standpoint of the building designer, building codes state inelastic goals that must be achieved. However, from the standpoint of the writers of the building code, the rules express a compromise between life safety and practicality. The materials that make up the floors and walls of buildings are rated in terms of how long they can contain a fire. The code contemplates the amount of time it will take for people to escape buildings of certain configurations and dictates construction types that will assure survival. The code addresses the geometry of escape routes and the numbers of people that will compete for them. The code could dictate higher standards but it has been judged that the increased costs of implementing them would not be justified by the marginal improvement in life safety.

At the outset of problem solving, we may attempt to set levels of goal achievement that we deem acceptable, but we must consider these to be tentative. We cannot know at the outset the extent to which pairs of goals are complementary or competing until we begin to generate solutions.

In committing to fixed goals before exploring a problem, we may also be guilty of setting the bar too low. There may be solutions that we had not imagined that exceed the standards that we contemplated in the abstract.

This perspective dictates that we find ways to retain flexibility in our targets. This may not be easy when procedures such as competitive bidding organize the problem solving process into discrete phases. For example, construction contracts usually require a fixed price bid, although uncertainties may remain until construction is actually underway. Uncertain parts of the work can be covered by allowances, permitting the contractor to charge for any excess over the stated allowance.

Strategy #3: Satisficing

A solution to a problem is feasible when its benefits outweigh its costs. To invest in the problem solving process, we must have an explicit or implicit sense that a feasible solution exists. As we move through the problem solving process, we should weigh the marginal utility of additional refinement of our solution.

In 1956, Herbert Simon coined the term *satisficing* to capture the notion that we do not seek perfect solutions to problems, but rather we seek satisfactory solutions. Since then, the notion of *bounded rationality* has largely replaced the model of man as a rational being. Simon's idea was that humans are limited in their ability to solve complex problems. They are limited in the time available to devote to the problem, they are limited in the information at their disposal, and they are limited in their cognitive tools. As a result, humans should be considered *satisficers*, seekers of satisfactory solutions rather than optimal ones. This view replaces the assumption underlying classical economic theory that people make optimal choices to maximize their benefit.

As problem solvers, what are we to learn from this awakening of economic theorists to the bounds of human reasoning? The principal lesson is that problem solving in the real world is an uncertain enterprise. We usually cannot know what the best solution might be. As we generate and develop alternatives, we can choose the best among them, but what other solutions lay beyond our view? How can we know what improvements may be yielded by an additional investment of time? We must find a balance between the persistent exploration of alternatives on the one hand and the awareness of the law of diminishing returns on the other. However, being conscious of our limitations should not lead to satisfaction with our first idea that passes the test of being *not wrong*.

Awareness of the limitations of our time and capabilities can help shape the way that we attack a problem. Effective exploration requires that we move quickly from place to place within a problem, generating alternative subproblem solutions without stalling into cul-de-sacs of over refinement.

We can apply Simon's idea of satisficing across the stages of problem solving, defined in Part IV. From the moment we declare that a problem exists, we should raise questions of feasibility. In the real world, there can be doubt. There are four feasibility stages that each problem must pass through:

- Integration of goals: Will the interested parties be able to resolve conflicting goals?

- Integration of solution: Can we find a solution where the parts fit together to meet the goals of the problem?

- Integration of action: Can the process of problem solving meet the time constraints of the problem?

- Resolution of resource conflicts: Can resources be made available to carry out the project?

Strategy #4: Be Ready to Redefine the Scope of a Problem

We can become so caught up in trying to solve a problem that we do not consider that its boundaries may be poorly drawn. As we invest in the development of a solution, our framing of the problem takes root, and it becomes increasingly difficult to modify.

Sometimes innovation is not possible on a small scale. A critical mass is required to support development of new technologies. An apt example is provided by a new way of building schools developed in California in the mid-twentieth century.

At the end of the nineteenth century, school classrooms were typically twenty by twenty feet. This was a convenient span for wood frame construction. By the 1950s classroom dimensions had grown to the thirty by thirty foot range, enabled by light steel and reinforced concrete construction. Classrooms of this size were symbiotic with an educational model of twenty to thirty students per classroom. It is hard to say whether the conventional model of a classroom was driven by the construction technology or the educational model of one teacher with twenty-five students.

In the 1950s, different theories of education were emerging. Notions of teachers working with small groups or lecturing to large groups were in conflict with the egg crate model of classroom design. In California, there was an explosion of school construction. This would be fertile ground for parallel development of new construction technologies and new teaching philosophies.

Ezra Ehrenkrantz was a young architect who had studied the development of industrialized building systems for schools in England after World War II. The Ministry of Education realized that the national demand for large numbers of quality school buildings could not be met by each local authority experimenting and trying to develop its own programs.[86]

Centralized action by the Ministry of Education led to significant innovation in school construction. When Ehrenkrantz returned to the

---

[86] Andy Thompson, *From Butler to Blunkett and Beyond, School Building in England and the Role of the A&B Branch.* Web publication at: http://www.oecd.org/dataoecd/41/42/2675804.pdf.

United States, the school building boom in California offered the potential to apply what he had learned in England. With the help of the Ford Foundation's Educational Facilities Laboratory, the School Construction System Development (SCSD) project was born.[87] Ehrenkrantz and his team convinced twelve California school districts to join together to buy school buildings as a single entity. This created a project of sufficient size to attract companies like Inland Steel to participate in the development of innovative building technologies. The specifications called for seventy-foot structural spans and flexible partitions. This would give educators the flexibility they needed to pursue a wide range of educational models. The specification also called for air conditioning, lighting, and electrical systems to be integrated with the structural and partition systems. These systems were to function as a kit of parts that would allow the architects for each school to develop a unique design that would fit the conditions of the building site and the needs of the school. Thirteen schools were built under the program.

The SCSD project was only possible by rethinking the boundaries that define the scope of typical building projects. Ehrenkrantz was able to translate an approach made possible by the urgency of construction after World War II into a collaborative effect not seen before in the United States. (See discussion on page 213.)

Strategy #5: Sensitivity Analysis

Sensitivity analysis determines the aspects of a problem that are critical to the quality of a solution. Determining the critical factors of a problem can dramatically simplify the search for good solutions.

Sensitivity analysis is an essential tool in development of computer simulation models. The purpose of a computer simulation is to explore the behavior of a system under hypothetical future scenarios. Factors that are critical to performance of the system define the landscape of scenarios to be evaluated. For example, in a supply chain model, there are hundreds of potential factors that can be studied, including distribution locations, transport options, reordering param-

---

[87] The history of the SCSD project is well documented in *SCSD: The Project and the School, a Report from the Educational Facilities Laboratory.* (New York, 1967).

eters, and supply interruptions. Sensitivity analysis is a process of testing each potentially critical factor to determine the extent of its effect on system performance. Since a landscape of potential scenarios is defined by the combinations of values of each factor, it is imperative to reduce the number of factors to a handful. For instance, if there were six factors with ten values each, one million scenarios would have to be tested.

In the search for alternative solutions, deciding what factors to explore is not unique to computer simulation. The way we frame problems points us to the variables we should manipulate. However, in computer simulation, the determination of critical variables is consciously exposed.

As problem solvers, a degree of humility will serve us well. The problems we face in work or in life are too complex, too ill-defined to yield to perfect answers. Good answers will do just fine.

PART VI   *Principle #6: Manage the Planning Fallacy*

In life, we learn that things take longer than expected, cost more than budgeted, and often fall short in delivering the benefits that we had hoped for. These realities were dubbed *the planning fallacy* by Daniel Kahneman and Amos Tversky in 1979. The more complex the project, the more that predictions of cost, time, and quality appear to be the result of wishful thinking. Chapter 21 takes a brief look at planning to set the scene for the discussion in Chapter 22 of why things go so wrong and what we can do about it.

Chapter 21   Planning and Procurement

Planning divides the work of problem solving into manageable tasks, defines the work to be accomplished by each task, and maps out task relationships. Procurement gets the resources required by each task. Together, planning and procurement make up the management of the problem solving process. In spite of our best efforts, reality seldom conforms to our best-laid plans. In this chapter, we will review the elements of planning and procurement as if rigorous project management will guarantee success. In Chapter 22, we will discuss why things can go so wrong in spite of our best efforts and what steps we can take to avert disaster.

The diagram in Figure 39 depicts a market-like representation of problem solving, much like we saw before in Chapter 17. Goals are the expression of demand that connects stakeholders to solutions. Actions are the expression of supply that connects resources to solutions.

Consider the problem of buying a house. We like the area we live in. We like the schools and parks. The location is convenient for work and shopping, but we have outgrown our current house and our income will support something better. Having decided that our current house is not meeting our needs, we have three broad options: renovate, buy an existing house, or build a new house. Each of these courses of action raises questions of feasibility. Can we modify our current house in a way that would meet our needs? If so, how would we manage the logistics of living on a construction site? However, renovating our current house would solve the location problem. Shopping for an existing house carries the lowest risk and the least logistical hassle if we can find the house we want. If we are to build a new house, where are lots available? How long would it take? What are the risks? Do we have the time to work with an architect and a builder to get the house that we really want?

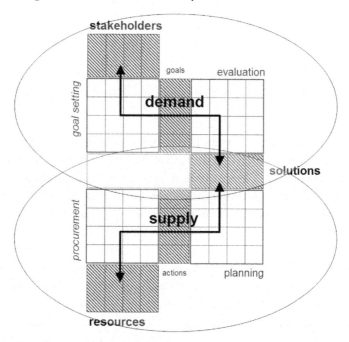

Figure 39: Market Model of Problem Solving

Beyond these obvious distinctions, our choice of approach determines the focus of the problem solving process. When we shop for a house, we have to provide a minimum of guidance to the real estate agent – number of bedrooms, location preference, and some notion of the feel of the house. If we are too specific, we may eliminate some interesting possibilities. As we go out and look at the houses that are available, we learn what our priorities are. This is a type of problem exploration. Members of the family do not have to agree on a cohesive set of goals; they can evaluate each house individually. Potential solutions to the problem can stimulate soul searching about what is really important. Seeing actual houses may be eye-opening. We may see room arrangements, views, use of outdoor space, or other design features that we would never have considered on our own. These considerations may outweigh the need for an exact fit between the characteristics of a house and our checklist of requirements.

If we chose to design a new house, we would have to come to agreement on requirements as abstractions. Although a designer might be able to coax us into incorporating one or another of her favorite features, we are still forced to think through what we really want in advance of seeing it realized. The hard part of designing and building a new house is making decisions about requirements in the abstract. This presumes a competent designer who can understand our goals and translate them into a design.

The renovation alternative is an act of imagination. We must be able to visualize what the current house could be. This is at once a technical problem and a needs problem. In renovation, there is a set of technical possibilities – going up, going out, giving up the garage, finishing off the basement – that must be assessed for feasibility. The technical possibilities then give rise to usage possibilities. As with looking at a new house, each potential solution triggers consideration of goals.

Framework for Assessing Planning and Procurement Alternatives

In Figure 40, the *alternative solution* axis refers to one alternative solution under consideration. The chart represents an alternative solution as a set of elements. During the course of solving a problem, alternative solutions are represented with increasing specificity. Two forces shape alternative solutions; the goals that define the problem, and alternative processes for planning and procurement.

At each stage of shaping an alternative solution, there is a balancing of the goals of the problem against the feasibility of implementation. When the implementation of a problem is highly constrained, we shape it to take advantage of available resources. When problems are rich in implementation options, we can more carefully focus on meeting the goals of the stakeholders.

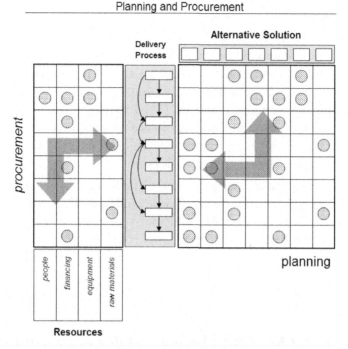

Figure 40: Interaction of Planning and Procurement

Christopher Alexander suggests that the structure of a problem emerges from its goals.[88] He suggests goals are the starting point of problem solving. In my view, problems often require substantial exploration to determine where the challenges and opportunities are to be found. Consider the challenge of designing a house in rural Wisconsin. We have some great ideas about siting the house to take advantage of view and terrain. We develop a schematic design and develop design details reflecting simple use of natural materials. Somewhere along the line, we discover that the few contractors willing to build in this area are in high demand. If they are willing to bid on the project at all, their prices are likely to be highly inflated.

---

[88] Alexander uses the term *requirements* rather than goals. His thesis that the structure of problems is determined by requirements is summarized in Chapter 9, pp. 116 – 131, *Notes on the Synthesis of Form*. (Cambridge: Harvard University Press, 1964).

We come across a family that has built a house in the area using factory built modules. As ghastly as this sounds, we visit the house and find it to be quite pleasant, with much the same scheme of materials that we had in mind. The total cost of their house was far lower than we were anticipating, given the contractor climate. To consider this option, we will have to rework the design of our house to fit the twelve-foot shipping constraint on factory built modules.

In this example, there is a strong interrelationship between the choice of technology – factory built modules – and certain key dimensions of the house. These factors constitute a subproblem that we should address early on in the design process. We should discover this issue and others like it through a process of problem exploration, before we make any decisions, even when they may seem compelling.

The above discussion gives us a rough model of planning and procurement. It may convey a sense that we should be the masters of the machinery of problem solving. However, the great challenge in planning and procurement arises from our focus on what we know. We harbor an idealized view of what will take place as we carry out our plans. The planning fallacy grows out of what we do not know – of the unanticipated wrenches that will be thrown into our well-oiled machinery. Managing the planning fallacy calls for us to engage strategies that recognize that things go wrong. Although we cannot focus on what we do not know, we can employ strategies that incorporate this reality.

Chapter 22   Getting Things Done

PROBLEM SOLVING PRINCIPLE #6:
MANAGE THE PLANNING FALLACY

The *planning fallacy* is the tendency of people to be overoptimistic about the completion time and potential benefits of a project. Daniel Kahneman and Amos Tversky proposed the term in a 1979 paper,[89] suggesting that people rely on their current optimistic vision of how events will transpire rather than rely on comparable past experience.

We underestimate the time it will take to complete tasks, and we overestimate the benefits that will accrue. This is true even when we undertake tasks where we have comparable experience. I know this to be true from personal experience. Throughout college, I had attributed my chronic *last-minuteness* to an admixture of procrastination and distractibility. There was always something more interesting to do than write a paper. In graduate school, a more intractable problem with time estimates came into sharp focus. First year of design school was like a boot camp. We were assigned a series of one or two week design projects, always due at midnight on Sundays. At the stroke of midnight, a faculty member cruised through the studio and collected the seldom-completed fruits of our efforts. The *charette*,[90] a last-minute intensive effort to complete a project, is a hallmark of archi-

---

[89] Daniel Kahneman and Amos Tversky, "Intuitive Prediction: Biases and Corrective Procedures." *TIMS Studies in Management Science 12*, pp. 313-327. June 1977.

[90] The term *charette*, meaning cart in French, originates in nineteenth century Paris. The work of architecture students was collected by a cart that was pulled through the student district in Paris. Students would ride on the cart in a desperate effort to finish their work. They were said to be *en charette*.

tectural design. I never learned to estimate directly the time it would take to produce the drawings for a project. I did learn that it always took at least twice as long as I felt it would take. I learned to multiply my intuitive estimate by two. With models, I used a factor of three. This practice has served me well to this day.

There are two basic strategies for combating the planning fallacy. The first is to set intermediate goals. The second is to look objectively at comparable projects done in the past, deriving a forecast from that experience.

Strategy #1: Set Intermediate Goals

For me, the ultimate in design *charette* was the architectural registration exams. In the 1970s the California test had seven separate exams to be taken over three days. The killers were the building design exam of twelve hours and the site-planning exam of five hours. By the time I got to the site-planning exam, I knew what had to be done. I decided that after one hour, my design concept must be complete. The remaining four hours would be dedicated to drawing the site plan. By hour one, my design was done. By hour four, I had completed the drawing of the buildings (a housing complex), the roadways, and the walkways. As I was contemplating how to spend the final hour, I noticed another exam taker still moving cardboard cutouts of buildings around on a sheet of paper. He was dead. During the last hour, I was embellishing. There is a technique called stippling, where, like a woodpecker, you make dots with the pencil to create shaded areas. Stippling makes an annoying noise, particularly in that it connotes to others the process of refinement of an already completed drawing.

Dan Ariely and Klaus Wertenbrock have studied the effectiveness of self-imposed deadlines in the battle against procrastination.[91] In a college course that required the writing of three papers, they compared the performance of two groups of students. For Group 1, they assigned deadlines for the papers spaced evenly through the semester. They allowed Group 2 to set their own deadlines for the papers. They had to decide on the deadlines during the first week of

---

[91] Dan Ariely and Klaus Wertenbrock, "Procrastination, Deadlines, and Performance," *Psychological Science.* Vol 13, No 3, May 2002; pp. 219-224.

the semester and could not change them. Grades on the papers were penalized for each day a paper was handed in late. Twenty-seven percent of the students in Group 2 set deadlines for all three of the papers at the end of the semester. Of course, these students could set their own personal deadlines however they chose. For example, if they felt that it would be wise to complete the papers early, they could do that and hand them in early. The majority of students in Group 2 spaced the deadlines out in roughly equal intervals, apparently feeling the need to be required to complete the first two papers earlier in the semester.

The authors compared the performance of the Group 1 students to the Group 2 *late completers* and the Group 2 *early completers*. They found that the closer a student was to having the required deadlines equally spaced, the better the performance on the work. Unsurprisingly, they also found that performance on a separate final project was affected by the deadlines. Students with all three deadlines at the end of the semester had an average grade of seventy-seven, compared to eighty-six, for the early completers.

Self-imposed deadlines can work for us if we establish clear consequence for not meeting them. For example, breaking a project up into phases with well-defined deliverables at the end of each phase can be effective, if the deadlines create a sense of urgency.

Strategy #2: Base Plans on Experience Not Projections

In an article appearing in the Harvard Business Review, Daniel Kahneman and Dan Lovallo suggest a process for overcoming chronically overoptimistic business forecasts.[92] They argue that companies should not want to remove the organizational pressures that promote optimism. Rather than trying to reign in the optimism of people directly involved in the activities being forecasted, they suggest that reliability can be improved by introducing a more formal forecasting process. They recommend a method known as reference-class forecasting:

---

[92] Dan Lovallo and Daniel Kahneman, "Delusions of Success: How Optimism Undermines Executives' Decisions," *Harvard Business Review*, Vol 81, No 7, July 2003.

It completely ignores the details of the project at hand, and it involves no attempt at forecasting the events that would influence the project's future course. Instead, it examines the experiences of a class of similar projects, lays out a rough distribution of outcomes for this reference class, and then positions the current project within that distribution.

A reference-class is a set of past projects with generally similar characteristics to the project at hand. A forecast is developed by placing the current project within the spectrum of completion times of the reference-class of projects. Lovallo and Kahneman call this taking the *outside view*. The forecasts that result from this approach are typically less optimistic than those generated from the *inside view* by people intimately familiar with the project.

Lovallo and Kahneman assert that most individuals and organizations would rather adopt the inside view, it being natural to focus on the project itself.

While understandable, managers' preference for the inside view over the outside view is unfortunate. When both forecasting methods are applied with equal intelligence and skill, the outside view is much more likely to yield a realistic estimate. That's because it bypasses cognitive and organizational biases. In the outside view, managers aren't required to weave scenarios, imagine events, or gauge their own levels of ability and control - so they can't get all those things wrong. And it doesn't matter if managers aren't good at assessing competitors' abilities and actions; the impact of those abilities and actions is already reflected in the outcomes of the earlier projects within the reference class. It's true that the outside view, being based on historical precedent, may fail to predict extreme outcomes - those that lie outside all historical precedents. But for most projects, the outside view will produce superior results.[93]

Strategy #3: Use Experience to Set Intermediate Goals

We can combine the reference-class approach and intermediate goals to achieve an effective problem solving strategy. For example, software development is renowned for late delivery. At SDI, we had

---

[93] Ibid, p. 7.

no magic formula for overcoming the unpredictability of project development time. However, for me there was always the pressing feeling that the project was running late from day one. This feeling was grounded in extensive experience in both software development and previous project work. In essence, I distilled the reference-class approach into a strategy of intermediate goal setting. This was not simply a matter of predicting how long a project would take but rather using past experience to drive a project to intermediate goals in its early stages.

When possible, I would do a substantial amount of development work during the period of courtship with the customer before we signed a contract. Although this was a gamble, it seemed more of a gamble to go into a software development contract without having completed a preliminary exploration. This early work would not only give us a head start on meeting our eventual deadlines, but it also would give us a better grasp of the scope of the work that had to be done. There is no substitute for the *feeling* that you are behind. This uncomfortable yet indispensable feeling results in reverse procrastination.

PART VII   *Principle #7: Employ Minimum Necessary Control*

In the world of work, customers and managers set the agenda; contractors and employees carry it out. This is not to say that the control of one person over another is total. In fact, a controlling entity might want to minimize the degree of control that it exercises in order to reduce unanticipated consequences. The science fiction writer Isaac Asimov captured this notion brilliantly in the novel *The End of Eternity*.[94] In his story, a group of Eternals who exist outside of time enter human history to make minimal changes to avert future disasters. They contrive to make the smallest changes possible in order to reduce or eliminate side effects.

In the world of families, parents want the best for their children but are constantly challenged to know how much control to exercise over their behavior, how involved to become in their lives. Fifty years ago, children in the United States were given considerable free time to play outside, learning to structure their own games, fend for themselves, and settle disputes. The ensuing generations of parents have taken a stronger hand in organizing the lives of the children. Sports teams, ballet lessons, and specialized camps have displaced free time. The merits of this evolution are worthy of debate.

Chapter 23 considers the range of control mechanisms from persuasion to brute force. Chapter 24 offers several strategies for seeking less control in order to minimize unintended consequences.

---

[94] Isaac Asimov, *The End of Eternity*. (New York. A Tor Book, 1955).

Chapter 23   Action and Control

Problem solving requires action. After all, we are changing the world, not just planning to change it. However, solving problems with direct physical action is the exception in most of our lives. More commonly, we achieve goals through interactions with others, both human and machine.

As with other components of the problem solving process, action does not necessarily maintain a fixed position within the problem solving process. Sometimes we may take the first steps in changing the world before we have fully decided where we are going. A classic example is *fast tracking* in construction. When completion of a building is under extreme time pressure, design and construction might overlap. Work on the foundations and structure of the building can begin before the design of other systems is completed.

Control

There are three broad reasons why we would want to cause others to act rather than take action ourselves. First, there is leverage. A group of people may be able to get more work done than an individual can. Second, others may be better qualified to do a task than we are; brain surgery comes to mind. Third, it may be the actions of others that we want to control. For example, local, state, and federal governments pass laws to improve driver safety. Parents attempt to control the behavior of their children.

We can sort the mechanisms of control into categories from carrot to stick.

- Persuasion: We can ask someone to help us out of kindness or because it is in their own best interest. Political campaigning comes to mind.

- Cultural norms: Much of our behavior is shaped by expectations by which culture guides our behavior.

- Incentives: We can create incentives, such as tax breaks, that reward the behavior that we are seeking.

- Contracts: We can enter into agreements where two parties exchange goods, services, or funds in a way that both parties benefit. Markets are a form of contract where goods and funds are exchanged.

- Employment: Employees agree to perform assignments within a broad job description in exchange for wages.

- Rules (policies): People and organizations may be in a position to control the behavior of those who fall under their influence. This is the relationship between schools and students, clubs and their members, retail establishments and their customers.

- Regulations: Regulations have the force of law but are normally written by administrative departments rather than legislatures. Regulations attempt to solve problems of health, safety, environmental quality, appropriate land use, and fairness.

- Laws: Governmental entities are empowered to pass laws to control the behavior of their citizens.

- Coercion: Slave owners, bullies, criminals, and armies can control their victims through physical force or the threat of physical force.

The Components of Control

Whatever the context, control is made up of four basic components, as shown in Figure 41. The household thermostat illustrates the interaction among these four components. First, the controller must have a goal. The goal of a thermostat is the temperature setting. In the simplest case, a human being sets a temperature, aligning a pointer with a desired temperature or toggling a digital set point. Second, the controller measures the state of the world in terms that it can compare to the goal. A thermometer within the thermostat continuously measures the ambient temperature. Third, the controller compares the measurement to the goal. In the language of control, the difference is called the *error*. Fourth, the controller sends a message to the system being controlled to make the state of the world more like the goal. This is achieved in thermostats in various clever ways, but the net result is a signal sent to a heating or cooling system that turns it on when the error is large and turns it off when the error is small.

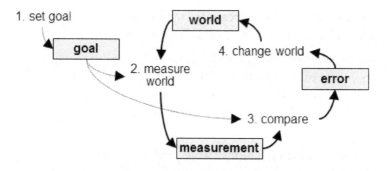

Figure 41: Components of Control

The goal may be as simple as the number on a speed limit sign or as complex as a contract for military hardware. The number on a speed limit sign is like the temperature setting on a thermostat. This is the goal set by the governmental unit responsible for the road. The speed of your car is the state of the real world that the governmental authority is trying to control. Unlike the thermostat, the controller is not measuring your speed continuously and sending you a signal when your error exceeds a certain limit. Rather, the authorities intermittently measure your speed with radar or other means. If they find sufficient error, you will receive a signal via squad car. Since you are more sophisticated than a furnace, you have internal control systems that are able to monitor your speed and shape it to conform to local regulations as you see fit.

Contracts play the same role as speed limit signs. The contract states the goal of the customer. The contractor is able to regulate its own activity to conform to the contract. The customer, like the local police, must be able to measure the actions of the contractor and compare them to the goals stated in the contract. This monitoring step may be done periodically during the course of contract execution or when the work is completed.

The Control Interface

In order to get someone else to do what we want her to do, communication is required. The controllee must know what to do and when to do it. In 1974, the US Congress passed the *Emergency Highway Energy Conservation Act*, setting a maximum national speed limit of fifty-five miles per hour. This was an attempt to reduce the problem of energy shortages in the early 1970s. The law induced state and local governments to change their speed limits. The control interface with drivers was the posting of new speed limit signs. Drivers learn through experience that certain latitudes can be taken with posted speed limits. On board radar detectors came into vogue. In this example, the communication between controller and controllee is a single number, easily understood by both.

The Agenda of the Controllee

Much of the problem solving we do is under the sway of other people. This does not mean that we entirely subjugate our own goals to those of others. When we are driving a car, we certainly share the goal of local and state authorities that we not get into an accident. However, we are willing to substitute our judgment for theirs as to what constitutes safe driving. In making our decisions as to, for example, speed, we have to integrate the goals implicit in the posted speed limit with our own goal of getting to point B in a timely fashion. Our passengers may even exert influence on us with regard to driving procedures.

At work, we have our own agenda. It may well be complementary to the directives of our supervisor or clients, but it may not be. For example, the question may arise, *how much is enough?*, when drafting a legal brief. All parties want a job well done. But incentives will affect behavior. For example, is the client paying by the hour? If so, the interest of the firm is that I do a thorough job, and profit will vary directly with the hours expended. The client, however, is concerned about exorbitant fees. In the circumstance where fees are based on the outcome of the work, incentives are quite different. The profits of the firm vary inversely with the hours expended. Of course, to get any income at, all there must be a successful outcome. In either case, I want to do a great job, but I also have two kids at home and a wife I haven't seen in a week. It is up to me, with some supervision, to integrate these influences and decide when enough is enough.

Chapter 24   Seek Minimum Necessary Control

It might seem to be against our nature to seek less rather than more control. To consider minimizing the control that we exercise is to recognize that we are not all-knowing. Humility will serve us well as we consider what actions to take.

PROBLEM SOLVING PRINCIPLE #7:
SEEK MINIMUM NECESSARY CONTROL

In order to reduce the probability of unwanted side effects, the effective problem solver gets things done with the least control that will achieve his objectives. Excessive control can lead to unanticipated consequences and unnecessary costs. This was the problem confronted by Isaac Asimov's Eternals. In the world that Asimov created, technicians had the ability to study the future to identify the *minimum necessary change* that would result in a desired modification in the course of events without substantial negative side effects. We mere mortals must rely on prediction to avoid these pitfalls.

Strategy #1: Exercise Control in Proportion to Need

Suppose we are hiring an individual to perform a task for us. There are many ways for us to specify what we want done. At minimum, both parties must clearly understand the statement of the work. It must provide a means of evaluating the quality of the work once it is done. The controller must realize that, although the controllee may be performing tasks to a certain extent under the controller's direction, the controllee has his own goals separate from those specified in the agreement between the parties. For example, if we hire a contractor to remodel our house, it is helpful to understand that he may have other projects in varying stages of completion. He is trying to balance out his workload in order to keep his employees and subcontractors continuously employed. If we needlessly constrain the project schedule in the construction contract, we will limit the number of contractors that are interested in bidding and will likely pay a surcharge that was unnecessary.

Communication is often the antidote to excessive or misdirected control. In the realm of government regulation, the regulator must have intimate knowledge of the operations being regulated in order to avoid unintended and unnecessary costs. The best sources of this knowledge are the people being regulated. Clearly one cannot *hand over* the writing of regulations to the regulated. The essential job of a regulator is to integrate the goals of regulation with real knowledge of the systems being regulated.

Strategy #2: Practice Benign Neglect

The term *benign neglect* was made famous by Daniel Patrick Moynihan, a US Senator from New York from 1977 to 2001. In spite of being a lifelong Democrat, Moynihan served as Richard Nixon's assistant to the president for urban affairs. Moynihan had taken a keen interest in immigration, ethnic diversity, and the state of the African-American family. During the late 1960s, Moynihan felt that the rhetoric of race relations had become so vitriolic that little progress on urban policy was possible. His call for a period of *benign neglect* was received with accusations of racism and indifference. Moynihan used the phrase in an internal memo to President Nixon as follows:

> *The time may have come when the issue of race could benefit from a period of "benign neglect." The subject has been too much talked about. The forum has been too much taken over to hysterics, paranoids, and boodlers on all sides. We may need a period in which Negro progress continues and racial rhetoric fades...*

Moynihan was espousing a strategy to let things develop on their own for a while – to observe but not to control.

As parents during the seventies and eighties, my wife and I were part of the trend toward managing our children's lives. But one incident comes to mind where I can claim to have sought minimum necessary control. I was returning from a business trip to upstate

Wisconsin one spring afternoon. My route took me past the high school where my son was a senior. Being an avid soccer fan, I decided to swing into the school to check out the soccer field to see if there might be a game. The entrance road was narrow and winding through a wooded area. As I approached the school, I saw that a group of people was standing near the road, looking toward a car that was stalled in the middle of a shallow stream. I slowed to survey the scene. There was my son Andrew pondering the situation. It was his car. I proceeded on to the parking lot and saw that, indeed, there was a soccer game underway. Concluding that there had been no injuries in the mishap, I walked over to the soccer field and took a seat in the lightly populated bleachers.

Some minutes after I arrived, my son's good friend Mark walked up and took a seat next to me. He expressed surprise that I was here. "Did you realize that Andrew had driven his car into the stream?" he asked. I said that I had noticed the car. I asked how they were going to get it out. Mark and Andrew had been returning from some important errand, and, according to Mark, Andrew might have been going a little too fast for the winding road. The car had just slipped off the road and slid sideways into the stream. During this conversation, I was doing my best to focus on the girls' soccer game. I told Mark that if they needed any advice, I would be here at the game.

After some time, the two boys returned to the soccer field. They had called a tow truck company but might have some difficulty paying for the service. I asked them to come back when it was time to pay the bill, and I would help.

For me, showing such restraint was a proud moment. I may have been aided by the sense that this incident was a good thing in the long run. With no injuries and no real harm to the car, my son had learned that he was not an invincible driver. There was certainly no way to blame the accident on someone else.

Strategy #3: Consider moving from Proscriptive to Performance Specifications

In the world of procurement, reducing the degree of control written into contracts has developed into an art. When we are not able to buy what we need *off the shelf*, we enter the world of contracts.

Even in small transactions, there must be an understanding of what goods or services the contractor will provide and what amounts the buyer will pay for them. The largest buyer of goods and services in the world is the US Department of Defense. For years, politicians have enjoyed taking cheap shots at the procurement frivolities of the defense department. Senator William Proxmire of Wisconsin originated the *Golden Fleece Award,* given annually to government programs that tested credulity. For example, in 1981, he gave the award to the Department of the Army for a study on how to buy Worcestershire sauce.

In spite of the impression given by such lampooning, the Department of Defense (DOD) takes the challenge of procurement very seriously. In 1993, *New Thinking and American Defense Technology*[95] called for *A Radical Reform of the Defense Acquisition System.*[96] A subsequent report of the US Army Materiel Command called for rethinking the way that military departments specify the products and services that they procure.

> *Performance specifications are at the heart of acquisition streamlining and reform. They permit greater contractor flexibility to develop innovative solutions and build in quality through process control and continuous process improvement. The government gets affordable, quality products and services from a strengthened national industrial base responsive to DOD needs. Use of performance specifications for systems and performance-based statements of work for services enhances competition and much needed force modernization.*[97]

Performance specifications capture the spirit of *minimum necessary control.* Rather than telling a contractor how to accomplish a task we want done, we codify our goals and let the contractor determine the best way to achieve them. This allows alternative methods of accomplishing a task to compete against one another. However, this

---

[95] Carnegie Commission on Science, Technology, and Government, *New Thinking and American Technology,* Second Edition, 1993.

[96] Ibid., p. 34.

[97] US Army Materiel Command, *Guide for the Preparation and Use of Performance Specifications,* 1999.

approach puts a considerable burden on the specification writer to design tests capable of verifying performance of proposed systems.

PART VIII   *Principle #8: The Real World May Fight Back*

Unintended consequences flow like water from the actions we take to improve our corner of the world. Problems exist in an ecology of natural and human systems. Our actions interact with the forces of this ecology. It is in the nature of ecologies that they seek balance. Changes in one part of the system bring on a rebalancing of the rest. Our actions change the world of others, sometimes intentionally, sometimes unintentionally. These others have a will of their own. They have their own agendas. They push back. For example, a state that increases taxes on certain categories of business creates an incentive for those businesses to move to another state. A state with charitable welfare programs with the goal of reducing poverty may attract individuals from other states that have less charitable welfare programs. To guard against unintended consequences, we must realize that the context of a problem is not static. It will react to the actions we take. We may find ourselves in a game like chess, where every move is met by a counter-move. However, in the game of getting things done, our opponent is often hidden from view, and the rules of the game are cloudy at best. We must seek out these opponents and rules in order to avoid the trap of playing a naively offensive game. Chapter 25 presents several cases that illustrate how organizational and industry frameworks resist change. Chapter 26 offers strategies for coping with the intransigence of established relationships.

Chapter 25   Existing Relationships Can Thwart Innovation

There's many a slip twixt cup and lip, according to the proverb. Our best laid plans are thwarted by unanticipated opposition. This holds true particularly for innovative ideas. The world appears not to welcome change. Even with ordinary tasks, unexpected roadblocks can divert our well-laid plans. Awareness of these forces can trigger specific measures to combat or co-opt them.

In previous chapters, we have seen many examples of the unanticipated reactions of context to problem solving actions. Newton characterized *reactions* as being equal and opposite to *actions*. Newton was describing the physical world. Our problem solving actions have a physical context to which Newton's third law directly applies. But we also operate in organizational and process contexts. These systems react to our actions in oblique ways, sometimes predictable and sometimes not.

The physical, organizational, and social contexts of problems are dynamically linked to the systems we want to change. The benefits predicted to flow from our problem solving efforts can be undermined by the reaction of the problem's context. The effective problem solver explores the links between the parts of the world he is going to change and the rest of the world that will react.

Problem solving happens within a framework of established relationships among people and organizations. Within organizations, this framework defines the roles of individuals and teams and sets the communications links through which information flows. Industry frameworks define supplier-customer relationships in a fashion that enables competition among entities that fill a particular role.

Organization and industry frameworks structure the way that we solve problems. They constitute a super-frame that breaks problems into parts that fit the roles defined by the framework. For example, when an experienced sales representative of a packaging equipment company calls on a prospective customer, say a toy manufacturer, he has a highly developed mental model at both the organizational and engineering levels. He knows that he will have to sell both the reliability of his equipment and the financial benefits of its improved performance over the company's existing systems. He has made many of these sales calls. Although organizations differ in their distribution of responsibilities, he has developed a knack for quickly determining the key actors.

From the customer side, the head of engineering is accustomed to assessing the capabilities of prospective suppliers. Although he has not used equipment from this company in the past, he has done his homework. The exchange of information between the salesman and customer follows a predictable course. Each is making a continuous assessment of the value of investing time in the relationship. For example, the salesman may be wary of the engineer leading him into making a proposal with no intent of proceeding with a project. Such a proposal may be of considerable value to the company in making future expansion plans. The engineer may have a different supplier of packaging equipment that he intends to use but is looking for a detailed proposal to keep that supplier honest. The salesman has been through this process many times. His first cut at a proposal may involve limited investment of his time. He may provide the toy company a list of technical questions to determine if they are serious about considering investing in new equipment.

This dance is repeated often throughout all industries. The points of connection between companies define markets, the places where products and services are bought and sold. Since suppliers tend to call on many customers, and customers often prefer to have alternative sources of supply, the supplier-customer interface tends to evolve toward standardization. Standardization of the supplier-customer interface allows industries to have interchangeable parts.

The roles of participants up and down the supply chain become well defined. These relationships form a structure that resists change.

We seldom can get much done without entering into the web of relationships that defines markets and society. When we go into a store or a lawyer's office or call on a business customer, we have expectations about what is about to happen. These expectations guide our actions and those of the people with whom we interact. It begins with an exchange of information and ends with the possibility of a transaction. Each party frames the relationship in a standardized way that streamlines the process. Much of the knowledge that supports problem solving defines how these relationships work. To *learn the ropes* of a business is to learn how relationships are framed with suppliers, other employees, customers, and regulators. These relationships form a structure specific to each industry.

For example, Figure 42 shows the traditional relationships among the parties in the design and construction of buildings.

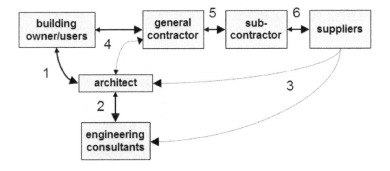

Figure 42: Conventional Building Industry Relationships

Relationship 1: The building owner hires an architect. Personnel at the architectural firm and within the building owner's organization form an interface for defining the problem, monitoring progress, and approving the design at predetermined stages.

Relationship 2: The architect retains appropriate engineering firms to develop structural, mechanical, and other system designs.

Relationship 3: The architect communicates with representatives of materials and component suppliers to support development of detailed design and specifications.

Relationship 4: Based on the architect's drawings and specifications, the owner selects a general contractor.

Relationship 5: As a part of the bidding process, the general contractor selects subcontractors.

Relationship 6: Based on the limitations of the specifications, the subcontractors select equipment and materials suppliers.

For this system to work, the interfaces between each pair of participants must follow both formal and informal rules of the road. Industry associations set standards for contracts among the parties.

Predictable relationships are useful. They define a modularity that allows industries to have interchangeable components. It is useful for people to have more than one source for goods and services. These relationships can also stifle innovation. New problems and opportunities may not map well onto these existing super-frames.

Case 1: Symbiosis Between a Problem and its Context

Human behavior adapts to its environment. For example, the buildings we inhabit, however inadequate they may seem, shape the way we live and work. We then perpetuate inadequate forms to fit these adapted behaviors. Sir Winston Churchill remarked:

We shape our dwellings, and afterwards our dwellings shape us.

This insight is true as far as it goes. But what happens next? After our dwellings shape us, we shape new dwellings to fit the shape of our adapted behavior. In this way, the design of dwellings becomes a self-perpetuating fit between form and function. This is true of many human artifacts. For example, consider the *QWERTY* keyboard design, shown in Figure 43. This arrangement of keys was designed to minimize the jamming of typing arms. The arms of adjacent letters would jam more easily than letters that were far apart, so pairs of letters that are commonly typed in sequence were separated.

212

Figure 43: QWERTY Keyboard

Typewriters with typing arms have not been in use for forty years, yet the QWERTY design remains. There are certainly better layouts in terms of typing efficiency; for example, the Dvorak simplified keyboard. The problem here is that there are so many people trained on the QWERTY keyboard, and there are so many keyboards with the QWERTY layout, that it is hard to make the transition. If it is true that typing on a Dvorak keyboard is more efficient and more easily taught than on the QWERTY keyboard, it must have also been true in 1867 when the QWERTY keyboard was originally laid out. The QWERTY keyboard design would only have been a good fit because the issue of keys jamming was more important than the issue of comfortable key locations. Behavior had to conform to the form dictated by technology.

Case 2: Inland Steel Building Systems

The structure of the building industry provides a framework for the interaction of many actors: building owners, architects, contractors, and manufacturers are the obvious roles. This framework provides great flexibility in that participants can come and go as long as they play their prescribed roles. However, rewriting the script can pose a daunting challenge, as illustrated by the following case.

In the mid-1960s, Inland Steel won the contract to build thirteen schools in California. The School Construction Systems Development Project (SCSD) was an innovative effort to bring large building component manufacturers, like Inland, into the production of integrated building systems. Inland brought together a team of building system producers and developed a compatible kit of parts for structure, heating and air conditioning, lighting, ceiling, and partitions. Individual architects in California used these systems in the design and construction of the thirteen schools. Inland built a plant in Milwaukee, anticipating that production of these systems would become a major part of their business. Three years later, Inland abandoned the concept. Why?

Inland's systems were designed on a five-foot grid. This was dictated by the specifications of the SCSD project. The rationale of the five-foot grid was to accommodate four-foot fluorescent light fixtures within recessed ceiling units. In order to sell the use of these systems, Inland representatives would have to sell the use of a five-foot grid to school architects early in the design process. This carried some risk for architects, since it would limit the number of suppliers that could compete on a project.

Inland Steel's building system called for a new set of marketing relationships. In building construction, there are well-established relationships among participants. In school construction, a school board and its committees hire an architect. Through a series of meetings, architects attempt to impress the board with their ability to bring the project in on time and within budget. The selected architect develops a design. During the latter stages of the design process, technical people in the architect's office meet with a continuous stream of building materials suppliers to make decisions about building details. This is where the sales force of Inland Steel building products sells the value of their conventional structural components. The architect's team would then incorporate decisions about building components and materials into their detailed drawings and specifications. One goal of these documents is to allow competitive bidding on as many components as possible.

These relationships were fundamentally incompatible with marketing the Inland Steel building system. The building system required early commitment by the architect to a five-foot planning grid and a set of integrated components only available through Inland. Inland's sales force was used to inhabiting the waiting rooms of architects' offices, seeking an audience with a crusty draftsman. They were hardly qualified to sell the concept of an integrated building system to

214

the architect during the initial stages of design. They were even less qualified to gain an audience with a school board to sell the idea that they should hire an architect who would be sympathetic with the use of pre-coordinated building components. Inland chose to market the system through its existing sales force. As a result, it failed to generate sufficient business to sustain the plant.

The essence of Inland's problem was that its innovative way of building required a substantial change in the organization of the building process. In order to solve the problem of lack of competition, Inland proposed to guarantee the price of building systems that they would supply perhaps 50 percent of the cost of the school. But the school boards and architects would have no benchmark to compare this to. We can only speculate about what Inland could have done earlier in the process had they focused on these barriers. Perhaps the building systems team could have fought harder with the management for an independent sales force.

Industry relationships such as these are what knit the strata of industries together. They are as hard to change as the arrangement of keys on a keyboard. The effective problem solver must recognize these constraints from the outset. Dealing with barriers presented by established relationships is a part of the Rubik's Cube that must be solved.

Case 3: Navy Barracks Project

In 1970, research-oriented building program people in the Pentagon wanted to look at using industrialized housing for Navy barracks. The Navy's typical way of designing barracks was to select one model from several standard barracks designs, then *apply it to the site*. This was efficient in that much of the working drawings and specifications were already done. Typically, these were concrete block buildings decorated with local materials. Use of factory-built housing would require fundamental changes in the building process.

In order for a range of technologies to be bid for the job, our team at Building Systems Development wrote performance specifications for the housing part. Performance specifications strive to avoid dictating a particular way of building by stating what function each building component must perform rather than how it is made. Housing system companies would have to collaborate with a local contractor to make a bid. There was substantial potential for confusion over who was bidding on what part of the work. We had planned to orchestrate a pre-bid conference, where potential general contractors and industrialized building suppliers could meet and assess each other's strengths and weaknesses. We were to be at the meeting to answer any questions about the process and issue clarifications where needed. In essence, we were defining a new set of interfaces between building owner, contractor, and principal supplier.

As the project moved into the design stage, the Navy transferred control from Washington to the regional engineering office in Charleston, South Carolina. This office had no research agenda and was disinclined to allow any deviation from standard procedures. As a result, we were not allowed to hold a pre-bid conference or communicate with the general contractor community in any way. Once the project was put out for bids, we were not allowed to communicate with potential bidders. The bids came in over budget. We talked to both the housing manufacturers and the general contractors, and it was clear that confusion had reigned when the bids were put together. We were not given a second chance.

During the initial feasibility assessment of this project, we should have insisted that standard bidding procedures be modified. Without the ability to modify standard procedures, we should have deemed the project infeasible. At the end of the day, it was not clear whether the research people at the Pentagon had the authority to waive standard bidding constraints. There was simply not sufficient focus on this aspect of the problem.

The two innovative projects discussed below shared the same fate of not anticipating the barriers down the road. On innovative projects, you are breaking new ground, rethinking the way things are done. You become absorbed in your new way of framing old problems, much like a scientist sequestered in his lab. The laboratory protects you from the realities of implementation. The laboratory might be a pilot project or simply the laboratory of the mind. But the transition from the laboratory to the real world can be harsh.

Case 4: Energy Investment Fund

In the early eighties, our firm, Syncon, developed an innovative way to finance energy conservation improvements. We created a pool of funds for financing conservation projects. Each investment would be paid back from a share of the savings that resulted. Only projects with savings that could be clearly measured were considered. Our target customers for the fund were small to medium-sized industrial firms in Milwaukee. We were successful in identifying potential projects. But there were two serious road blocks. First, there was a catch-22. After initial skepticism, the customer would recognize that the return on investment would have to be very good in order for only part of it, say 50 percent, to justify investment by an outside entity. They would reason that if the idea is that good then they, the customer, should make the investment and reap the entire benefit. Unfortunately, they would be short of cash at the moment, but they would put the project into next year's budget. At best, this would mean that the project might be completed in two years. By that time, the project would have nearly paid for itself. More realistically, once we left the scene, they would lose interest and the project would never get done.

The second barrier was the threat that we posed to the person within the organization who had failed to recognize this money saving opportunity. This was more likely to happen in larger firms. This person had many avenues available to thwart our involvement in the project. He may or may not have been able to pick up the ball and run with it. Our failure was in not recognizing the importance of identifying such a person and co-opting him by giving him credit and partial control over the project.

Case 5: Furnace Replacement Program

In 1980, the Wisconsin Gas Company retained Syncon to test the shared savings idea to fund residential furnaces. The gas company would pay for the installation of a high efficiency furnace in exchange for a share of the savings over a five to seven year period. The residential customer would get a free furnace and a somewhat reduced gas bill. After the shared savings period, the customer would get all of the savings. We installed over one hundred furnaces and declared the pilot program a success. The actual installation was done by local heating contractors who gave us a fixed installation cost per furnace. This was a win-win situation, or so we thought. We had not anticipated the reaction of the handful of high profile local contractors, who were making substantial profits on installing high efficiency furnaces. It was easy for these firms to get the Wisconsin Public Service Commission to put a stop to full-scale implementation. The gas company was cast as meddling in private enterprise. End of program. This was all done very quietly, no hearings, no discussion.

Our patron at the gas company was a rather forward thinking vice president, but he made the same mistake that we made, getting immersed in the details of the pilot project without preparing for opposition downstream. We may have been able to thwart the opposition of the local contractors had we brought the Public Service Commission into the project at an early stage.

Each of the examples in this chapter illustrates failure to anticipate the inflexibility of established relationships. Each of these projects has the flavor of the novice chess player absorbed by his offensive strategy, neglecting his opponent's inevitable reaction.

Chapter 26   The Real World May Fight Back

As we solve problems, our focus is on that part of the world that we intend to change. We inhabit a mental model of the world that puts our concerns front and center, relegating related contextual considerations to the periphery. It is easy for us to neglect the effect that our actions have on systems that are not our primary concern.

When we make changes in the world, particularly when we innovate, we may be upsetting the balance of forces. These forces will adjust, sometimes in ways that directly thwart our goals.

PROBLEM SOLVING PRINCIPLE #8:
THE REAL WORLD MAY FIGHT BACK

Problem solving occurs within a framework of established relationships among people and organizations. These relationships form a structure that resists change. Innovative ideas may require the reinvention of these relationships.

Strategy #1: Adopt the Outside View

Businesses often neglect the potential reaction of their competitors when they plan the introduction of new products. Lovallo and Kahneman point to this blind spot as one component of over-optimistic forecasting, leading to many business failures.

One of the key factors influencing the outcome of a business initiative is competitors' behavior. In making forecasts, however, executives tend to focus on their own company's capabilities and plans and are thus prone to neglect the potential abilities and actions of rivals.[98]

The effective problem solver must be able to step outside of his problem-centric representation in order to gauge the reaction of external forces. Lovallo and Kahneman call this the *outside view*.

Competition comes in many forms. In the case of the Energy Investment Fund, discussed in the previous chapter, we had two sources of competition within each potential customer. First, we were competing with the customer's belief that they could do the project themselves, earning *all* of the savings. Second, when we proposed innovative energy saving projects, we were implicitly threatening the individual within the enterprise who was responsible for energy efficiency. Without strategies for defusing these two sources of competition, our proposals were doomed to failure.

The Shared Savings Program we developed for the Wisconsin Gas Company was also sidetracked by unanticipated competition. Our pilot program was a success. So much so that local contractors could see that their large profit margins might be threatened if the program were implemented full scale. They suggested to the Wisconsin Public Service Commission that the gas company was undermining private enterprise. Had we been wearing our effective problem solver hats, we would have anticipated this move. We should have brought the Public Service Commission into the project during the pilot phase.

The following case provides a small example of a problem solver adopting an outside view. For nine years, I was on the design review board in Shorewood, Wisconsin, a suburb of Milwaukee with a population of 14,000. The board was made up of five citizens, at least two of whom had to be either a design professional or a real estate broker. Our mandate was to review projects in the village to determine if they negatively impacted the value of adjoining properties. Most of our work reviewed modest commercial and home improve-

---

[98] Dan Lovallo and Daniel Kahneman, "Delusions of Success: How Optimism Undermines Executives' Decisions," *Harvard Business Review*, Vol 81, No 7, July 2003. p. 5 (in reprint).

ment projects. From the applicant's perspective, we were an unwelcome impediment to their efforts to improve their building. In reality, in almost all cases, projects were approved with one or another small improvement. We were, in essence, providing free design consulting.

Only in rare cases did applicants accept that the review was a part of their problem solving process. Such was the case with Mr. Ng, an entrepreneur who planned to convert a gas station into a Chinese restaurant. There were many problems with his application, requiring numerous meetings with not only our board but also the planning commission. His approach was markedly outside of the norm. He asked for help. He fashioned a collaborative spirit at meetings where substantial changes were required of his design. Ultimately, he won approval for the restaurant. East Garden went on to be a welcome addition to the Shorewood landscape.

Broadly speaking, any government body that seeks to constrain the behavior of citizens can expect resistance. As in the case of the Design Review Board, the goals of citizens clash with the goals of government bodies. When one state raises the legal drinking age, liquor stores crop up on the other side of the border with adjoining states. Increased sales taxes create added incentive for Internet purchases. Tightening environmental requirements for manufacturing can drive businesses to source materials from overseas.

The effective problem solver, like Mr. Ng, looks past the boundaries of his immediate problem to anticipate how its context will react. Like chess, we cannot become preoccupied with our side of the game. Unlike chess, the intersection of human problems is not typically zero sum. If we can put the goals of all sides on the table, an integrated solution may be available with a substantial net benefit. Regulatory actions taken blindly can result in worse than a zero sum outcome.

Strategy #2: Bring the Interface Within the Scope of the Problem

An interface is the point of connection between two components of a larger functioning system. In order for components to be interchangeable, interface rules define the configuration of each component at its point of connection.

For example, standard light bulbs and lighting fixtures work together because the base of the bulbs and the sockets in the fixtures obey the rules defined by the E27[99] specification developed by Thomas Edison. Interfaces are not *things*; rather, they are rules that define the relationships between components of a larger system.

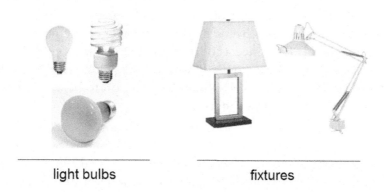

| light bulbs | fixtures |

Figure 44: Bulbs and Fixtures Have a Well-Defined Interface

If you want to manufacture a standard light bulb, you must design it to screw into the socket of a standard lamp. If you manufacture digital storage devices, they must connect via USB cable to a computer. Most industries are composed of interconnected companies with standardized interfaces. This allows multiple companies to compete to fill a well-defined role. These roles are defined as much by the communications links through which buying and selling are done as by the specifications of the products and services.

Imagine that you are a light bulb manufacturer. Imagine that you have discovered that a major efficiency improvement can be achieved that would require increasing the size of the base of the bulb (the screw-in part). Common domestic light bulbs have the E27 base. It would be futile to market the new light bulb without consideration of

---

[99] Named after Thomas Edison, the screw fitting is twenty-seven millimeters in diameter.

its incompatibility with existing lamps. What to do? There are two basic alternatives. First, offer an adapter that would fit between the bulb and the lamp. This might be problematic where there is not sufficient space within the lamp to accommodate the adapter and the new bulb. Second, sell the bulb with a lamp. This is the approach taken by low-voltage fixtures such as those found in track lighting.

The obstacle presented by the light bulb interface is a metaphor for barriers to innovation in many fields. For example, in construction, the competitive bidding – the interface between architect and contractor – can stifle innovation. Innovative construction methods developed by contractors often have design implications. Architects are leery of adopting design elements that only one contractor is able to carry out. Design-build firms combine architectural and construction services, eliminating competitive bidding based on detailed design documents. This requires redefinition of the firm's relationship to the building owner, since a commitment must be made to the project at an early stage.

Strategy #3: Reorganize

Sometimes, reorganization can reduce or eliminate barriers to effective problem solving. In 1977, President Jimmy Carter signed legislation that created the US Department of Energy (DOE). The energy crisis of the mid-seventies spawned the thinking that the problems of energy supply and demand were sufficiently intertwined that the various energy related commissions, administrations, and subdepartments scattered throughout the federal government should be brought under one roof. This step followed by only three years the consolidation of agencies dealing with nuclear power. According to the DOE Web site:

The Department provided a framework for a comprehensive and balanced national energy plan by coordinating and administering the energy functions of the federal government.

The passage of time has proven that administrative reorganization cannot always solve the politics of policy development. Nonetheless, the intent of this move recognized that the existing organizational framework stood in the way of coordinating energy policy. Previously, energy related issues such as conservation were seen as subsidiary to the missions of existing departments such as Housing and Urban Development, Agriculture and Transportation. The creation of DOE was an effort to align organizational frameworks with the structure of the problems they were intended to solve. Only the perception of a crisis could bring on such a disruptive change.

On September 11, 2001, suddenly the hard problem, *the problem that must be solved*, became protecting the country from the prospect of repeated terrorist attacks. In 2003, twenty-two agencies of the federal government were consolidated into the Department of Homeland Security (DHS). As with DOE, DHS was created in response to a crisis. The existing federal bureaucracy was viewed as standing in the way of developing an integrated security plan.

These examples illustrate the powerful connection between organizational frameworks and the problems they are intended to solve. The desire for integrated strategies pulls us in several directions. The Department of Transportation would very much like to maintain an integrated strategy for dealing with the challenges of transportation. How can that be achieved when transportation-related energy and security issues have been reassigned to other departments?

Strategy #4: Work Outside the System

Many companies organize departments along functional lines, such as sales, accounting, engineering, manufacturing, and logistics. This encourages coordination of these functions and maintenance of standards of practice. Each department maintains a common way of looking at the problems it faces. These shared mental models are functional frames in that they focus on aspects of a problem that fall within the purview of a particular area of knowledge or skill. Christopher Alexander makes a powerful case that our ability to creatively solve problems can be undermined by subdividing the problem into inappropriate conceptual categories.

Detailed analysis of the problem of designing urban family houses, for instance, has shown that the usually accepted functional categories like acoustics, circulation, and accommodation are inappropriate for this

224

problem. Similarly, the principle of the "neighborhood," one of the old chestnuts of city-planning theory, has been shown to be an inadequate mental component of the residential planning problem.[100]

When an organization takes on a new activity, deciding where it fits within the organizational structure can be a challenge. New initiatives often start as projects, staffed by people borrowed from various departments. The project team may report directly to a high-level manager rather than a department head. Eventually, the time comes to create a permanent organizational place for the new activity. At one extreme, it could be spun off as a separate business, replicating many of the functional departments of the parent company. At the other, it could be integrated into the existing structure with current personnel taking on new responsibilities.

Many companies face the challenge of integrating the sales function for new products into existing lines. Often, the greatest asset of a company is its sales force. Over the years, salespeople build relationships of trust and reliability with customers. When a company adds a new product to its offerings, through either innovation or acquisition, it is natural to launch it within the existing sales structure. Customers wish to control or even reduce the number of suppliers they have to deal with. The last thing they want is to have to interact with more than one representative from a single company. There are several clear advantages of working within existing departments:

- Use existing employees rather than hiring new ones
- Avoid committing to new staff when rate of sales growth is uncertain
- Use existing customer contacts rather than having to establish new ones
- Cross-pollinate sales of new and old products

---

[100] Christopher Alexander, *Notes on the Synthesis of Form*. (Cambridge: Harvard University Press, 1964) p. 66.

Under some circumstances, these advantages are outweighed by two key obstacles:

- Although the new product may superficially seem to be in the same category as the existing line, there may be significant differences. Sales people may need a deeper understanding of a new and innovative technology in order to overcome customer resistance to products they have not used in the past.

- The decision by the customer to adopt a new product may not lay with the customer personnel with whom the sales force is accustomed to dealing. New relationships might be easier to establish with a highly motivated, product-specific sales force.

Strategy #5: Expand Your View of Stakeholders

We can avert disaster by recognizing the interests of people potentially affected by our problem solving efforts. Expand the definition of stakeholders to include not only those directly involved in the problem but also those whose world may be changed by potential solutions.

It may not be possible to identify secondary stakeholders until potential solutions are considered. For example, in Dallas a high-rise condominium project is causing considerable controversy. The highly reflective glass on the south side of the forty-two-story building is directing sunlight from unexpected angles into the adjacent Nasher Sculpture Center. The New York Times reported, "No one knows quite what to do. The condo developer and the museum are at loggerheads. Fingers are being pointed. Mr. Piano (the museum's architect) is furious. The developer's architect is aggrieved. The mayor is involved. A former George W. Bush administration official has been asked to mediate."

This controversy could not have been anticipated until the building design was well under way. The lesson here: each solution may bring additional stakeholders into the problem.

In order to anticipate the reaction of others to our problem solving efforts, we must adopt an ecological perspective. This may require seeing the problem situation from their perspective. Put another way, we must imagine how the people affected by our actions frame the problem. Perhaps we need a corollary to Miller's law, discussed in Chapter 7. To understand how a person will react, we must see the world through her eyes.

PART IX   *Educating Problem*
Solvers

The principles of effective problem solving described in this book are applicable across a wide range of human challenges. The more demanding the problem, the more we need the principles. Our daily trip to work can be managed by autopilot until a fallen tree wakes us up. In the workplace of the twenty-first century, the balance between the routine and demanding will continue to shift toward the demanding. Every child will not become an innovator. But we can hope for every child to become a responsible citizen striving to understand the complexities of community issues, striving to look beyond the platitudes and simple answers that mask the difficult questions of our time.

In my view, the most effective teacher of these principles is experience. But to learn from experience, we need to develop habits of reflection and self-criticism. Experience in problem solving does not start with our first job. We are solving problems from a very young age, difficult problems at that. Every day, children face the challenges of being a child, of finding their way with others, of shaping their ideas about things. Then they go to school. In the classroom, meaningful problem solving is put aside in favor of highly structured learning tasks. The opportunity is lost to build on their experiences.

Gurus of education, such as Howard Gardner at Harvard, see this century as presenting new challenges to education at all levels. He argues that the educational philosophy of one hundred years ago was attuned to the need for an educated elite with a general population having only basic literacy skills.

Nowadays, however, almost any function that can be executed through the application of regular procedures will sooner or later be computer-

228

*ized. To be attractive to employers, an individual must be highly lit-
erate, flexible, capable of troubleshooting and problem-finding, and not
incidentally, able to shift roles or even vocations should his current position become outmoded.*[101]

Yet, even one hundred years ago, John Dewey called for an education grounded in problems of the real world. He contrasted formal
education with the apprenticeships by which most people learned a
trade in the nineteenth century. Dewey argued that formal education
could become remote and dead, too abstract and bookish to be useful
in the real world. He contended that the limited knowledge acquired
in societies without formal education had the advantage of usefulness.[102]

The goal of education should be long-term understanding, not
short-term performance on tests. College graduates lament how little
they have retained from college courses, even within a year or two of
taking them. When I was in graduate school, calculus was required as
a prerequisite for taking courses in structural design. However, it was
so readily accepted that few of the students retained any working
knowledge of calculus that the professor tried to teach without it. The
irony here is that analyzing structures would be a fantastic vehicle for
teaching calculus. But, of course, that opportunity had been lost.

Conventional classroom education has not been a breeding
ground for a problem solving perspective. In order to have the
opportunity to develop problem solving skills, we have to actually
engage in real problem solving.

In the following chapters, I will share some observations about
why teacher-centric education fails to nourish effective problem
solving skills and about the promise offered by new directions that
call for problem based learning.

---

[101] Howard Gardner, *The Disciplined Mind* (The Penguin Group, New York,
1999) p. 43.

[102] John Dewey, *Democracy and Education, an Introduction to the Philosophy of
Education.* (Macmillan Company, 1916) Republished as an e-document by
the Penn State Electronic Classics Series. p. 12.

Chapter 27 The Problem With Education

There is much debate about how to educate our young people to be problem solvers in the twenty-first century. In the conventional educational paradigm, teachers present chunks of knowledge that students are expected to learn. To supplement these presentations, students execute homework assignments and do assigned readings. Educational programs tend to be broad and shallow, driven by state and federal standards that are intended to leave no child behind.

Traditional educational practices fail to foster reflection, self-criticism, critical investigation, curiosity, or validation. Traditional education is built around the conveyance of knowledge from the teacher to the student. Emphasis on testing reinforces the priority given to command of a broad range of facts rather than a deep understanding of concepts. This emphasis is reflected in the cycle of assignments, exercises, and tests that are given in an academic vacuum. There is no connection to experiences where the knowledge might take deeper root. In traditional school, problems are well defined; there is little need for research, and the problem statement has all of the information required to find a correct answer. Well-defined problems are their own reality. This promotes the notion that a problem is a reality of its own.

At all levels of education, teachers are recognizing the value of ill-defined problems. Ill-defined problems require students to confront the context of the problem. Information is missing. Students must develop problem statements of their own. Interaction with a real or pseudo client is required. Students must identify the unknowns of the problem. They must investigate the context of the problem. All of this provides the opportunity to observe that the definition of a problem must be extracted from the real world. The problem exists in the real world, but the problem statement is something different. It is imperfect; it is a model.

In the real world, we have to decide what tools to use to make sense of problems. Not in school. In school, we are handed problems on a silver platter. When taking algebra, we are given algebra problems. Even though a *word problem* might attempt to disguise the problem's nature, we know which math tool we are supposed to use since the problem is given while we are learning that tool. One of the challenges of problem solving in the real world is figuring out how to look at the problem and deciding what thinking tools to use to generate solutions. This part of problem solving is stripped away by well-defined problems in school.

In the real world, we have to forage for information to support the development and evaluation of alternative solutions. In school, we are given the information we need to solve problems.

Because we are seldom given latitude to shape the process by which we solve problems in school, little time is devoted to reflecting on the process – where we made mistakes, what alternative approaches we might have taken. Our natural inclination to being curious is discouraged.

These shortcomings of our approach to educating problem solvers came into sharp focus for me when I taught architecture. Students came to us as juniors in college. They were thrown into a design studio having taken two years of liberal arts courses. We might start with the design of a simple facility, say a park structure. To give the process a taste of reality, we would meet with a park official who would fill the role of client. Based on these discussions and a selected site, each student would be asked to develop a building program, stating goals and site considerations. They would then proceed to develop a design. Many students were stunned by the fact that they were not given a clear statement of the problem. They were further stunned by the lack of a *correct* answer. The idea of using criteria that they had developed to evaluate their solutions was a new experience. It didn't seem to help to remind them that this is what they do all the time in confronting the problems of everyday life.

The starkest shortcoming was the lack of self-criticism. Students would often be satisfied with a so-so solution. They would ask,

"What is wrong with this one?" A history of accepting the parameters of a problem as given facts had stifled their creativity. The definition of a problem was not to be challenged. This is a hazard in design, where clients routinely express goals by giving examples of solutions that they have experienced. The student tends to take the examples as sacrosanct rather than digging to reveal the client's real goals that the examples were given to illustrate.

The problem with traditional teacher-centric education is that students must put aside their embryonic problem solving skills when they step into the classroom. In real life, students confront a wide band of challenging problems that call for exploration, experimentation, and creativity. In school, they must practice passivity, test taking, and the parroting back of the lessons of the day.

Chapter 28   *Problem-Based Learning*

At all levels of education, the effectiveness of the *teacher talks - students listen* paradigm is being challenged. The notion of education consisting of an accumulation of facts is giving way to a more student-centered approach. For example, in Singapore, the mantra of the Ministry of Education is *Less Teaching More Learning*. Under several guises, the new approach focuses on the initiative of the student to define problems, inquire, explore, and generate solutions. The teacher is recast as a mentor, selecting appropriate problems, guiding the student's efforts, and helping the student assess progress.

In problem-based learning (PBL), the learning process is driven by a problem designed to mimic the complexity of problems encountered in the real world. Students are responsible for determining the information they need to be able to generate solutions. Teachers become research facilitators rather than delivering course content through lectures. Students typically work in teams, again mimicking patterns of work in the real world. Brainstorming and concept mapping encourage students to explore problems before setting a course toward a solution.

In PBL, emphasis is placed on documentation of the research and problem solving process. Students keep individual records of their research, making verbal and written reports as the problem solving effort unfolds. Significant time is devoted to reflection on the problem solving process, for example, the value of exploration and false starts. Where possible, students are cast in the role of real world problem solvers. A defining hallmark of PBL is that the problems are not easy. They do not have perfect answers. Often the goals of the problem are ill-defined, and the context presents a moving target.

In the late 1960s, problem-based learning was pioneered by Howard Barrows at the medical school at McMaster University in Hamilton, Ontario, Canada. According to Barrows, PBL has six core characteristics:[103]

- Learning is student centered

- Students work in small groups

- Teachers act as facilitators or guides

- Problems form the basis for organized focus and stimulus for learning

- Problems stimulate the development and use of problem solving skills

- New knowledge is obtained through self-directed learning

By the early 1990s, use of PBL principles was widespread at medical schools with four schools, including Harvard, having converted their entire curriculum to PBL. By 2004, 70 percent of 123 medical schools surveyed used PBL, but only 22 percent used PBL for over 25 percent of their preclinical curriculum.[104]

Traditionally, the preclinical years of medical school are taught in lecture and lab courses very much like college courses. PBL courses are radically different. Small groups of students, four to twenty, meet with a faculty advisor or tutor. The group is given a set of facts that describe a biomedical problem. A typical case is chosen to illustrate an area of basic science to be studied. The students analyze the case and generate a set of issues in the form of questions. The group of students drives the questions and conducts research to answer them.

---

[103] Howard Barrows, "Problem Based Learning in Medicine and Beyond: A Brief Overview." In Wilkerson and Gijselears, *New Directions for Teaching and Learning*, no.68. *Bringing problem-based learning to higher education: Theory and Practice.* 1996. San Francisco. pp. 3-13.

[104] Scott Kincade, "A Snapshot of the Status of Problem-Based Learning in US Medical Schools," 2003-2004. *Academic Medicine*, Vol 80, No 3 / March 2005.

At each meeting of the group, students report on their research and generate new questions. Students keep individual logs on the process of the group and on their own research. PBL stresses critical evaluation of the problem solving process.

PBL at the Undergraduate Level

The use of PBL in colleges is widespread. Three college professors at the University of Rhode Island have written a practical guide that gives a good feel for how PBL actually works.[105] One of the authors, Libby Miles, describes her approach to orchestrating an introductory writing course. She puts each writing assignment into a real world context. First, students write an application for an internship at a local congressman's office. A series of assignments cast the student in the role of congressional staff writing answers to constituent letters. A later project calls for designing a page on the congressman's Web site stating his position on a controversial issue. Miles describes writing as a process of creating and revising drafts in a series of stages as new information is discovered and versions are presented in class for criticism. She characterizes her classroom as follows:

> *If you were to walk into my classroom, you would not hear the typical sounds of productive work but instead the chatter of cell phone conversations, electronic beeps as instant messages pop up on computer screens around the room, and the tapping of keyboards and clicking of mice as students Ask Jeeves and Google and then exclaim, "I found him" and "Aw, I was soooo wrong!"*

Another of the authors, José Amador, is a professor of soil science at the University of Rhode Island. He uses PBL in all four of his undergraduate courses. He stresses the importance of learning to work in a problem solving context much like his students will face when they get into the professional world, whether they be consultants, regulators, technicians, or researchers.

---

[105] Jose Amador, Libby Miles, C.B. Peters, *The Practice of Problem Based Learning, A Guide to Implementing PBL in the College Classroom*. Anker Publishing Co., Bolton, Mass. 2006.

Their work will require that they collaborate with professionals from different walks of life, that they integrate knowledge from a wide variety of sources, and, perhaps most importantly, that they will have to solve messy, open-ended, poorly structured problems with real consequences.

Amador plays the role of mentor, resisting the temptation to answer student questions directly, preferring to answer questions with questions. He listens carefully as teams discuss problems, getting a better sense of what is going on in their minds than when he gave traditional lectures.

The third author, C.B. Peters, teaches an introductory sociology course to a class of five hundred students. He uses a mixture of PBL and conventional approaches. In both cases, the class meets in a large lecture hall. When in PBL mode, small groups of students arrange themselves helter-skelter around the room as they work on problems. Peters will occasionally interrupt the mayhem to offer guidance based on what he is hearing as he cruises from group to group. Before adopting the PBL approach, Peters was pleased with the overall success of his course but felt that something was missing. In lecture mode, he would often describe a problem, allow a short period for students to ask questions and offer comments, and then he would present his thinking on how to solve the problem.

PBL offered me a way to keep my students engaged in the "doing" of sociology over an extended period. Because I think that's what introductory courses ought to do — get students to do the discipline, not merely learn about it.

The three authors discuss at length problems arising out of group work – group formation, free riders, and individual evaluation. They also stress the importance of the problems used in PBL. Problems must challenge the students but not frustrate them. They must be ill-defined, forcing students to cope with shaping the scope of the problem. Problems must be complex but manageable within the time allotted.

Architecture schools have taken a PBL approach for over a century. From day one, students are given design problems taken from real world experience. Problems start with meetings either with real world clients or faculty playing the role of client. Students must learn the process of extracting a set of building requirements from client meetings. As with other phases of design, they learn by doing. The process of generating design alternatives is typically not taught. Students produce sketches of preliminary designs and are then visited by faculty who offer criticism, often harshly. Separate courses are taught on structures, mechanical systems, and professional practice. Sadly, these courses are seldom integrated into design projects. Furthermore, architecture students are seldom asked to keep journals and reflect on the process of problem solving. Such reflection is a keystone of the PBL movement.

Peer Instruction

In 1990, Eric Mazur had been teaching introductory physics at Harvard for seven years, with exceptional student ratings. He then discovered that his teaching was not improving his students' conceptual understanding of physics. This revelation came through a test developed by David Hestenes, a professor of physics at Arizona State University. He tested students' understanding of the most fundamental concepts of physics. It had been administered to thousands of students in the southwestern United States with dismaying results. When Mazur gave the test to his students before and after his introductory course, it showed that there had been little improvement in understanding fundamental concepts. While reviewing the results with his students, on a whim, he asked them to discuss a problem among themselves. This was in a large lecture hall with hundreds of students. Within minutes, they had figured it out, after he had spent ten minutes trying unsuccessfully to explain it. For Mazur, this was the birth of *peer instruction*.

Over the ensuing decade, Mazur and his colleagues refined the peer instruction approach, centering it on conceptual questions called *ConcepTests*. Short presentations focusing on a central point are followed by a ConcepTest that probes students' understanding. After working on the test for one or two minutes, the students then discuss it in small groups. Mazur urges the students to try to convince their fellow students of the correctness of their own approach. These discussions last two to four minutes. The instructor roams around the room to get a sense of where further explanation might be needed.

Testing of student comprehension has shown that peer instruction results in substantial improvement over the traditional lecture format. Peer instruction is not full-blown problem-based learning, in that it does not incorporate ill-defined problems and student-driven research. However, its success highlights the value of working in teams, an integral component of problem-based learning.

PBL in K-12

In 1995, The National Academy of Sciences, through its National Research Council, published *National Science Education Standards* to provide guidance for the teaching of science from kindergarten through twelfth grade. The core idea driving the standards is:

> *Inquiry into authentic questions generated from student experiences is the central strategy for teaching science.*

The standards stress that students learn best by *doing* science rather than being told about it. This echoes basic principles of the Montessori teaching philosophy, emphasizing the children's exploration of the world around them.

There is no better example of rethinking K-12 education than what is happening in Singapore. The new mantra of the Ministry of Education is *Teach Less Learn More*. Singapore is moving away from teacher- and textbook-based acquisition of knowledge to student-centered inquiry and problem-based learning. For example, a problem given to secondary school kids at a CHIJ[106] school asked them to develop an itinerary for a one-day tour of the Little India district of Singapore for target groups of tourists. Taking two to three weeks, the project required teams to study the Indian culture, do field trips to Little India, design a tourist itinerary, design a brochure, and make a presentation to the Singapore Tourism Board to sell them on their proposal.

---

[106] Convent of the Holy Infant Jesus schools are eleven all-girls Catholic schools in Singapore.

Effectiveness of PBL

Over the years, there have been substantial efforts to evaluate the effectiveness of PBL versus conventional education. In the short term, PBL is more effective for procedural knowledge while conventional methods are more effective for factual knowledge. In the long term, PBL is more effective for both factual and procedural knowledge. For example, researchers drew the following conclusion from a synthesis of several hundred separate studies comparing PBL to traditional teaching methods.

> *... several value statements can be made about the effectiveness of PBL that were supported by the majority of the meta-analyses reviewed: PBL instruction was effective when it came to long-term retention and performance improvement. PBL students were overall slightly underperforming when it came to short-term retention. Ultimately, the goal of instruction should be performance improvement and long-term retention. Therefore, preference should be given to instructional strategies that focus on students' performance in authentic situations and their long-term knowledge retention, and not on their performance on tests aimed at short-term retention of knowledge.*[107]

A core principle of problem-based learning is that the student explores and defines the requirements of the problem. This process of constructing a model of a real world (or pseudo real world) situation provides fertile ground for understanding the limits and pitfalls of modeling. The number one lesson is that models are not reality.

Problem-based learning in its many forms emphasizes the keeping of journals, daily logs, intermittent reports, and after the fact evaluations by students. This process of reflection, or self-criticism, is valuable training, requiring the student to take a step back from his work to consider its effectiveness.

---

[107] Johannes Strobel and Angela van Barneveld, "When is PBL More Effective? A Meta-Synthesis of Meta Analyses Comparing PBL to Conventional Classrooms." *The Interdisciplinary Journal of Problem-based Learning*, Vol 3, No 1, 2009.

Chapter 29   Learning Problem Solving Principles

Problem-based education provides students a firm foundation for learning the principles of effective problem solving presented in this book. Integration of each of the eight principles into the practices of PBL is discussed below.

Principle #1: Mental Models are Not Reality

Throughout the educational process, knowledge is often presented as factual; there is no distinction drawn between the representation of a past or present condition of the world and the world itself. Nowhere is this more apparent than in the teaching of history. Historical *facts* are actually constructed by historians. Who are these people? What are their agendas, their worldviews? Secondary education is taught from secondary sources that mask the origin of historical representations. The process of historiography is rarely taught.

Under the pressure of covering broad spectrums of material, topics are *looked at* rather than explored. Exploration could expose students to the existence of alternative views of subject matter. When we are confronted with contrasting, even conflicting, alternative representations of the real world, we may come to appreciate that we are, in fact, looking at representations, not the real world itself.

Learning the scientific method further supports the idea that most of our representations of the world are actually like scientific hypotheses, calling for testing ideas through experimentation. The essence of the scientific method is to try to disprove hypotheses, not to confirm them as guided by the instinct of confirmation bias.

Well-defined problems are their own reality. When we are given problems in school, there is no need for research because the problem statement has all of the information required to find a correct answer. This promotes the notion that the problem is a reality of its own.

PBL introduces ill-defined problems where the student has to confront the context of the problem. Information is missing from the problem statement. Students must define the problem for themselves. This requires interaction with a real or pseudo client. Ill-defined problems require that students identify unknowns. They require investigating the context of the problem. All of this provides the opportunity to learn that a problem statement must be extracted from the real world. The problem exists in the real world, but the problem statement is something different. It is imperfect. It is a model.

In a preliminary course on computer programming, the following problem statement was given:[108]

> *Develop a program to calculate the net wage of a store's sale assistants. These sale assistants are paid a wage plus sales commission after deductions, such as income tax.*

The problem statement is intentionally incomplete. The instructor functioned as the client for the program. He encouraged the students to ask any questions that they required for clarification of the problem. Program solutions were subjected to a test to determine completeness. If the program was not fully functional, the student was told the manner of failure and allowed to revise the program. Eighty percent of the students ignored the existence of a client and proceeded directly to writing programming code. The authors concluded, "This behavior stems from the habit of dealing with well-defined problems."

In PBL, the use of ill-defined problems is often combined with an emphasis on recording the process of problem solving through

---

[108] Andrea Mendonca, Clara de Olieira, Dalton Guerrero, Evandro Costa, "Difficulties in Solving Ill-defined Problems: A Case Study with Introductory Computer Programming Students." *39th ASEE/IEEE Frontiers in Education Conference*, October 2009, San Antonio Texas.

journals and intermediate reports. Dewey again had it right when he equated our assessment of the consequences of our actions with thought itself.

> *Thought or reflection ... is the discernment of the relation between what we try to do and what happens in consequence. No experience having a meaning is possible without some element of thought.*[109]

The table below suggests opportunities within the PBL framework to introduce the seven strategies of Principle #1 that were presented in Chapter 7.

Principle #1: Mental Models are Not Reality			
	Page	Strategy	PBL Mechanism
Strategy #1	44	Be aware of the fallibility of mental models	Peer instruction
Strategy #2	44	Seek disconfirming evidence	Applying methods of science - experimentation
Strategy #3	45	Be open to criticism and self-criticism	Working in teams
Strategy #4	46	Strengthen your System 2 deliberative muscle	Keeping journals
Strategy #5	47	Employ Miller's law	Listening to the way others frame problems; working in teams
Strategy #6	47	Recognize your level of expertise	Post-project assessment, journals
Strategy #7	49	Validate mental models	Working in teams

---

[109] John Dewey, *Democracy and Education, an Introduction to the Philosophy of Education*, Macmillan Company, 1916. Republished as an e-document by the Penn State Electronic Classics Series. p. 150.

Principle #2: Be Willing to Reframe the Problem

In the real world, we first have to recognize that a problem exists. In school, problems are given to us. In the real world, we have to decide what tools to use to make sense of problems. In school, problems are assigned in the context of learning a tool we are expected to use. There is only one right way to frame a problem, since the frame is the tool we are trying to learn. Until we learn that our current representation of a problem is only one of potentially many models, we will not think to reframe the problem when the current representation is failing us.

Periodic self-assessment gives us the opportunity to reframe a problem. This notion builds on Principle #1. First, the problem solver must be aware that his current mental model is not the only possible representation. It is a tool that may or may not be working. If it's not working, alternative tools must be sought. The discipline of self-assessment can lead to rejection of the current framing of the problem.

Principle #2: Be Willing to Reframe the Problem			
	Page	Strategy	PBL Mechanism
Strategy #1	80	Hunt for helpful ideas	Team interaction
Strategy #2	83	Be aware of your progress	Keep journals
Strategy #3	84	Be curious - seek real understanding	Ask lots of questions & explore possibilities
			Explain concepts to others
Strategy #4	87	Be skeptical of expert opinion – even your own	Critically assess team members ideas
Strategy #5	88	Think metaphorically	Use brain storming sessions

Several features of PBL expose students to the usefulness of reframing. First, PBL classes usually organize students into teams. Team members work both in the group and independently, developing competing ways of framing the problem. The team must select one or more initial frames and then make periodic assessments of which model of the problem is providing an effective path toward a solution. Peer instruction as practiced in the teaching of physics at Harvard brings this benefit into sharp focus.

In addition, in PBL, problems unfold over days or weeks. As student research develops new information, changing perspectives can displace earlier models of the problem. PBL's emphasis on student logs of their work offers the opportunity to track changes in the way the team looks at the problem.

Principle #3: Seek Understanding Through Exploration

Howard Gardner wants the educational process to produce "human beings who understand the world, who gain sustenance from such understanding, and who want – ardently and perennially – to alter it for the better." He argues that questions are more important than answers, that knowledge and understanding should evolve from the constant probing of important questions.[110]

Exploration is a hallmark of all of the forms of PBL. However, the focus is often on exploration of information sources, expanding knowledge of the problem domain. Little emphasis is given to exploration of the structure of the problem itself. This type of exploration is found largely in design problems where competing interests within the problem vie for limited resources such as space, time, and money.

An effective vehicle for developing exploration skills is to explain subject matter to others. Several projects discussed in Chapter 28 illustrate the potential of learning from teaching. The project in Singapore, where high school students developed a guide to an ethnic neighborhood in Singapore, challenged the students not only to research the character of the neighborhood but also to consider how this information should be conveyed to tourists. The PBL writing class virtually puts student writers into the office of a congressman, requiring that they communicate the congressman's perspective to third parties through answering constituent letters, writing speeches, and developing Web site material. One format for PBL projects in

---

[110] Howard Gardner, *The Disciplined Mind* (The Penguin Group, New York, 1999).

science is for students to prepare demonstrations of basic scientific principles for various audiences such as parents and other students.

Principle #3: Seek Understanding Through Exploration			
	Page	Strategy	PBL Mechanism
Strategy #1	105	Relax constraints	Emphasis on exploring and understanding a problem before locking into solutions
Strategy #2	106	Think outside the box	
Strategy #3	108	Do not fall in love with your first idea	
Strategy #4	109	Be able to relinquish good solutions	
Strategy #5	109	Look at multiple solutions to each part of the problem	
Strategy #6	110	Seek out the hard parts of a problem and explore solutions to them	
Strategy #7	111	Move quickly through all parts of the problem. Then do it again. And again.	
Strategy #8	113	Conduct experiments	Encourage use of experiments to validate hypotheses
Strategy #9	114	Be flexible as to the granularity of your mental models	Reflection on how a team has modeled a problem can yield insights into the components from which the model was built
Strategy #10	117	Allow good solutions to emerge from understanding of a problem from both the top and the bottom	Post-problem assessment should plot the path taken to a solution.
Strategy #11	121	Let creativity happen without seeking it	

Exploration requires time. If we are to give kids the time to explore problems, we must be willing to live with a reduced number of problems. There is only so much time. We must accept that a reduction in subject matter coverage is warranted by the value of learning to explore with an open mind. PBL projects provide an opportunity to stress persistence, patience, and curiosity. Students must learn to be comfortable with early stages of a project where possibilities are being expanded rather than constrained.

Principle #4: Create Maps of Complex Problems

The notion of creating maps of problems fits comfortably in problem based learning. Linda Torp is chief education officer for Success Lab, Inc. in Chicago. Sara Sage is an assistant professor of secondary education at Indiana University. They both have extensive experience in constructing curriculums for problem-based learning in mathematics and science. They have compiled a guide to PBL curriculum development.[111] Under the heading *Mapping the Terrain of Problem Possibilities*, they argue that mapping is an invaluable tool with multiple applications for PBL.

> *Once you can see and examine the terrain of these possibilities, look for areas of conflict or dissonance… Are political, social or interpersonal conflicts apparent? What pulls you in, sparks a need to know, and begs for resolution? Do multiple stakeholders have a vested interest in the problem?…We look for situations that have multiple solutions. Most problems – especially in the real world – rarely have one right answer.*

Problem maps can take many diagrammatic forms but have the common purpose of guiding the exploration of the breadth and depth of a problem before making decisions that will limit possible solutions.

Complex problems involve people with different roles. Each role has a perspective that reflects aspects of the problem with which the

---

[111] Linda Torp and Sara Sage, *Problems as Possibilities: Problem-Based Learning for K-16 Education*, Association for Supervision and Curriculum Development, Alexandria, VA, 2002.

person is contending. Role-playing games are an effective tool for getting students to adopt a role driven perspective on a problem situation. When I was teaching construction management to graduate students in architecture, we used role-playing games that centered on stressful construction problems. Each problem defined four or five roles, including building owner, architect, construction manager, contractor, and supplier. We gave a general description of the situation to each student. We then gave separate descriptions for each role, including objectives and facts specific to the role. Their task was to meet as a group and agree on a course of action to resolve the problem.

For example, a storm may have just collapsed a construction crane, damaging several structural members. Replacing the members as originally designed would result in considerable time delays. Alternative solutions would require design alterations. Each alternative course of action has implications for all of the participants in the game. Students would begin the game self-consciously trying to adopt the personas of their roles. However, after a short time, they would play their role with enthusiasm.

Principle #4: Create maps of complex problems			
	Page	Strategy	PBL Mechanism
Strategy #1	154	Map goals	Use of concept maps
Strategy #2	158	Create Planning/ Evaluation Maps	
Strategy #3	160	Map the relationship between elements of a solution and Program Activities	
Strategy #4	161	Map resources	
Strategy #5	162	Recognize the need to shift among representations of the problem	Team members can assume roles with different representations of the problem – role-playing games

I was so pleased with the results of these games that I adopted a role-playing approach to the final exam for the course. The exam took the students through a series of meetings regarding a construction project. At these hypothetical meetings, the student was asked questions and had to propose courses of action to deal with the problem of the day.

Principle #5: The Perfect is the Enemy of the Good

Nowhere are the shortcomings of conventional education more starkly revealed than in the notion that problems have one and only one correct answer. This idea is inculcated into us from an early age. We learn our math tables. We are tested for our knowledge of historical facts. We are seldom, if ever, challenged by problems that are ill-defined or that have multiple paths to a solution. In the real world, the cost of solving a problem one way or another may play a big role in determining which path to take.

To solve real problems, we have to define our goals and assign them priorities. This is how we are able to assess alternative courses of action. Solutions are not right or wrong, but better or worse as scored by our goals. But in school, problems have a correct answer. Not only is there a correct answer, but there is also a correct way to get to the answer. Generally, creativity has no place in problem solving in school. In the real world, we can never be sure whether we have found the best solution. We have to decide when to stop looking for something better. Not so in school, where there is one right answer; you are either right or wrong. The school is an environment that fosters a lack of self-criticism.

Conceptualizing problem solving as a quest for perfect answers can burn us at both ends of the quality spectrum. On the one hand, we may deem a barely acceptable solution as *not wrong* and therefore *correct*. On the other hand, we may find that an exceptional solution still embodies compromises, failing to meet all goals at the highest level, and therefore is not *correct*. These extremes were on display when I taught architectural design to college juniors. When a student asks "What is wrong with this solution" he has fallen into the trap of thinking that a solution that is not *wrong* is therefore *correct*. Other students would become tied down to working out one particular

248

design detail and lose track of their progress toward an overall solution.

	Page	Strategy	PBL Mechanism
Principle #5: The Perfect is the Enemy of the Good			
Strategy #1	177	Develop a clear statement of goals	Use of ill-defined problems forces the students to ask questions and resolve conflicting interpretations of the problem
Strategy #2	179	Understand the nature of goals and be ready compromise	
Strategy #3	181	Satisficing	Monitoring progress can force closing in on a solution
Strategy #4	183	Be ready to redefine the scope of a problem	The goals of ill-defined problems can evolve as information is collected and solutions are explored
Strategy #5	184	Sensitivity analysis	Evaluating progress should include factors that are critical to a solution of a solution

There is a cognitive dissonance that arises out of our training in school to seek *correct* answers and the need for self-criticism described in the prior chapter. Self-criticism is required when we have to choose from a range of potentially viable alternatives.

PBL stresses the importance of ill-defined problems. Students are drawn in to shaping goals, sorting out what is important and what is not.

Principle #6: Manage the Planning Fallacy

The core of the planning fallacy is that we can easily imagine things going well on a project. Imagining unanticipated roadblocks is far more difficult because they are, well, unanticipated. The antidote to the planning fallacy is experience. Young professionals minimize the importance of experience, largely because they have so little. They favor thinking things through anew rather than relying on the results of past efforts. This phenomenon amplifies the planning fallacy.

Learning about the planning fallacy requires experience. Students in architecture school learn the difficulty of completing projects within a tight schedule. The value of experience is multiplied when students assess projects after the fact. When PBL incorporates student logs and post-problem review and assessment, there is an excellent opportunity to compare plans with actual results. In the real world, post-project assessments are seldom conducted unless the project has led to litigation.

PBL case studies can provide the opportunity to assess the problem solving successes and failures of others.

Principle #6: Manage the Planning Fallacy			
	Page	Strategy	PBL Mechanism
Strategy #1	193	Set intermediate goals	Planning, monitoring, and evaluating the work includes setting schedules, evaluating results, and learning about the planning fallacy
Strategy #2	194	Base plans on experience not projections	
Strategy #3	195	Use experience to set intermediate goals	

Principle #7: Employ Minimum Necessary Control

Problem solving in the real world often involves controlling the actions of others. Even in professional schools, this aspect of problem solving is minimized or completely neglected. Problem solving can involve a chain of decision makers, each limiting the range of options available to the next actors in the chain. Overwrought decisions at one level can hamper the quality of decisions at the next level. This effect is widely recognized in the realm of government regulation. Evoking the results that the regulator is looking for, without hampering the performance of the actions being regulated, requires supreme knowledge of the practices being regulated. Such knowledge is seldom in the hands of the regulator. The only path to effect minimum necessary regulation is extensive dialog and collaboration between the regulators and the regulated. This notion is anathema to interest groups that are steeped in the goals of regulation without appreciating the negative effects of overregulation. Role-playing games can be effective in exposing the need for collaboration in determining the extent and nature of control.

Principle #7: Employ Minimum Necessary Control			
	Page	Strategy	PBL Mechanism
Strategy #1	203	Exercise control in proportion to need	Learn from applying PBL principles in teaching younger students
Strategy #2	204	Practice benign neglect	
Strategy #3	205	Consider moving from proscriptive to performance specifications	Role-playing games

We can view the entire experiment of PBL as an exercise in minimum necessary control. The PBL teacher is a mentor, providing guidance and support only as needed for the student to navigate the waters of each problem.

Principle #8: The Real World May Fight Back

Problem solving in school entails few unexpected side effects. Experiences outside the classroom offer more opportunity to reflect on the realities of getting things done. Extracurricular activities at school often face unexpected obstacles such as need for funding, competition for facilities, and schedule coordination. Off-campus activities such as community service can also provide opportunities to observe the unexpected.

There are many real-world cases that can be studied where problem solving has been derailed by unintended consequences. The efforts over the years of the US Corps of Engineers to control the Mississippi River would provide rich examples.

Even in professional schools, problem solving is isolated from the realities of organizational context. Design schools create the possibility of developing the first six principles, since they traffic in ill-defined problems. However, students are isolated from the issues that arise as designs are taken into the real world of implementation.

Internships offer the potential to learn from real world problem solving. Unfortunately, interns are commonly hijacked to perform menial tasks within the organization. Structured internships focusing on project assessment could provide invaluable experience to the student and useful feedback for the organization.

In the teaching of science, PBL offers the potential for students to develop an ecological perspective, where they understand that changes in one part of a system are met by rebalancing of related parts. Having an ecological perspective on the behavior of systems will serve students well in assessing barriers to getting things done in the real world.

The way that we are traditionally taught about the physical world does not help us develop this dynamic perspective. For example, in architecture school, I was introduced to the basics of human comfort. We feel cold or warm for two reasons. First, cold or warm things may be touching us, and heat moves to or from us through conduction. This may be cold or warm air, seats, water, or anything else that contacts our skin. Second, we feel warm because warm objects like the sun or a fire radiate heat to us. Conversely, we radiate heat to cold surfaces such as large windows on a cold night. But I wondered how our bodies know that the cold surface is there in order to radiate to it. Of course, it does not. All surfaces radiate heat in all directions. The amount of heat they radiate is a function of their temperature and their surface color and texture. When we stand in a cozy cabin with our hands to the fireplace and our backs to the picture window, we are radiating equally in both directions. However, the fireplace is radiating more heat to us than we are radiating to it, so we have a net gain. Very pleasing. The window, on the other hand, is radiating less heat to us than we are radiating to it, a net loss.

	Page	Strategy	PBL Mechanism
Principle #8: The Real World May Fight Back			
Strategy #1	219	Adopt the outside view	Experiences outside the classroom offer opportunities for students to develop case histories of projects that have contended with resistance to change.
Strategy #2	221	Bring the interface within the scope of the problem	
Strategy #3	223	Reorganize	
Strategy #4	224	Work outside the system	
Strategy #5	226	Expand your view of stakeholders	

Problem-based learning provides fertile ground for learning principles of effective problem solving. In addition to being actively engaged in solving problems, students must learn to reflect on their efforts; they must learn to be self-critical.

To become effective problem solvers, even to become effective citizens, students need to strive to understand. Information is readily available on the Internet to confirm even the most thinly supported belief. Students need to reach beyond their confirmation bias to understand the complexities of the twenty-first century world. The burden on educators is not to inculcate curiosity; kids are born with that. Educators must design learning experiences that allow the students' natural curiosity to flourish.

Appendix 1   Design by Natural Selection

Design by natural selection is a method of generating design solutions for problems that lend themselves to rapid evaluation of the quality of individual design instances. In a sense, the process of natural selection explores a landscape of potential solutions looking systematically for a path to higher quality.

In the fall of 1965, in my third year of graduate school in architecture, I was moved to take a course in the math department called Design by Natural Selection. The professor, Brad Dunham, was a senior researcher at the IBM facility at Yorktown Heights, New York. Unlike most math courses, this one had no prerequisites other than that the student be immersed in some field other than mathematics and have some background in computing.

The course content was a summary of projects that Dunham had been involved in at IBM. Most were failures. He lauded the learning potential of failed projects. One that was not a failure was the design of a logic component for the IBM 360 series of computers. Other design teams at IBM had failed to come up with a mathematical algorithm for designing the optimal component configuration. Dunham took a different tack. He used a design approach that evolved good solutions through natural selection. Starting with a randomly selected design, Dunham's computer program would make a random change and see if the new solution was an improvement over the old. If so, the change would be accepted, if not, the change would be rejected. This process was repeated until the design converges on a good solution.

	Front entry	Rear entry	Door	Circ	Desk	Fresh	Flowers	Lawn	Mowers	Door	Powder	WC	Counter	Work space	Door	WC						
			Office							Women			Cash		Men		Aisle					
	1	2	3	4	5	6	7	8	9	10	11	12	13	14	15	16	17	18	19	20	21	22
1		0	6	0	0	25	0	0	0	0	0	0	30	15	0	0	50	0	0	0	0	0
2			4	0	0	3	0	20	20	10	0	0	0	0	10	0	0	0	0	0	0	0
3				50	10	0	0	0	0	15	0	0	5	15	15	0	4	4	0	10	0	0
4					50	0	0	0	0	0	0	0	0	0	0	0	0	0	0	0	0	0
5						0	0	0	0	0	0	0	0	0	0	0	0	0	0	0	0	0
6							50	6	0	0	0	0	0	0	0	0	10	30	15	0	0	0
7								0	0	0	0	0	0	0	0	0	10	0	0	0	0	0
8									50	0	0	0	0	0	0	0	0	10	30	15	0	0
9										0	0	0	0	0	0	0	0	10	10	5	0	0
10											50	0	0	0	0	0	0	0	0	0	0	0
11												50	0	0	0	0	0	0	0	0	0	0
12													0	0	0	50	0	0	0	0	0	0
13														50	0	0	15	3	0	0	15	15
14															0	0	15	3	0	5	0	0
15																50	0	0	0	0	0	0
16																	0	0	0	0	0	0
17																		50	20	10	20	20
18																			50	0	10	10
19																				30	10	10
20																					10	10
21																						50
22																						

1 Tabular set-up showing the numerical "pair importance values" that will determine the spatial relationships between various areas in a retail flower shop.

Reprinted from *Progressive Architecture,* August 1967, pp 110-11

Figure 45: Flower Shop

Dunham found that this process is not as simple as it sounds. First, it is essential that designs be easily scored, since the process will require many iterations, perhaps millions. Second, Dunham found that the path to good solutions is seldom a straight line. To illustrate, imagine we are in a hilly landscape and our goal is to get to the highest point. In essence we are "designing" our location in the landscape. Of course, we are blind and have no way to evaluate if a direction will take us toward higher ground without actually moving in that direction. So we take a step at random. Did we get higher? Then keep that move. Did we get lower, then reject that move. But what if we ascend a very small local hill? How would we know that this is not a good solution? Dunham developed tricks for testing for local peaks. It turns out that the size of each move is critical.

In the spring semester of that year, I set out to apply Dunham's natural selection approach to architectural design. The test case, a flower shop, was simple in the extreme, consisting of seven spaces made up of twenty-two elements. In the model, these elements could be arranged in any pattern in a rectangular grid. The score of any given arrangement was calculated by measuring the distance between each pair of elements and multiplying by a *pair importance value*, as shown in Figure 45; the lower the score, the better the design. For adjacent elements, the distance is zero. As in Dunham's projects, a simple scoring system is an essential element of the design by natural approach. The results illustrated in Figure 46 show snapshots of the design as it evolved from an initial state, shown at the top of the illustration, to a state where no improvement was found. This evolution required 3,474 random moves, reducing the score from 4,993 to 230.

These simple experiments took an entire semester to complete. In 1966, computer programs and input data were created on IBM punch cards and submitted to a computer center to be run. A day later, I would get the deck of cards back with large printout sheets, usually with only a few lines indicating that the program did not run, often because of a typo on one of the punch cards. Debugging even a simple program was agony.

Over the ensuing forty-five years, techniques of design by natural selection have become far more sophisticated. Rather than a single thread of changes from one version of the design to the next, populations of designs are represented. Each generation, superior individuals from the population are selected to interbreed, creating the next generation of the population.

Figure 46:

Sample Designs Progressing Toward Low Score

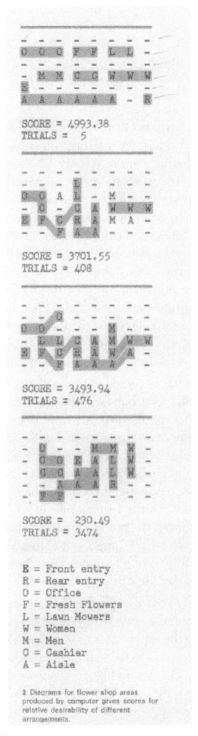

SCORE = 4993.38
TRIALS = 5

SCORE = 3701.55
TRIALS = 408

SCORE = 3493.94
TRIALS = 476

SCORE = 230.49
TRIALS = 3474

E = Front entry
R = Rear entry
O = Office
F = Fresh Flowers
L = Lawn Mowers
W = Women
M = Men
C = Cashier
A = Aisle

2 Diagrams for flower shop areas
produced by computer gives scores for
relative desirability of different
arrangements.

Appendix 2 Pill Probabilities

To predict how systems will behave, we build mental models. In these models, we attempt to capture the critical factors that dictate the dynamics of the system. This is what industrial engineers do for a living. In order to make operations flow more efficiently within organizations, they try to understand how operations work. The first step is to describe the aspects of the operation from which dynamics arise. These descriptions often take the form of mathematical equations or simulations. Once a model is built, it must be validated. Does it replicate what happens in the real world? First time around, the answer is usually no. So the description must be refined and the model fine-tuned. Several cycles of model building and validation might be required for the model to reach a useful level of predictive power. This excursion into pill probabilities is an illustration of the process of description, modeling, validation, and refinement.

It has occurred to me to wonder about the likelihood of getting a half pill when I shake a pill from the container that holds my blood pressure medication. My prescription calls for one half pill per day. The pills are oblong shaped with a crease down the middle to make breaking them in half with one's fingers possible, if not convenient. A new bottle of pills comes with a ninety-day supply – forty-five pills. At first, of course, there are no half pills, so the probability of getting one is nil, but as I break pills in half and consume one half, I return the other to the bottle. Gradually the number of half pills increases to the point where, bingo, out comes a half pill, no surgery required. So I set about trying to understand the dynamics of this process over the ninety-day life of the prescription.

My goal in exploring the pill selection problem was to be able to estimate the mixture of full pills and half pills at any given time during the ninety days that it takes to consume the bottle of pills. The first step was to try to understand the range of possibilities that could occur. The plot in Figure 47 shows the starting point in the upper left corner with forty-five full pills in the bottle on day one. The possible

258

outcomes are bracketed by two extreme cases. Line **A** shows the scenario where if there are any half pills in the bottle, they are taken. This results in a full pill being broken into two half pills every other day, one half being consumed on that day and the other half on the next. In the other extreme case, only full pills are selected as long as any remain. This scenario is shown Line **B**, where all of the full pills have been broken into half pills by day forty-six. (The number of half pills is not shown for these two cases).

The two lines marked **C** show a single scenario where pills are randomly selected. In this case, full pills are selected on each of the first ten days. By day thirty-one, there is the same number of full and half pills. By day seventy-five, all of the full pills are gone. Again, this is one random path through the ninety-day period.

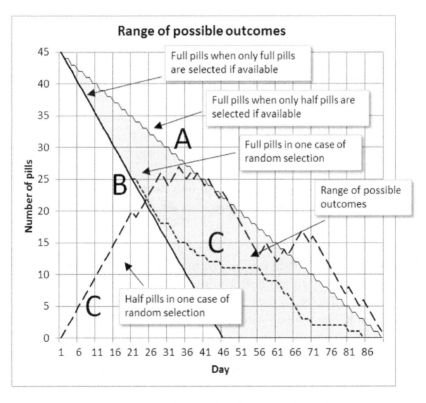

Figure 47: Pill Selection Possibilities

At this point, I need to clarify what I mean by *random*. We might think of running into a friend in a foreign country as a random event. In this usage, random means completely unpredictable; the probability of such an event is impossible to estimate. I am using random in the sense that a flipped coin lands randomly on either heads or tails. I know that there is a 50 percent chance of either outcome; I just don't know which it will be in any given toss. To be clear about the nature of randomness in our pill scenario, I will resort to the time-tested bag of marbles. Let's start with a bag of forty-five black marbles and a separate supply of forty-five white marbles. I ask you to reach into the bag of black marbles and pick one *at random*. At the start of our operation, you will pick a black one, because that is all that is there. When you pick a black marble, you put it into the discard bin and replace it with a white marble. After the first step in the process, the bag will have forty-four black marbles and one white one. You now reach in and select another marble. If it is black, which will likely be the case, you again set it aside and replace it with a white marble. If we repeated this entire experiment many times, every once in a while the second marble will be the white one. The probability of this happening would be one chance in forty-five, much like the chance of getting number twenty-two on an American roulette wheel is one chance in thirty-eight (thirty-six numbers plus zero and double zero). When you do grab a while marble from the bag, be it on the second try or whenever, you put it directly into the discard bin and proceed to the next step. As the process continues, the probability of picking a white marble increases with the increasing proportion of white marbles in the bag.

Now consider the three scenarios depicted in Figure 47. To actually achieve scenario **A** in our bag of marbles metaphor, you would have to be very lucky indeed. Each time there is a white marble in the bag, you would have to pick it. As discussed above, the first white marble would be mingling with forty-four black marbles. You would have one chance in forty-five of picking it, or about 2 percent. Once you cleared that hurdle, there would be only blacks for the third draw. On the fourth draw, there would again be a single white marble in the bag along with forty-three black ones. To continue along the path described by scenario **A**, you would have one chance in forty-four. Of course, it is extremely unlikely that you will continue to pick these lone white marbles. In fact, the chances are one in one billion-billion. The same odds are against you for following scenario **B**, where you only pick black marbles until they have all been replaced by white ones. Scenario **C** is a single actual case where the selection at each step was made at random based on the proportion of marbles in the bag or, should I say pills in the bottle. In this one case, note that the first ten selections were full pills. But what can we learn from a single case such as scenario **C**? The answer is, not much. We need to look at a large sampling of cases to develop an understanding of the shape of the operation.

Before we proceed, it is worth considering the relationships among a series of random events. The well-known *gambler's fallacy* is the belief that in a series of random events, the outcome of one event will affect the events that follow. For example, at roulette, if the color red comes up five times in a row, the next turn of the wheel has a more than even chance of resulting in a black. This is not true when the events are independent of one another, as with roulette and coin tossing. We can represent the results of tossing a coin ten times as a set of Hs and Ts. Consider the following two results of ten coin flips: HHHHHHHHHH and HHTHTTTHTH. Which of these two sequences is more likely to occur? The second example looks more realistic, since it is representative of a jumble of heads and tails. It looks more random. However, the probability of these two sequences is exactly the same as $1/2^{10}$, or about one chance in one thousand.

Our pill scenario is made the more interesting by the fact that, unlike flipping coins or spinning a roulette wheel, prior events in the sequence do affect the probability of later events. Each time we draw out a black marble, a white marble is added to the bag, and drawing a black marble the next time becomes less likely. This is a kind of self-regulating system, driving the content of the bag toward an equal number of black and white marbles.

Having developed a preliminary understanding of the dynamics of this process, the next step was to try to characterize the probable paths that random selection of pills would take. My preferred tool for this kind of analysis is Excel. A random path, like the one shown in Figure 47, can be generated using spreadsheet formulas. By generating a large set of random paths, a general picture of likely paths can be developed. The chart in Figure 48 shows the average percent of half pills for a set of five hundred random trials. 95 percent of the trials fall within the confidence range shown. In addition, the chart shows thirty of the five hundred results.

We now come to a critical step in the modeling process, validation. It happens that I did this analysis on day seventy-three in the life of my current bottle of pills. I checked the contents of the bottle and found eight full pills and two half pills – 20 percent half pills. Checking the chart in Figure 48, this state of affairs is far outside the 95 percent confidence interval. After a brief review of the logic behind my analysis, I came to one key assumption as the source of this disconnect between the model and reality. The model assumes that each time a pill is selected, the probability of selecting a large or small pill is proportional to the number of each in the bottle. Under this assumption, if there are sixteen large pills and sixteen small pills in the bottle, I would have a 50 percent chance of shaking out a small pill. But as I thought about my actual pill-shaking behavior, the plot thickens. As I shake pills from the bottle to my hand, I try to have just one pill come out; sometimes I succeed, but other times more than one comes out. If several come out, and there is a half pill among them, I maneuver the full pills back into the bottle, retaining the half pill. If only one pill comes out, if it is a full pill, I might shake a bit more to see if a half pill comes out. I am by no means poring over the entire contents of the bottle looking for half pills. However, I do allow myself one or two extra shots at scoring a half pill, thus avoiding having to split a full pill. (This behavior achieves nothing more that postponing the inevitable splitting of forty-five full pills; nonetheless, it is what I do.)

The discovery of such quirky behavior is common in industrial engineering. Such behavior may only be discovered by a model based on assumptions that do not capture real world behavior. In some cases, identifying such quirks is the payoff of the analysis. Such discoveries may call for corrective measure that can substantially improve operations. In our example, we are not looking to improve the pill consumption process; we just want to understand it.

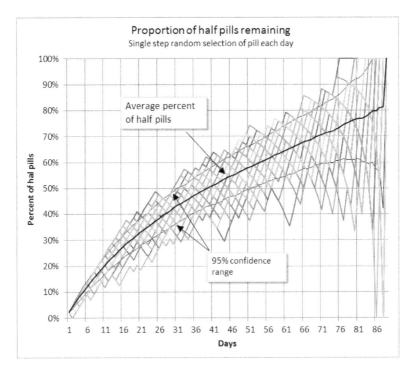

Figure 48: Probable Paths for Proportion of Half Pills

In order to move my model toward greater validity, I added a variable to each pill selection step. Rather than basing the probability of getting a half pill on a single selection attempt, I allowed for multiple attempts. Each day, the model would allow up to three random selections from the current contents of the bottle. Each attempt, the probability of getting a half pill would be based on the proportion of half pills in the bottle. Making up to three attempts would substantially improve the odds of getting a half pill. The chart in Figure 49 shows the probable percent of half pills with three selection attempts. This result seems more realistic when compared to my single data point of eight large pills and two small ones.

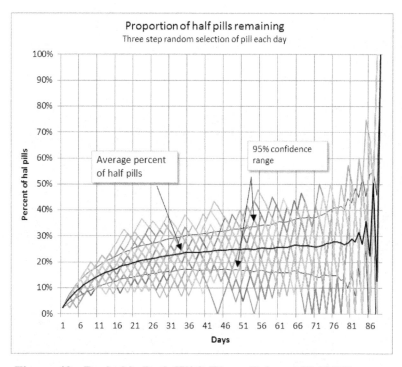

Figure 49: Probable Path With Three Tries at Half Pill

Figure 49 does not by any means represent a *correct* model of my actual pill selection behavior. At best, it is an approximation. More importantly, the process of description, modeling, validation, and remodeling has led to a substantial understanding of the dynamics of the operation. It also serves to illustrate the importance of the validation step. At the outset of framing a problem, it can be difficult to know what the critical descriptive factors might be. In some settings, collecting detailed information can be costly and time consuming. Model building is, of course, reliant on descriptive information, but it can also help us discover what information is critical. We should build the validation step into our problem solving process. Dissonance between models and reality should not be taken as a failure but rather as a step in the process of discovering the aspects of the problem that are critical to development of understanding.

Appendix 3   Truss Design

This appendix presents a short primer on structural analysis of a truss, elaborating on an example presented in Chapter 15. The key concept here is *free body analysis*, whereby components of a system can be defined in any manner that supports the method of analysis.

Statics is the analysis of structural systems that are not in motion, that are, in a word, static. These are the systems that hold up buildings, bridges, dams, and other structures that we want to remain stationary.[112] In reality, there are dynamic considerations in the design of such structures brought on by wind and earthquake forces, but for our purposes, we can set those considerations aside.

The underlying principle of statics is that objects that are not in motion must not have any net forces on them. That is, any force acting on the object must have an equal force acting in the opposite direction. This is one instance of the application of Newton's first law of motion:

> *Every object in a state of uniform motion tends to remain in that state of motion unless an external force is applied to it.*

The state of uniform motion that we are talking about in statics is the state of no motion. Take the case of you sitting in your chair. Let's presume for the moment that you are not moving. We know that you have a force on you; the earth is pulling you with the force of gravity. From Newton's first law, there must be an equal and opposite force pushing up; otherwise you would be moving toward the center of the earth. That force is provided by the chair. When we talk of *net* force, we are adding up the forces that are acting along the

---

[112] Stationary structures are subjected to the dynamic loads of wind, earthquakes, and in some cases traffic. These forces are neglected in this discussion.

same axis. The axis in this case is the vertical axis. We have to assign a sign to these forces as a function of their direction. We could call the downward force of gravity a negative force, and the upward force of the chair a positive force. The sum of these two forces is zero; otherwise you would be moving in the direction of the net force.

We need to take one more baby step here before we can walk. Please bear with me. Sometimes the forces that keep things from moving are not directly opposing one another. Take the hanging weight in Figure 50.

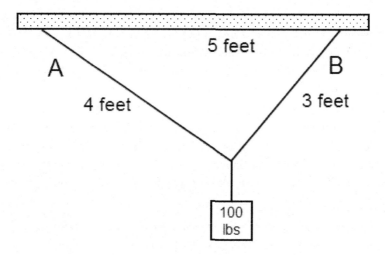

Figure 50: Weight Supported by Two Ropes

The one hundred pound weight is supported by two ropes. Nothing is in motion, so there must be an upward force on the weight to oppose the force of gravity. We can tell from looking at the picture that if the ropes and the connections are strong enough, they will support the weight; in other words, this is a plausible physical situation. To solve the problem, we must look at the vertical and horizontal *components* of the forces in the two supporting ropes. In Figure 51, I have shown the horizontal and vertical components of the forces in ropes A and B. I think we can agree on two things about the components just from observation. First, A_h must equal B_h. Since these are the only horizontal forces on the weight, if they were not equal, the weight would be moving sideways. Second, $A_v + B_v$ must be equal and opposite to the one hundred pound force of gravity.

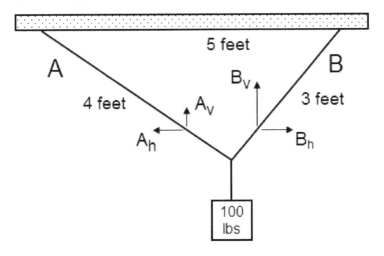

Figure 51: Components of Supporting Forces

These facts are not yet sufficient to solve for the forces A and B. The forces A, A_h, and A_v have a special relationship. They are proportional to the length of the sides of the triangle that they form. This relationship is indicated in Figure 52.

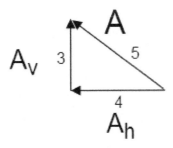

Figure 52: Components Proportional to Sides of a Triangle

This may make some intuitive sense if you image that the weight is hanging only from rope A, as shown on the left in Figure 53. In other words, rope A is vertical. There would then be no horizontal component to force A. If we pulled on A slightly to the right, there would be a slight horizontal component developed in rope A to the left to oppose the horizontal pull to the right.

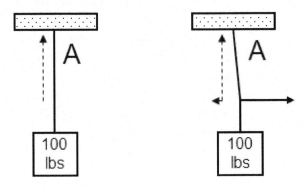

Figure 53: Introducing Small Horizontal Component to Force A

I want you to trust me that these force components are proportional to the sides of the triangle formed by the angle of the rope. This trust buys you not having to slog through several more pages of exposition on this subject.

So now we can solve for forces A and B in Figure 51.

$$A = 5/3 * A_v; \qquad A_v = 3/5 * A$$
$$A = 5/4 * A_h ; \qquad A_h = 4/5 * A$$
$$B = 5/4 * B_v; \qquad B_v = 4/5 * B$$
$$B = 5/3 * B_h ; \qquad B_h = 3/5 * B$$

Since $A_h = B_h;$ $\quad 4/5 * A = 3/5 * B;$

Since $A_v + B_v = 100;$

$$3/5 * A + 4/5 * B = 100;$$

Surely you recognize these as simultaneous equations that can be handily solved. Again, I'll spare you the process:

$A = 60; \quad A_v = 36 \quad A_h = 48;$
$B = 80; \quad B_v = 64 \quad B_h = 48;$

Now we are prepared to engineer static systems. All we have to remember from the above is that if we have only two unknown forces acting on a system, in our example, the forces A and B, and we know the direction of all of the forces acting on the system, then we can solve for the unknown forces.[113]

A classic problem in statics is the truss. We are designing the bridge shown in Figure 54 to support the three hundred tons of load shown in the drawing. The bridge supports can only provide upward support, not sideways. It should be fairly clear that each of the bridge supports must provide an upward force of half of the total vertical load, or one hundred fifty tons each.[114] But what about the forces in the eleven structural members that make up the bridge? Take a moment to look at the drawing and speculate about the forces in each of the truss members.

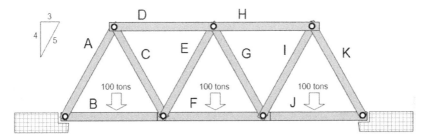

Figure 54: Bridge Truss Design Problem

Members B, F, and J are acting like beams, each supporting one hundred tons. They each require fifty tons of upward support at each end. The remaining members only have forces acting at their end points. These members are either in compression, acting like col-

---

[113] All of these examples are two-dimensional. Real-world engineering problems, of course, have to be concerned with forces in the third dimension perpendicular to our sheet of paper.

[114] We are neglecting the weight of the bridge itself.

umns, or in tension, acting like ropes. Each joint is a pin connection. This means that there are no rotational forces transmitted through the joints. This is common in truss design.

Here is where we introduce the concept of the *free body diagram*. We were able to determine the forces holding up the bridge, since we know that the bridge is not moving, and the only external force on the bridge is the three hundred tons pushing down. To draw this conclusion, we are looking at the bridge as a whole. To analyze the forces in the members that make up the bridge, we will have to look at its parts. But here's the trick: we need not look at parts in the sense of the parts from which the bridge is built. We can figuratively carve out any part that will help us with our analysis. In Figure 55, we have selected a section around one of the joints. If we think about the part of the bridge that has been selected, it must obey Newton's first law, just as any object must.

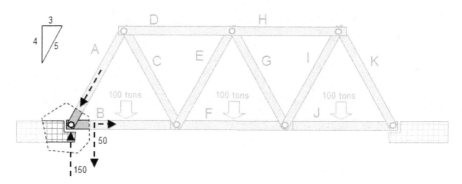

Figure 55: Defining Joint AB as Free Body

We know that there is an upward force at the bridge support of one hundred fifty tons. We know that there is a downward force in member B of fifty tons because member B is supporting one hundred tons, fifty tons at each end. There are two unknown forces, the force in member A and the horizontal force in member B. We can solve for these as we did with the hanging weight. Member A must have a vertical component of one hundred tons downward to offset the net upward force of one hundred tons from B and the support. But in order for A to have a downward component of one hundred, it must have a force along the axis of A of one hundred twenty-five tons, as shown in Figure 56. This is because these two forces have a ratio of four to five, as shown in the triangle to the left of the figure. This leaves a horizontal force in A of seventy-five tons. The only way to offset the leftward push of A is to have an equal and opposite rightward pull in member B.[115]

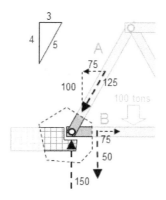

Figure 56: Forces in Joint AB

Having solved for the forces in member A, we can move to the ABD joint. (We will only take this one additional step in the analysis, so please stick with it.) But first, let's be sure we understand what is going on in member A. The diagram in Figure 57 shows that the one hundred twenty-five ton force that member A applies at the bridge support joint is opposed by an equal and opposite force of the bridge support on member A. If we look at the forces applied to member A, the one hundred twenty-five tons applied at the bottom must be opposed by an equal and opposite force at the top. This force, in turn, is opposed by an equal and opposite force upward from member A. Member A is in *compression,* much like a column in a building.

---

[115] The bridge support itself will typically be designed to allow horizontal movement of the bridge so that it can expand and contract. Therefore, the support does not apply any horizontal forces on the bridge.

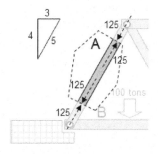

Figure 57: Forces in Member A

Now let's look at the ACD joint. The vertical force pushing up through member A can only be opposed by a downward force in member C, as shown in Figure 58. Member D, being horizontal, cannot exert a force up or down. The diagram in Figure 59 shows that member C must be pulling down and to the right with a force of one hundred twenty-five.

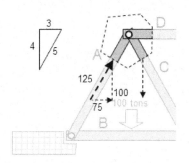

Figure 58: Define the ACD Joint as Free Body

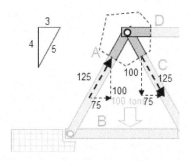

Figure 59: Analysis of Forces in Member C

Both members A and C are trying to move joint ACD to the right. The joint will move to the right unless member D provides an opposing force of one hundred fifty tons, as shown in Figure 60.

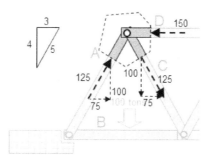

Figure 60: Analysis of Forces in member D

Let's step back for a moment and see what we have discovered. Member A is pushing up on joint ACD; it is in compression. Member C is pulling down on joint ACD; it is in tension. In essence, joint BCEF is hanging from member C. If we look at the bridge as a whole, we will see the forces shown in the diagram in Figure 61.

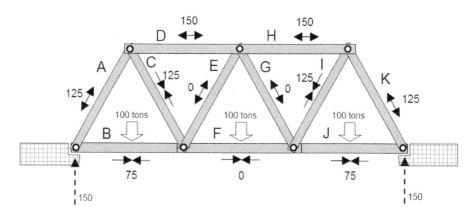

Figure 61: Complete Solution

You must agree that these results are interesting. The middle of the bridge is hanging from members C and I. E and G have no force at all, while D and H, which seem to be the most remote members from the action, are taking the largest forces. You might wonder why members E and G are in the design at all. Their function is to stabilize the ends of D and H in the center of the bridge. Otherwise, they would constitute one member twice as long, with a greater tendency to buckle.

There are several lessons to be learned from this exercise. First, systems do not have *inherent* component parts. We can define parts however we want in order to serve the purpose of understanding the behavior of the system. In this case, one might think that the parts of this bridge are obvious, the members A through K. Yet we defined parts by drawing boundaries around joints in order to do static analysis. We could not have done that on a member-by-member basis. This freedom, the freedom to break problems up into parts that support understanding, is an essential tool in solving complex problems.

Second, the way we frame a problem allows us to apply specific problem solving rules.

Third, sometimes solving the easy parts of a problem first makes sense. We start by solving those joints with the fewest unknown forces. This is loosely analogous to putting a jigsaw puzzle together, where we start with the easiest pieces to identify, the edges. Each piece that we fit with another piece makes the remainder of the puzzle a little bit easier. Caution: this is a dangerous rule to apply generally to problem solving.

Appendix 4   Furnace Test Procedure – Wisconsin Gas Company

This appendix reproduces Appendix J of the Report on the Pilot Project of the Shared Saving Program, an energy conservation project of the Wisconsin Gas Company, 1984. In order to evaluate the potential energy savings for each home heating system, a standard procedure was developed for field personnel. We can look at this procedure as a FRAME for collecting the information needed to predict the savings that would result from a new furnace. As is evident from thirteen changes in the procedure documented below, the procedure evolved as we applied it to a variety of situations. Frames are practical things. Their function is to guide us in creating mental models in order to predict the outcomes of our actions. They are subject to continuous improvement as suggested by this example.

The following discussion traces the development of the seasonal efficiency test procedure as it evolved during the fall of 1983. The first approach involved two parts.

1. Steady state combustion efficiency test using the Bacharach flue gas analyzer, measuring oxygen percent and net temperature of gasses leaving the furnace.

2. Test of off-cycle losses measuring the temperature of air in the plenum supplying air to the house. This test required an estimate of the heat stored in the heat exchanger during the warm-up cycle and the heat delivered to the house during the cool-down cycle. The difference was lost up the stack during cool-down.

Problem #1: Small errors in reading temperatures during warm-up or cool-down led to large percentage errors in the difference between heat absorbed during warm-up and heat supplied to the house during cool-down .

Change #1: Rather than measuring heat lost during cool-down indirectly, as the difference between heat stored and heat supplied to the house, the test was modified to measure directly the heat lost up the stack. Since the oxygen method of measuring flow in the stack is not available when the burner is not firing, several alternative flow measuring approaches were tried. Pitot type measuring instruments, designed for measuring flow in ducts, are ineffective at the low rates of flow encountered in furnace stacks. A hot wire anemometer was tried, but stack temperatures were too high for the instrument to give accurate readings. We then adopted use of a draft gauge, using flow formulas that the Wisconsin Gas Research Department has used in prior stack flow tests. Draft readings, converted to flow, were then combined with temperature readings to give heat flow up the stack during the cool-down period. On-cycle and off cycle flow readings were also used to determine infiltration of outside air into the house to make up stack flows. An infiltration factor of 0.7 was used, as in the DOE AFUE test, to account for the fact that stack flows result in reduction of exfiltration as well as addition of infiltration.

Problem #2: Extensive hand calculation of heat flow during off cycle based on draft and temperatures during one-minute time intervals.

Change #2: Equations used in the AFUE procedure were adopted to project cool-down temperatures and flows based on readings at three points in time.

Problem #3: In order to project average seasonal efficiency, it is necessary to extrapolate from the conditions of the test day to conditions for an average day.

Change #3: Average off time is calculated using the heating factor, furnace size, and measured *on time*. Average furnace room temperature is determined on the basis of measured furnace room temperature and the difference between outdoor temperature and average outdoor temperature of twenty-nine degrees. Average infiltration loss is based on the difference between average furnace room temperature and average outdoor temperature.

Problem #4: During warm up, furnaces operate at higher efficiency than during steady state, since the cooler heat exchanger results in better heat transfer and therefore cooler flue gasses.

Change #4: By measuring stack temperatures and flows during the warm-up period, the warm-up gain can be determined by comparing these temperatures and flows to steady state temperatures and flows. The AFUE method for projecting curves from a limited number of readings was also adopted for calculation of warm-up gain.

Problem #5: Calculation of the off-cycle loss as a percent of total use requires a projection of the average furnace *on time.* This was originally done by gradually increasing the thermostat setting until the furnace went on. At this time, the weather was too warm to wait for the natural on-cycle. We found that *on times* would be typically somewhat longer with this manual method as compared to a natural on-cycle.

Change #5: Where possible, we record the low voltage signal to the gas valve overnight, thus recording burner on and off time. If this is not possible, we time at least two on-cycles that occur naturally (without manually turning up the thermostat).

Problem #6: In several cases, the heat flow measured at the furnace outlet and in the stack after the draft diverter did not match, indicating error in one or more of the temperature or oxygen readings.

Change #6: It was determined that the thermometer used in the stack (with a three hundred degree limit) was giving a false reading. We had been substituting a higher range thermometer when higher temperatures were indicated, but on several occasions the thermometer indicated temperatures substantially below three hundred when they were actually above. In addition, the slow response time of the thermometer integral with the Bacharach analyzer gave falsely low readings of furnace exit temperatures during the warm-up period. We are now using a new high range fast response thermometer for all temperature readings.

Problem #7: In many cases, gas flows in the stack indicated by the oxygen readings were substantially below those indicated by draft readings. This error ranged from a few percent to nearly 100 percent. We discovered that in many cases there are restrictions in the cross sectional area of the stack at its point of connection to the furnace or draft diverter.

Change #7: We have measured the minimum cross-sectional area of the stack and recalculated flows based on this reduced area and draft readings. This proves to be an uncertain approach to calculating flows for two reasons. In some cases, it is not possible to determine this area. Furthermore, the rate of flow through an orifice of complex shape does not follow the equation for flow in a pipe of equivalent diameter. Therefore, we are using the flow determined by oxygen analysis to calibrate the draft readings taken when the burner is off.

Problem #8: Approximately one-half of the furnaces retested show inconsistencies in combustion efficiencies as measured at the furnace outlet. This appears to occur in cases where there is one large port rather than several smaller sectional ports. In such cases, temperatures and oxygen readings taken at this port vary greatly both from place to place and moment to moment.

Change #8: In all cases where furnaces were tested, efficiency as determined by temperature and oxygen readings in the stack (after the draft diverter) were consistent within 12 percent averaging about 6 percent. This includes readings taken on days with extremely differing outdoor temperatures. This consistency appears to result from the mixing of flue gasses, which occurs by the time they reach our test point in the stack. We are therefore now determining combustion efficiency on the basis of stack temperature and oxygen readings.

Problem #9: Seasonal efficiency on an average day does not necessarily reflect average seasonal efficiency for the full year. Notes in the DOE AFUE test book indicate that consideration was given to projecting furnace performance on the full range of days using bin temperatures but this was found to yield essentially the same result as using average conditions. We have found that under certain circumstances, bin temperature analysis yields a significantly different seasonal efficiency. For instance with low efficiency furnaces that are small relative to heating factor and run on a short on-cycle, bin temperature analysis may yield a seasonal efficiency 3 to 4 percent higher than using an average day.

Change #9: Since we take the bin temperature approach as reflecting more accurately the actual performance of a furnace during the course of a year, we now use this number (usually higher) rather than the result for an average day.

Problem #10: Analysis of the results of retests has shown that our original assumption that burner on-times are dictated by the thermostat anticipator is not true in all cases. Furnaces with longer burner on-times tend to run even longer as the outside temperature falls.

Change #10: We developed a method to project burner *on times* based on tested on-time, outside temperatures, and furnace size. This approach is described in a separate report - "Burner On-Time".

Problem #11: Furnaces with very large heat exchangers tend to operate at higher temperature ranges throughout their operating cycle as temperatures get colder and the heat exchanger does not fully cool-down by the start of the next burner on-cycle. This is not taken into account by our current evaluation procedure.

Change #11: We determined that for a full-scale program, the procedure would be modified to accommodate gravity units, but for the duration of the pilot program, this change would not be made. To protect the company and the customer against incorrect estimates of savings, a modified billing procedure was developed, reflecting only estimated savings rather than actual usage of the new furnace. This approach is discussed in the section on billing.

Problem #12: Higher flue drafts caused by low outdoor temperatures result in an overestimate of infiltration losses when tests are performed on very cold days.

Change #12: A draft adjustment factor was added on page four of the customer worksheet to reduce or increase stack flow based on the temperature on the test day compared to each temperature category in the analysis.

Problem #13: Near the end of the pilot program, it was discovered that stack flows were being inaccurately estimated because incorrect information was provided on the constituents of the natural gas currently being supplied by the company.

Change #13: Several key fuel-related variables were added to the first page of the worksheet as determinants of combustion air/fuel ratios and flue gas/fuel ratios. A third level of modeling was required to take the results of a single furnace test and extrapolate how it would perform throughout the year. Tests might be performed on a mild day where the furnace would go on once per hour, or our team might visit a house when the furnace was off for only brief periods of time. We developed a model that predicted furnace off times each month of the heating season, based on the results of a single test.

Appendix 5   A Pyramid of Oranges

This problem was posed to me in 2004, a time when I was absorbed by the question of how problem solving unfolds. Since I had worked the problem on a white-board in my office, I decided to record the process with as much fidelity as short-term memory permitted. It is a short story of the quest for understanding.

Two weeks ago, I got a phone call from a tennis buddy posing a mathematical problem. He asked me to imagine a stack of oranges with a square base, four on a side. The second layer is three on a side, on up to a single orange at the top. The question: How many oranges are in the stack? Of course, this is readily solved as the sum of the squares of four, three, two and one or sixteen plus nine plus four plus one. The total is thirty. The mathematical problem is to derive a formula for the total number of oranges as a function of the number along one side of the base.

I'm sure I would not be writing this story if I had not solved the problem, although the reader may question whether my derivation of the equation should really be considered a solution or just a lucky guess. The telling of the story has been triggered by a couple of factors. First, I worked the problem out loud on the white-board in my office, so I could retrace my steps. Second, I went back to the problem after I had presented the solution to try to come up with a logical derivation of the solution. And third, my mind has lately been preoccupied with a sort of meta review of my thought processes. This amounts to nothing more than an after-the-fact attempt to describe the course taken by a thought process and to fit its productions into some larger mental framework.

As I tell the story, I will try to guard against excessive after-the-fact embellishment. One of the hazards I face is distinguishing between the thoughts as they happened and the story-telling thoughts that try to connect the original piece of work to its roots.

It's 9:30 am, and the phone rings. The paced voice of Steve Preston is recognizable half-way into the first word. "I've got this great mathematical problem from a friend of mine, a professor of mathematics at Princeton. Visualize a stack of oranges with four on each side of the bottom level then three, two, and one at the top. The question is how many oranges in the stack. But not just for this case, but for any number. Now take your time on this one. See you at the match." We had a tennis match at 11:30.

Pass 1: Look at the Pattern of Numbers

My first instinct is to look at the solution to the problem for the first several cases and look for a pattern. The solutions for numbers one through five are shown in the table below.

Number	Oranges on Layer	Total Oranges
1	1	1
2	4	5
3	9	14
4	16	30
5	25	55

Obviously, the gap between values for total oranges is the perfect square that has been added at the base, but this does not lead to any obvious equation for total oranges.

Pass 2: Simplify From Three to Two dimensions

Seeing no path to an equation for total oranges in the pattern of solutions above, my next thought is to simplify the problem from three to two dimensions – the bowling pin approach.

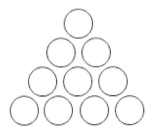

Figure 62: Bowling Pins

Number	Bowling pins on layer	Total bowling pins
1	1	1
2	2	3
3	3	6
4	4	10
5	5	15

I came up with an equation for total bowling pins by a process I cannot recollect; we could say it was trial and error.

Eq 1: $[N * (N + 1)] / 2$

After the fact, I stumbled across a rather elegant graphic path to this solution, as shown in Figure 63.

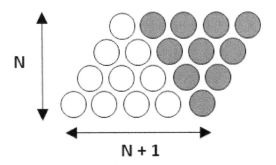

Figure 63: Two Sets of Bowling Pins

So what do bowling pins tell us about oranges? For one thing, the area of a triangle of base N is

Eq 2: $(N*N)/2$

Comparing equation 2 to equation 1, the number of pins is greater than the area of a triangle of equal size. The drawing in Figure 64 shows that a significant portion of our ten bowling pins extends outside of the area of a triangle of the same base. As the number of bowling pins along the base increases to infinity, the percent extending beyond the inscribed triangle approaches zero.

Figure 64: Number of Pins Larger Than Area of Triangle

Pass 3: Volume of a Pyramid

Not seeing a direct link between the equation for the number of bowling pins and the number of oranges, I returned to three dimensions. At this point, I pull out the recollection that the volume of a cone is one-third of the volume of the cylinder in which it is inscribed. I think that the same might apply to the pyramid of oranges and the cube in which it is inscribed.

I try to visualize the pyramid within the cube, and see the missing pieces. How can I match the missing pieces to a volume twice the size of the pyramid? No luck. I turn to calculus. If we plot a curve with the height of a continuous pyramid along the X axis and the cross-sectional area of the pyramid along the Y axis, the equation is:

Eq 3: $Y = X^2$

The plot in Figure 65 gives the cross-sectional area of a pyramid at X distance from its top. The volume of the pyramid will be given by the area under this curve, in other words, the sum of the cross-sectional areas. The area under this curve is given by the integral of the function that defines the curve.

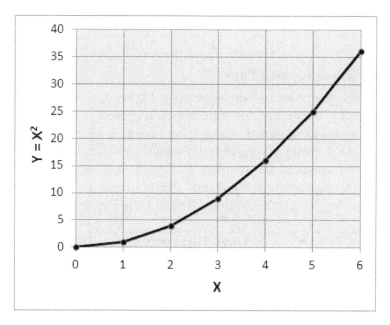

Figure 65: Area of Pyramid Cross Section as a Function of Height From the Bottom

The equation for the integral x to the power n is as follows:

Eq 4: $\int x^n = x^{n+1} / (n+1)$

So the equation for the volume of a pyramid with a height equal to one side of its base is:

Eq 5: Volume $= x^3 / 3$

Pyramid Height	Area of Base	X³	Volume: X³/3
1	1	1	0.33
2	4	8	2.67
3	9	27	9.00
4	16	64	21.33
5	25	125	41.67

Pass 4: Searching for a Pattern

I reach this point and am again stuck. I know that in the case of bowling pins, the area of the superimposed triangle is less than the number of bowling pins. For the same reason, I am sure that the volume of a pyramid will understate the number of oranges in a stack. I decide to compare the number of oranges to the volume of a pyramid. To deal in whole numbers, I decide to multiply the number of oranges by three rather than dividing X cubed by three.

N	N³	Three Times Number of Oranges	Difference
1	1	3	2
2	8	15	7
3	27	42	15
4	64	90	26
5	125	165	40

My goal now is to see a pattern in the difference. I want to start with three times N cubed and subtract an amount that is a function of N. This next step is inspired by the bowling pin solution. The expression $N * (N + 1)$ suggests a parallel in three dimensions. After trying a couple of possibilities, I land on $N^2 * (N + 1)$, in other words, $N^3 + N^2$. I compare this to the actual number of oranges times three in the table below.

I recognize the numbers in the difference column immediately as the number of bowling pins in triangular formation. Why this would be is not immediately apparent; nonetheless, I have my equation when I add the equation for bowling pins to $N^3 + N^2$ and divide the sum by three.

N	$N^3 + N^2$	Three Times Number of Oranges	Difference
1	2	3	1
2	12	15	3
3	36	42	6
4	80	90	10
5	150	165	15

Eq 6: Oranges in three pyramids = $N^3 + N^2 + [N*(N + 1)]/2$

This can be tidied up as:

Eq 7: $N^3 + (3*N^2)/2 + N/2$

The last step is to divide by three to get to the number of oranges in one pyramid.

Eq 8: $N^3/3 + N^2/2 + N/6$

Pass 5: Proof

On my morning walk the next day, I turned to the question of proof. I knew that the formula worked for the cases of N = 1 through N = 5, since I had worked those out by hand. I had also confirmed that the formula worked for cases up through N = 40, by setting up the solution for these cases in Excel. So I knew that the formula worked before I delivered it the day before. But this was not proof that it worked for all cases of N.

I turned to the tried and true method of induction for the proof. The induction method says that if you can prove a proposition about numbers for the case of N = 1 and you can prove that if the proposition is true for any number N, then it is true for N+1, you have a proof that it is true for all numbers. This follows from the fact that given the second part of the proof, if the proposition is true for N = 1, then it is true for N = 2. But in the first part of the proof, we would have established that it is true for N = 1, therefore it is true for N = 2. But if it is true for N = 2, then it is true for N = 3, and so forth for all of the countable numbers.

So, given our equation, we can prove that it is true for N = 1 by solving the equation and comparing to an actual count of the oranges.

In a pyramid with one orange on a side, there is one orange. When we substitute one for N in the equation below:

Eq 9: $\qquad N^3 / 3 + N^2 / 2 + N / 6$

We get:

Eq 10: $\qquad 1/3 + \frac{1}{2} + 1/6 = 1$

This was the easy part. Now for the induction part. I am going to show that if the above equation is true for the number N then it is true for the number $M = N + 1$. We know that in the real world of orange pyramids, the difference between one pyramid with base of M on a side and one with base of N on a side is that a square base of M by M oranges that have been added to the bottom of the N pyramid. The difference between three N pyramids and three M pyramids will be $3M^2$, as shown below. I'm using three pyramids since the equation is a bit simpler.

Eq 11: $\qquad$ **3 N pyramids + 3 * M^2 = 3 M pyramids**

Now we put in the equation for the number of oranges in three pyramids of N and M on a side:

Eq 12: $\qquad N^3 + (3 * N^2) / 2 + N / 2 + 3 * M^2 =$

$$M^3 + (3 * M^2) / 2 + M / 2$$

If the above equation is true, then we have proven by induction that our equation holds for all values of N. The equation below consolidates the expressions with M on the right side.

Eq 13: $\qquad N^3 + (3 * N^2) / 2 + N / 2 =$

$$M^3 - (3 * M^2) / 2 + M / 2$$

To simplify the next steps, multiply through by two:

Eq 14: $\qquad 2 N^3 + 3 * N^2 + N = 2 M^3 - 3 * M^2 + M$

Now we can substitute $N + 1$ for M as follows for the three expressions on the right hand side of equation 14.

Eq 15: $\qquad 2 M^3 = 2 (N + 1)^3 = 2 N^3 + 6 N^2 + 6 N + 2$

Eq 16: $\qquad - 3 M^2 = -3 (N + 1)^2 = - (3 N^2 + 6 N + 3)$

Eq 17:   **M   = N + 1.**

Now we can substitute the expressions from equations 15 through 17 into equation 14 as follows:

Eq 18: $2 N^3 + 3 * N^2 + N = (2 N^3 + 6 N^2 + 6 N + 2) - (3 N^2 - 6 N - 3) + (N + 1)$

Consolidating the values on the right side of the equation, we get:

Eq 19: $2 N^3 + 3 * N^2 + N = 2 N^3 + 3 N^2 + N$

This proves that the hypothesis in equation 11 is true.

But Why Does it Work?

It was only the *idea* of using induction that occurred to me on my walk; the details required pencil and paper. But even knowing that this proof would work out, I was still left feeling a bit empty handed. I was lacking the visual proof provided by the bowling pin solution in Figure 63. So I started over, imagining three pyramids with a base of three on one side and a cube, a square, and a triangle with bases of three on the other.

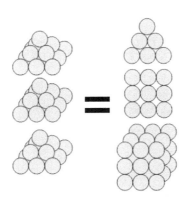

Figure 66: Graphic Equivalent of Equation 6

One can verify by eyeball that the three pyramids in Figure 66 have the same number of oranges as the cube, square, and triangle on the right. This is the graphic equivalent of Equation 6.

Applying the same principle of induction, let's move from this case where N = 3 to the case of N = 4. On the left, we will be adding three squares that are four by four oranges at the bottom of the three pyramids. On the right, we will be adding three faces to the cube that are four by four as shown below in Figure 67.

But these three faces have fewer oranges than the three four by four squares added to the pyramids, since the faces of the cube have some oranges in common. The dark gray, or left, face of the cube is claiming all sixteen of its oranges and matches one of the bases of the three pyramids. The black, or top, face shares four oranges with the dark gray face, so we look to the bottom of the triangle to provide the missing four oranges, making up the base of the second pyramid. The white, or front, face of the cube has only nine oranges of its own, since it shares oranges with both of the other newly added faces. The new edges of the square provide the seven oranges required to make of the third four by four base. As N grows from four to five and so on, each step of the way, the triangle and square will have grown to fill in for the oranges that are shared by the faces of the cube.

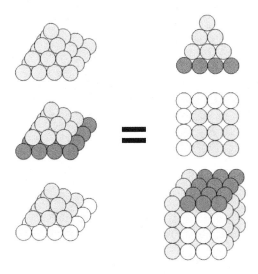

Figure 67: Transition From Base of three to Base of Four

Figure 68 shows how we get from N = 2 to N = 3.

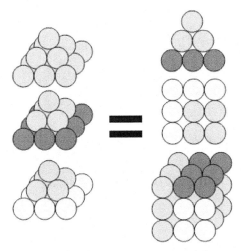

Figure 68: Transition From Base of Two to Base of Three

Figure 69 gets us from N = 1 to N = 2.

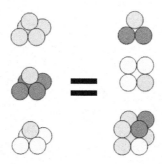

Figure 69: Transition From Base of One to Base of Two

Figure 70 establishes that in the case of N = 1, three pyramids have the same total number of oranges as a cube, a square, and a triangle.

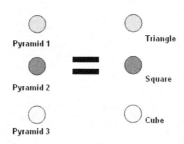

Figure 70: Base of One

Appendix 6   Pascal's Triangle

The story in this appendix was written in August 2005 at the time the events in the story took place. I was sufficiently lost in my quest to understand this problem that it seemed ripe for documentation. At that time, this book was a glimmer in my eye. This is the story of searching for a frame. I explored several ways of framing the problem without satisfaction. In the end, the clouds parted and a very simple model emerged.

This piece is about problem solving. It is about the interplay between a problem and the tools that might be used to solve it. The problem in question is about numbers. I'd like to think that there are some people who share my fascination with the magic of numbers, but maybe you're not one of them. So why read on? There is the mere suggestion in these pages that the search for a solution in this case might shed some light on a broader class of problem solving. You might classify this problem in the broad class of: "College Board Questions" as does my lovely wife. What I'm trying to capture is the search for a way of looking at a problem that yields not only a solution but also understanding.

The approach is to present the steps that I went through, from problem discovery to failed efforts to solution without understanding, to new tools, and finally to understanding.

Each section begins with an italicized summary that would allow the faint of heart to skip the details.

Step 1: The Problem of Counting Sit-ups

I love to count things. There are many variations on counting. When I get into elevators, I like to find words of eight letters. Bathrooms challenge me to estimate the number of tiles on the walls or floors, and then count them to check out the estimate. I used to count basketball hoops while driving in rural Wisconsin. Finding hoops is spiced up by holding my breath between hits. Same applies to finding flag holder gizmos on houses while walking to work in Milwaukee.

I'm not sure why counting to twenty-five recurs in my life. I like to walk with my eyes closed from time to time. Twenty-five steps is an ambitious goal in all but the most open spaces. I have been doing my morning sit ups in groups of twenty five since I had serious back problems in the early eighties. I like to vary the way I count to twenty-five. I think that seven-six-five-four-three is my favorite. It recently occurred to me to count the ways of counting to twenty-five. Pursuit of this question led to this little monograph.

In this section, my first attack on the problem is to look at a simpler version. I break the simpler version into parts, briefly have a false sense of progress, and eventually run out of steam. The main contribution of this first step is clear definition of the problem.

First, we should have a clear statement of the problem:

How many ways can one divide the counting from one to twenty-five into segments? Each segment can have from one to twenty-five numbers.

Of course, a general solution to this problem must answer the question for any number, not just twenty-five.

Breaking the Problem Into Parts

It seems altogether logical to look at this as a set of subproblems. There is one way to count to twenty-five in one segment:

1, 2, 3…25.

There are twenty-four ways to count to twenty-five in two segments:

294

Segment 1   Segment 2
1;   2, 3, 4…25
1, 2;   3, 4, 5…25

…

1, 2, 3…23; 24, 25
1, 2, 3…24; 25

How many ways can I count to twenty-five in three segments? Here's where it gets more interesting. This is also where I decided that a simple version of the problem would be easier to explore. Let's count to six in three segments. I'm also going to get away from the numerical counting in favor of groups of dots. Table 1 gives the alternatives for this case. I'm going to use the expression 6/3 to refer to six things counted in three segments.

Table 1: Count to Six in Three Segments (6/3)						
	Segment					
Case	**1**	**2**	**3**	**4**	**5**	**6**
1	••••	•	•			
2	•••	••	•			
3	•••	•	••			
4	••	•••	•			
5	••	••	••			
6	••	•	•••			
7	•	••••	•			
8	•	•••	••			
9	•	••	•••			
10	•	•	••••			

So I pondered this case. How could I get from here to the case of 25/3? There is a pattern here. There is one case with four in the first segment, two cases with three in the first segment, three with two, and four with one. The total number of cases is the sum of

1+2+3+4. There is a general formula for the sum of the numbers from 1 to n:

Sum of numbers from 1 to n = n * (n+1) / 2.

If I could prove that this is true for all values of n, then the solution for 25/3 would be

Sum of numbers from 1 to 25 = 25 * (25 + 1)/2 = 325.

At this point I've got two problems: prove that the above formula works for all numbers and determine how this logic applies to counting in four or more segments. I decide to focus on the case of four segments.

Table 2: Count to Six in Four Segments (6/4)						
	Segment					
Case	**1**	**2**	**3**	**4**	**5**	**6**
1	●●●	●	●	●		
2	●●	●●	●	●		
3	●●	●	●●	●		
4	●●	●	●	●●		
5	●	●●●	●	●		
6	●	●●	●●	●		
7	●	●●	●	●●		
8	●	●	●●●	●		
9	●	●	●●	●●		
10	●	●	●	●●●		

Table 2 shows the ten cases where six items can be counted in four segments. The pattern is less obvious here than in the 6/3 case. When three are taken in the first segment, there is only one case. When two are taken in the first segment, the total is 1 + 2, a pattern that can be seen in the second segment. When one is taken in the first segment, the pattern in the second segment is clearer still, $1 + 2 + 3$. Reducing this pattern to a formula is more complex than in the 6/3 case and does not bode well for five, six or more segments.

At this point I stalled out.

Step 2: Try Some Familiar Tools: Permutations and Combinations

My next approach was to try to recast the problem into a problem of combinations or permutations. Permutations and combinations are methods of counting the ways that items can be selected from a group of items, such as dealing a hand of cards from a deck. I tried to formulate the counting sit-ups problem as a combinations problem but failed. As we will see later, I should have tried harder.

To proceed, we need a brief refresher on this little corner of high school math. Permutations and combinations deal with counting the ways in which items can be selected from a group.

A simple example of a permutations problem is to determine the number of ways that a specified number of cards can be dealt from a deck. Let's say we have a deck of ten cards made up of the ace through ten of hearts. We deal a hand of two cards. How many ways can these two cards be dealt? A single permutation would be the three dealt first and the four dealt second. If the four is dealt first and the three is dealt second, that is a second permutation. If we do not care about the order in which they are dealt, then we are counting combinations.

The number of permutations of ten cards taken two at a time is ten times nine. There are ten ways that the first card can be dealt. For each of these, there are nine ways that the second card can be dealt. If a third card is to be dealt, then for each of the ninety ways that the first two can be dealt, there are eight ways to deal the third card – a total of seven hundred twenty permutations for ten cards taken three at a time.

If we call the number of cards N and the number dealt M, then the expression for the total permutations is:[116]

Permutations of N things taken M at a time = N! / (N-M)!

As I recall it from high school, the number of combinations is derived from the number of permutations. In our example where we deal hands of three cards, each combination of three cards has six permutations. For example, if I were dealt the two, three, and four of hearts, they could be arranged in the following ways: 2-3-4, 2-4-3, 3-2-4, 3-4-2, 4-2-3, and 4-3-2. This can be computed using the above equation with N = 3 and M = 3.

With N = 3 and M = 3,   N! / (N – M)! = 3! / 0! = 6

The seven hundred twenty permutations in our example of ten cards taken three at a time are made up of one hundred twenty combinations with six permutations for each. To compute the number of combinations from the number of permutations, divide the total permutations by the permutations within the selected group. This latter number is M!

Combinations of N things taken M at a time = N! / (N-M)! / M!

Since I have a passable knowledge of these rules, my challenge was to recast the problem of counting sit-ups into a problem of combinations. I couldn't make it fit. Dividing the counting of a sequence of numbers into segments just did not conform to my range of possible permutation or combination problems. Square peg, lots of non-square holes.

---

[116] The "!" symbol connotes "factorial," meaning the product of all numbers from the specified number to one. For example, 5! = 5 * 4 * 3 * 2 * 1 = 120. Note that 0! Equals 1.

Step 3: Brute Force

Looking for another angle of attack, I decided to calculate the total number of ways to count sit-ups for small values of N, where N stands for the total number of sit-ups.

Table 3: Number of Cases for N = 1 to 6						
	Segments					
N	1	2	3	4	5	6
1	1					
2	1	1				
3	1	2	1			
4	1	3	3	1		
5	1	4	6	4	1	
6	1	5	10	10	5	1

Some problems yield to brute force, where one simply counts all possible outcomes. Table 3 counts the possible segments (shown in the columns) for the number of items being counted (N) equal to one through six (shown in the rows).

For example, in row 4, column 2 has a value of three. This says that there are three ways to count to four in two segments. (They are 1-3, 2-2, 3-1.) I came up with these values by systematically counting all of the possibilities. This approach works for small values of N, but not for larger values, such as twenty-five.

Pondering Table 3, I eventually noticed that each cell is the sum of the cell above and to the left. This is illustrated in the three high-lighted cells, where $10 = 4 + 6$. Of course, the first column has no left, so it is equal to the cell above. On further inspection, I noticed a more amazing pattern: the sum of each row is a power of two. For the rows one through six the sums are 1[117], 2, 4, 8, 16, and 32. Wow. Suddenly, if this holds for all numbers, my problem is solved by the simple equation:

Total cases = 2 $^{(n-1)}$

---

[117] Remember that any number raised to the zero power is one.

If this is true for all values of N, then the total number of ways to count to twenty-five is $2^{\wedge 24}$ or 16,777,216.

But why would this be true, and how could I prove it?

Step 4: Proof by Induction

Having discovered that the total ways to count sit-ups seemed tied to powers of two, I set out to prove it. My tool of choice for proving propositions in logic or math is induction. Broadly speaking, induction is the process of deriving general truths from the truth of specific examples. Mathematical induction employs a specific technique of getting from the truth of instances to the truth of a broader class of statements. As satisfying as it is to complete a proof of this sort, I find that it adds little to my understanding of why the counting of sit-ups should be related to powers of two.

The premise that induction works is a basic assumption (*primitive*) in mathematics. Attempts to reduce mathematics to a minimum number of primitives in the late nineteenth century distilled out five assumptions; one of them is that the principle of induction works.

Mathematical induction: If a statement can be proven true for the number 1, and it can be proven true that if the statement is true for any number N, it is true for N+1, then the statement is true for all numbers.

So, how do we apply induction to our problem of counting sit-ups? Our hypothesis from page 299 is that the total was to count up to a number N is $2^{(N-1)}$. If we can show that for any number N the number of cases for N+1 is twice the number for N, then we have the core of an induction proof. To state this more clearly:

If

[a] Cases for N+1 = 2 times cases for N, and

[b] Cases for N = 1 is 2^{N-1}, then

[c] Cases for all N = 2^{N-1}

Example of Mathematical Induction

Prove that for all numbers N,

(a) $1 + 3 + 5 + ... + (2N-1) = N^2$

For example, for N = 4: $1 + 3 + 5 + 7 = 16 = 4^2$

[1] First we must show that the equation is true for N = 1. Since (2N-1) = 1, we are left with $1 = 1^2$.

[2] Now we must prove that if it is true for any number N, it is true for N + 1. Let's say that M = N+1. Starting with the premise that equation (a) is true for N, we must now prove that it will be true for M.

(b) $1 + 3 + 5 + ... + (2M-1) = \qquad M^2$;

We now substitute (N + 1) for M in (b):

(c) $1 + 3 + 5 + ... + (2(N+1) - 1) \quad = \qquad (N + 1)^2$

(d) $1 + 3 + 5 + ... + (2N+1) \qquad = \qquad N^2 + 2N + 1$

We know that $(N+1)^2 = N^2 + 2N + 1$. (quadratic equation).

Let us look at the number in the series on the left just before the last number. It will be two less that the last number, or 2N + 1 – 2, or 2N – 1;

(e) $\underline{1 + 3 + 5 + ... (2N - 1)} + (2N + 1) = \quad \underline{N^2} + 2N + 1$

But notice that the underlined portions on each side are equal, since our premise is that equation (a) is true. Since we are adding equal amounts to each side of a valid equation, the equation continues to be valid. Therefore, if equation (a) is true, equation (e) is true.

Since we have shown that (a) is true for N = 1, it must be true for N = 2. And since it is true for N = 2, then it is true for N = 3. And so on. This is proof by induction.

The argument below will show that if we assume that the proposition is true for N = 4, it is then true for N = 5. This is meant to represent that if one assumes that the proposition is true for any number N, it is true for N + 1. A specific example is being used to make the discussion more concrete.

Table 4 gives all cases for counting to four with any number of segments from one to four.

Table 4: Count to Four in Any Number of Segments = Eight Cases						
	Segment					
Case	1	2	3	4	5	6
1	••••					
2	•••	•				
3	••	••				
4	•	•••				
5	••	•	•			
6	•	••	•			
7	•	•	••			
8	•	•	•	•		
9						
10						

We are now going to derive all of the ways to count to N + 1 (N + 1 = 5 in our example). First, as shown in Table 5, we will add a single element as a new first segment to each of the cases for N given in Table 4.

There are two facts that we must show to be true for these eight cases for counting to N + 1:

1. Each case is unique. If each of the eight cases in Table 4 is unique, then it is obvious that the cases in Table 5 are also unique.

2. If the cases in Table 4 represent every way to count to four, then the cases in Table 5 represent every way to count to five in which the first segment has one element. This falls a little short of obvious. Let's restate the process. We are asked to count to five by starting with a segment of one element. Once we have taken the one el-

ement for the first segment, we have N - 1 elements (in our example, four) remaining. How many ways can we count to four? Our premise is that these are all given in Table 4, and therefore, have been reproduced in Table 5.

Table 5: Cases for N+1 = 5; With a First Segment of One Element Added to the Cases for N = 4						
	Segment					
Case	1	2	3	4	5	6
1	○	●●●●				
2	○	●●●	●			
3	○	●●	●●			
4	○	●	●●●			
5	○	●●	●	●		
6	○	●	●●	●		
7	○	●	●	●●		
8	○	●	●	●	●	
9						
10						

In Table 6, we show that eight additional unique cases can be generated from the cases in Table 4 by adding one element to the first segment in each case. There are three facts we must show to be true about the cases in Table 6:

1. Each case in Table 6 is different from all other cases in Table 6. This seems obvious since our premise regarding Table 4 is that each of its cases is unique. Adding one element to the first segment of any two cases that are different will result in different cases. Therefore, all pairs of cases in Table 6 must be different.

2. Each case in Table 6 is different from each case in Table 5. Since all cases in Table 6 have more than one element in the first segment, and all cases in Table 5 have one element in the first segment, there are no duplicates between Table 5 and Table 6.

3. Now the tough nut: we must show that if all cases for N elements are included in Table 4, then all cases for N + 1 elements are included in Tables 5 and 6.

Table 6: Cases for N+1 = 5; With One Element Added to the First Segment of Each of the Cases for N = 4						
	Segment					
Case	1	2	3	4	5	6
1	○●●●●					
2	○●●●	●				
3	○●●	●●				
4	○●	●●●				
5	○●●	●	●			
6	○●	●●	●			
7	○●	●	●●			
8	○●	●	●	●		
9						
10						

For any number of elements N, cases can be generated with a number of segments from one to N. We will refer to the number of segments of a particular case as M. We will look at three values that M can take on.

For M = 1, there is only one case that has N elements. This is created in Table 6, row 1, by adding one element to the case where M = 1 from Table 4.

For M = N, there is only one case that has N segments with one element in each. This is created in Table 5, row ,8 by adding one segment of one element at the front of the case from Table 4 with four segments of one element each.

For all values of M between one and N, there are multiple cases for each value of M. For example, in Table 4, three cases are given in for M = 3. They are in rows 5, 6, and 7. What we will show now is that for any value of M between one and N, every case for N + 1 will be found in Tables 5 and 6. Let's use M = 3 as our example. In Table 7, each case with three segments in Table 4 spawns three variants with an added element. This is so because a new element can be added to any of the three segments.

Table 7: All Possible Ways to Create Cases with Three Segments by Adding One Element				
Variant	Table 4 Case	Segment 1	Segment 2	Segment 3
1	5	○●●	●	●
2	5	●●	○●	●
3	5	●●	●	○●
4	6	○●	●●	●
5	6	●	○●●	●
6	6	●	●●	○●
7	7	○●	●	●●
8	7	●	○●	●●
9	7	●	●	○●●

These are not necessarily unique cases; in fact, there are duplications in variants 2, 4; 3, 7; and 6, 8. Table 7 is not meant to produce unique cases but rather all possible cases for three segments.

What we need to show now is that all of these possibilities are covered by the cases in Tables 5 and 6. Let's divide these variants into two groups: those that begin with segments of one element, and those that do not. We have already shown that Table 5 includes all possible cases that begin with a segment of one element. Variant 5 is Table 5, case 2. Variants 6 and 8 are Table 5, case 3. And variant 9 is Table 5, case 4.

Now we deal with the variants where the first segment has more than one element. We must show that each of these appears in Table 6. Pick any variant with more than one element in its first segment, say variant 2. Remove one of the elements from the first segment. We now have a case for N = 4, which must appear in Table 4, if our premise is true that all cases for N = 4 appear in Table 4. It is, in fact, case 6 of Table 4. We can now create a case in Table 6, by adding an element to the first segment, reproducing variant 2. This turns out to be case 6 of Table 6. Thus, although variant 2 in Table 7 was not originally generated by adding an element to the first segment, we have demonstrated that it is identical to a case in Table 6 that was generated by adding an element to the first segment of one of the cases in Table 4.

We have shown here that for any number of segments, M, all possible cases for N + 1 elements have been created by the methods that created Table 5 or Table 6.

So what have we proven? If all of the cases for N elements are listed in Table 4, then Tables 5 and 6, each with the same number of cases as Table 4, list all of the possible cases for N + 1. In other words, *if we have identified all of the cases for N elements, then there will be exactly twice as many cases for N + 1 elements.*

In Table 8, we express the number of cases for each N as a power of two. Since the number of cases for N = 1 is one, it conveniently works that $2^{(N-1)}$ equals one. Since the number of cases for each value of N + 1 is two times the number of cases for N, we can express the number of cases for each N + 1 as $2 * 2^{(N-1)}$. This is $2^{(N)}$.

Table 8: The Formula		
N	Cases	$2^{(N-1)}$
1	1	$2^0 = 1$
2	2	$2^1 = 2$
3	4	$2^2 = 4$
4	8	$2^3 = 8$
5	16	$2^4 = 16$

But we know that the number of cases for N = 1 element is $2^{(N-1)} = 1$. Therefore, we know by induction that the number of cases for N = 2 is $2^{(2-1)} = 2$, and so on for all of the positive integers.

Step 5: Pascal's Triangle

As problems do, this problem had been occupying space in the back of my mind for some weeks. In passing, I mentioned to a friend my discovery about the table of numbers where each number is the sum of the two numbers above. He said, "Oh, you mean Pascal's Triangle." It turns out that Pascal's triangular arrangement of numbers provides a direct way to visualize problems of combinations. This eventually took me back to the counting sit-ups problem with a more powerful way to reframe the problem as a problem of combinations and to better understand its underlying structure.

I had never heard of Pascal's triangle. So I hit the internet. Blaise Pascal was born on June 19, 1623, in Clermont-Ferrand, France. By the age of seventeen, Pascal had written an essay on conic sections that, according to my sources, caught the attention of none other than Rene Descartes. The breadth of his interests and accomplishments in mathematics, physics, engineering, art, philosophy, and religion is mind-boggling. But here we are only interested in Pascal's Triangle.

In expanding the mathematical expression $(x + 1)^{\wedge n}$, Pascal noticed that the coefficients of the terms take on a lovely pattern.

$$(x + 1)^{\wedge 0} \quad = 1;$$
$$(x + 1)^{\wedge 1} \quad = x + 1;$$
$$(x + 1)^{\wedge 2} \quad = x^2 + 2x + 1;$$
$$(x + 1)^{\wedge 3} \quad = x^3 + 3x^2 + 3x + 1;$$
$$(x + 1)^{\wedge 4} \quad = x^4 + 4x^3 + 6x^2 + 4x + 1;$$
$$(x + 1)^{\wedge 5} \quad = x^5 + 5x^4 + 10x^3 + 10x^2 + 5x + 1;$$

Keeping in mind that the coefficient of the first term in each expression is one, we can arrange the coefficients, without the powers of x, in the triangle of numbers shown in Figure 71. This is Pascal's Triangle.

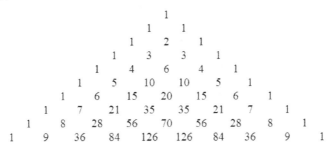

Figure 71: Pascal's Triangle

307

This pile of numbers has several interesting properties. We can see that each number is the sum of the two numbers directly above it. The reason for this becomes evident when we compute an example from the equations above.

$$(x^3 + 3x^2 + 3x + 1) \ast (x + 1) =$$

$$
\begin{array}{rcl}
(x^3 + 3x^2 + 3x + 1) \ast x & = & 1x^4 + 3x^3 + 3x^2 + 1x \\
+ \quad (x^3 + 3x^2 + 3x + 1) \ast 1 & = & \underline{ 1x^3 + 3x^2 + 3x + 1} \\
& = & 1x^4 + 4x^3 + 6x^2 + 4x + 1
\end{array}
$$

Note that each coefficient is the sum of the coefficients above it. For example, the second coefficient in the result is four. It is the sum of the first and second coefficient in the 1-3-3-1 row. This summation can be tracked in row five of Pascal's Triangle.

Calculator of Combinations

Pascal's Triangle leads us to a different way of thinking about combinations. Let's consider the case of a deck of ten cards, the ace through ten of hearts. In the discussion of combinations above, we posed the question as follows: How many ways can we deal three cards from a deck of ten? Now let's restate the question. If we arrange the cards in the deck from ace to ten, then how many ways can we deal the entire deck into two piles, one with three cards and one with seven cards? Stated this way, we have a decision to make with each of the ten cards. In Figure 72, one example of this process is represented by the shaded path where cards three, five, and six are dealt into the pile of three – the hand – and the other seven are dealt into the reject pile. At each step, when we move to the left we are rejecting the card; when we move to the right, we are keeping it. In order to end up with three cards kept, we must move to the right exactly three times. This will always take us to the fourth number in the last row, with one hundred twenty possibilities. The first position in the last row represents keeping no cards. The last position in the last row represents keeping all ten cards. There is only one path for each of these results.

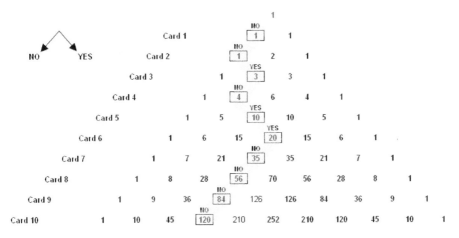

Figure 72: Tracing Path Through Pascal's Triangle

Ponder for a moment the meaning of each position along the shaded path, each with its own number. If we look at the position after card five is dealt, the number ten represents the number of alternative paths by which we could have arrived at this point. Restated, this is the number of ways that we could have selected two cards from a deck of five. Each position in the triangle represents a solution to its own problem of combinations, the row indicating the number of cards, the position across the row representing how many have been selected. Keep in mind that the first row represents selecting no cards.

I find this fascinating in several ways. Pascal's Triangle shows me a very familiar problem in an entirely new way, satisfying in its own right. But this new way is cool because it frees combinations from being derived from permutations. In the conventional formulation, we look at the permutations of ten things taken three at a time. Then we compute how many permutations actually consist of the same items arranged in a different order. In the Pascal's Triangle paradigm, we are directly modeling combinations with no reference to permutations. Free at last.

Step 6: Walking to Work

As fascinated as I was with Pascal's Triangle, I felt I needed a real-world scenario to more directly illustrate its mechanics. So I came up with the "walking to work" problem. This was a key step in developing a "process view" of combinations, a link back to the problem of counting sit-ups.

When we lived in Milwaukee, I frequently walked to work, a distance of about a mile. The streets were laid out in a grid, a simplified version of which is in Figure 73.

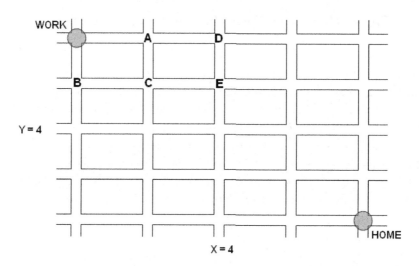

Figure 73: Walking to Work

The question arises: How many ways can one walk from home to work through these streets? Every path to be considered must traverse eight blocks. In other words, there are no detours allowed that would take me away from the destination.

At most intersections, there is a choice of which path to take. For example, at intersection C, I could go to A or B. The intersections lying along the edge, such as A, B, and D are the exceptions. Once I have arrived there, I have no further choices.

Now for the key to the problem. At any intersection, such as C, the total number of paths to the work intersection is the sum of the paths from the next intersections. For example, since both A and B have only one path to work, the total for C will be the sum of A plus B, or two. From intersection E, I can go to C or D. The total paths from C is two and from D is one, so the total for E is three.

This logic leads to the road map given in Figure 74, and a solution of seventy for the four-by-four grid of blocks.

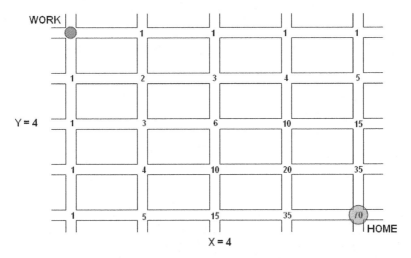

Figure 74: Number of Paths From Each Intersection

The walking to work problem is an instance of Pascal's Triangle. The number on the upper left corresponds to the top of the triangle. But how does this help us understand why the numbers reflect combinations as shown above? The trip to work required me to walk eight blocks. Exactly four of the blocks that I walk must take me toward the left. At any intersection, I can chose to move to the left or not, until I run out of my four blocks moving left, then I must move to the right the rest of the way.

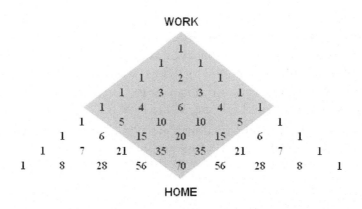

Figure 75: Walking to Work – Pascal's Triangle

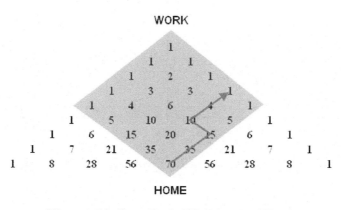

Figure 76: One Path Walking to Work

We can view the walking to work problem as a sequence of choices between going left and going right at each intersection. There are eight decision points, starting with the home intersection. This is the same as dealing eight cards, where each card can go into a hand or into a discard pile. But the hand must end up with four cards. Each card is a decision point.

In the walk to work, we can consider going left as comparable to dealing a card into the hand. Once we have gone left four times, we have reached the boundary on the left and must go right for the remainder of the trip. This is the same as having dealt four cards; all remaining cards must go into the discard pile.

Step 7: Walking to the Beach

The walking to the beach problem brings us closer to seeing how counting sit-ups, walking to work, and Pascal's Triangle are all singing the same tune.

How many ways can one walk from home to the beach, if one does not care where on the beach that one arrives? This question is captured in Figure 77. The shaded area shows that it is an extension of the walking to work problem. There are seventy ways to walk to the point in the middle of the beach. There is only one way to walk to the points on the far north and far south.

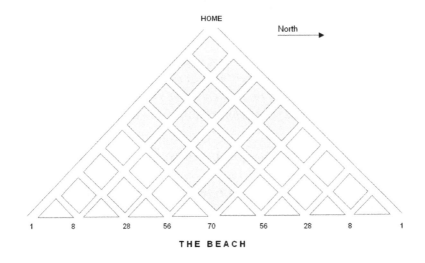

Figure 77: Walking to the Beach

The numbers across the bottom are drawn from the ninth row of Pascal's Triangle. The destination that is one block north of the south end of the beach with eight possible paths is easy to understand, since there are eight places to traverse the one-block move to the north. The other destinations require some more serious counting, or one could simply fill out Pascal's Triangle.

The total of all routes to the beach is 256, or two to the eighth power. Why is this so? As with the walk to work, we have eight decision points on the walk to the beach. The difference is that the walk to work was bounded by streets on the left and on the top. On the walk to the beach, we have two choices at every intersection. There are two choices at the home intersection. For each of these, there are two choices at the second intersection. Each successive decision point, the number of possibilities doubles. Since there are eight decision points in this example, the total routes are 2 x 2 x 2 x 2 x 2 x 2 x 2 x 2 = 256. This is the sum of the numbers along the beach side of the diagram.

Step 8: Understanding the Counting of Sit-ups as Combinations

With my newfound perspective on combinations, I returned to counting sit-ups. The key to this new perspective is viewing combinations as a series of choices defined by the total number of selections to make and the number of decision points where they can be made.

We can use the walking to the beach grid as a way to show alternatives for counting sit-ups. In Figure 78, two alternatives are shown, dividing the counting of sit-ups into segments. The first alternative is three segments: 3-4-2. The second is seven segments: 1-1-1-2-2-1-1.

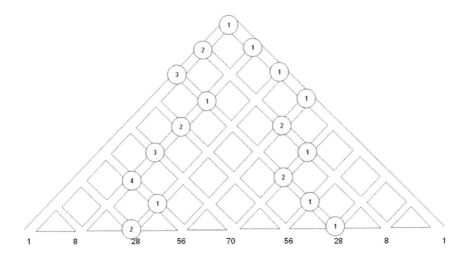

Figure 78: Counting Sit-ups

The numbered circles represent individual sit-ups; their number indicates their position within a segment. Each move to the right is a decision to start a new segment. Each move to the left is a decision to continue the current segment. As with the walk to the beach, there are eight decisions to be made and 256 ways to make them. However, nine rather than eight sit-ups are represented in this example. This results from the fact that the first sit-up has no related decision; it must be the first sit-up in a segment, regardless of how long the first segment is.

We have now arrived at a simple and elegant way to frame the problem. After we have done the first sit-up, we have twenty-four decisions to make. Do I continue with the current segment, or do I start a new one? Every combination of these twenty-four decisions produces a different set of segments. The number of ways we can make these decisions is two times two times two ...twenty-four times. Therefore, the formula for alternative ways to count sit-ups is $2^{\wedge [N-1]}$. If we are counting twenty-five sit-ups, there are 16,777,216 ways to divide the count into segments.

315

Appendix 7   *Procurement Planning*

This appendix reproduces a report entitled "A Framework for Developing Procurement Plans on CORPS Construction Projects." The report presents a conceptual map of the flow of information and decisions on building projects. The purpose of the map was to identify critical factors that affect procurement – the process by which the Army goes about organizing the building process.

Mr. Mike Carroll
US Army Construction Engineering
Research Laboratory
Interstate Research Park, Newmark Drive
P. O. Box 4005
Champaign, IL 61820
September 22, 1981

Dear Mike,

Attached is our report in fulfillment of Requisition Request Number CERL-FS-81-85. As we have discussed on past occasions, and as discussed in our letter of August 19, 1981, we have substantially broadened the scope of the report from the original intent of focusing on procurement as relates to Systems Building Technology.

Goals of the Report

As we understand it, the impetus for the report has come from the perceived need for a means of making decisions about procurement early in a building project so that the selection of certain "predesigned" technologies can at least be considered. These technologies are inaccessible in the traditional design bid-build process since the A&E's design details conflict with those of the technology. These technologies are referred to as either industrialized building or systems building. The idea has been put forward of a "selector mechanism" whereby a procurement model is selected based on the nature of a specific building project.

As pointed out in the draft, however, there are many factors that affect the choice of procurement approach beyond the availability of certain technologies. Experience in the building industry over the last twenty years, particularly in the private sector, has led to substantial procurement flexibility as a result of the pressures of time, interest rates, regulation, increasing complexity of building site conditions, and other factors. In the draft report, this has led quite correctly to treatment of procurement issues across the board, rather than those factors that relate only to building systems. At the early stages of a building project, when the direction for procurement is set, all salient factors should be taken into account, not only those that deal with technology questions. Otherwise the selector mechanism might lead to bad procurement decisions and the whole effort would have been counterproductive. This suggests that the title of the report should be changed from "Procurement Procedures for Systems Construction" to something like "An Approach to Procurement Planning."

Industrialized Building

The image conjured by the term "industrialized building" is of mass production, standardization, off-site fabrication, and a high ratio of capital to labor. However, none of these characteristics is necessarily in conflict with the traditional building process. The real conflict with traditional building practices arises from the effort of building producers to rationalize building design, to develop designs reflecting their understanding of the most sensible way to put the building together. Rationalization does not inherently imply the trappings of industrialization cited above. The Veteran's Administration study attached to the draft report provides an excellent example. Integrated lighting/ceiling systems are no more mass produced, standardized, off-site fabricated, or capital intensive than conventional hung ceilings. They are simply a more rational design, integrating the product designs and installation procedures of several trades that are usually designed and installed separately as specified by the A&E. The development of such rationalized designs requires a team effort among the building producers; it does not occur as a byproduct of competitive bidding. The greater the extent to which the producer team has developed a complete building package, the greater the conflict with traditional practice where the architect's detailed design decisions will preclude its use. The need for competitive bidding is, of course, a major barrier; otherwise, the A&E could copy the design of the building system.

A broader question is raised by this discussion. Who is in the best position to make decisions about the way the parts of a building fit together? Is it the A&E, the contractor, the subcontractor, or the manufacturer? As suggested by the VA example, this question need not be answered with a broad stroke on each project, but can be addressed specifically for each building element. In fact, the specification writer is continually deciding what decisions should be made by the A&E and what should be left to the building's producers. From the British perspective, we in the US leave considerable design latitude to the subcontractors and manufacturers for development and review in shop drawings. Subcontractors in many trades have very capable engineering staff, and manufacturers have extensive capability in product engineering. The owner's objective is to have a building design incorporating his goals for time, cost, and quality while at the same time reflecting the best available thinking on how to put the building together. The selector mechanism, to be responsive to this objective, must orchestrate the procurement process so that design responsibility is allocated to the appropriate members of the building team.

Our report deals with a topic of great importance to the CORPS, and we feel that it presents a practical and professional review of the ingredients of procurement planning and their relationship to the other areas of project decision making. It is not within the scope of this report to carry out extensive research on procurement alternatives but rather to present the experience readily available to the SYNCON team in a clear conceptual framework. It has also not been within the scope of our contract to review current CORPS procurement practices to determine the procurement framework within which projects must be carried out, and where such a framework may limit effective procurement planning. Such a review is certainly in order and would probably best be carried out by CERL or other CORPS professionals.

Putting this report together has been rather more of a creative exercise than we originally planned. We have welcomed the opportunity to bring together into an integrated picture many of our concepts, insights, and experiences about procurement. If we can be of further assistance on later stages of this project or in other CERL research efforts, please call on us.

Best regards,

SYNCON CORPORATION
David J. Parsons, AIA
Vice President

Introduction

The purpose of this report is to sketch out a procedure for developing a project procurement plan. The debate over procurement in the building industry has revolved around three basic approaches to procurement that have been popular over the last ten years, namely, the traditional design-bid-build approach, construction management (CM), and design-build. Although many key procurement issues are raised by these three approaches, we have found them an inadequate starting point for assessing alternative procurement processes on particular projects. The following problems arise from the use of these stereotypes:

- They tend to be applied to projects as a whole rather than to elements within projects. It has to be recognized that a mix of approaches can be used as called for by the elements within a project.

- Several aspects of procurement have become associated with each of the models that need not be (i.e. fast-track scheduling with the CM approach; building systems with the design-build approach; prescriptive specifications with the traditional approach).

- Often, the decision to take one of these three approaches is a straw man, since one or both of the alternatives is obviously ruled out by regulatory constraints or project schedule requirements. In such cases, the real question is: What variations should be used within the model that has been selected?

- In the industry, there is wide variation in the use of these terms. We have found projects where the terms CM and design-build have been used interchangeably.

For these reasons, we would like to see procurement planning specify management tools rather than broad models. These tools can be applied to projects as a whole or to elements within projects. Procurement, as will be spelled out in greater detail in later sections of the report, is defined as consisting of four component parts:

- definition of roles

- determination of project phasing

- choice of procedures for selecting participants to fill each role

- selection of control methods that ensure that the responsibilities taken on by each participant are fulfilled.

A model of project decision making is presented below that puts procurement planning in the context of four other project decision areas: ASSESSMENT OF OWNER OBJECTIVES, RESOURCE ANALYSIS, ACTIVITY ANALYSIS, and DESIGN. Once the model is presented, each of the five areas is discussed. Lastly, a variety of procurement responses is given to a series of problem areas.

The principal conclusion of this report is that a procurement plan cannot be produced automatically as a function of project characteristics at the beginning of the project. The project characteristics, including owner's goals and the construction environment, can only influence procurement planning as it develops in parallel with project design, resource analysis, and activity analysis. These decision areas must be developed together through several phases, since the development of information and decisions in each area depends on information produced by the others.

Project Decision Making Model

Procurement planning will be treated in this report as one of five areas of analysis and decision-making essential on construction projects. The five areas are: ANALYSIS OF OWNER'S GOALS, RESOURCE ANALYSIS, DESIGN, ACTIVITY ANALYSIS, AND PROCUREMENT PLANNING. Each of the five areas both produces information used by the other four and uses information produced by the other four. In addition, GOALS and RESOURCE ANALYSIS take information external to the project, process it, and pass it to the other analysis and decision areas. The first of two external sources of information, INFLUENCES ON THE PROJECT, includes the goals for the project at all levels within the owner organization, as well as the influence of the community in which the project will be located and the influence of regulatory agencies such as EPA, OSHA, and the like. The second external source of information is the CONSTRUCTION ENVIRONMENT, or the building industry itself, including contractors, labor, and professionals, the building site, and the site context including weather, access, and supporting infrastructure.

The outputs of the five decision areas are the FACILITY DE-SIGN, the PROCESS DESIGN, and the PROCUREMENT PLAN. These are the products of the latter three decision areas: DESIGN, ACTIVITY ANALYSIS, and PROCUREMENT PLANNING.

The model of project decision-making that has been developed for this report is shown on page 323. It has the following elements: rows, columns, activity cells, information exchange cells, external inputs, external outputs, and feedback loops. These elements are discussed below.

Rows - Each row of the matrix is associated with one of the five analysis and decision making activities, for instance, row three is associated with DESIGN and contains in its informational cells the inputs into that activity.

Columns - Each column in the matrix is associated with one of the five analysis and decision-making areas, for instance, column two is associated with RESOURCE ANALYSIS and contains in its informational cells the outputs of that activity.

Activity Cells - The five analysis and decision making activities are represented in the matrix by cells with a heavy border. The inputs into the activity are indicated by horizontal arrows pointing into the cell. The outputs of the activity are indicated by vertical arrows leaving the cell.

Informational Cells - The twenty cells other than the five activity cells represent the information that is exchanged among the five activities. Information in each cell is the output of the activity in its column and the input into the activity in its row. The informational cell is not intended to represent an activity in and of itself but simply to represent information being transferred from the activity in its column to the activity in its row.

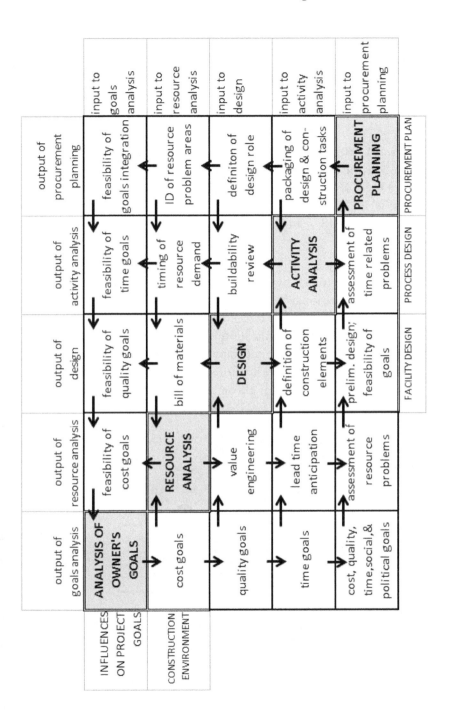

External Inputs - The two areas of external input to project decision making are located in the upper left part of the page. The first area, INFLUENCES ON THE PROJECT, is filtered through ANALYSIS OF OWNER'S GOALS to the other four decision areas. The second area, the CONSTRUCTION ENVIRONMENT, is filtered through RESOURCE ANALYSIS.

External Outputs - The products of project decision-making are indicated in the lower right part of the page. These are the FA-CILITY DESIGN, the PROCESS DESIGN, and the PROCUREMENT PLAN. They are produced by DESIGN, ACTIVITY ANALYSIS, and PROCUREMENT PLANNING respectively.

Feedback Loops - Every pair of activities defines a loop within the matrix. Since there are five activities there are ten such loops, each with two informational cells and two activity cells. For instance, as shown below, DESIGN produces a bill of materials that gives RESOURCE ANALYSIS an indication of the project's demand for materials, products, contractors, and suppliers. RESOURCE ANALYSIS, in turn, provides feedback to DESIGN in the form of value engineering and an indication of those design parameters that are dictated by available resources.

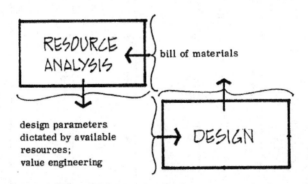

Analysis of Owner's Goals

In order for project management to make decisions both in the design and procurement areas that are coherent, the concept of management by objectives should be followed.

This requires that a consistent set of project goals be developed. Often, only one or two goals are highlighted on building projects, for instance a target completion date or a project budget, with others being left to the interpretation of project management and the design team. In such an approach, the project team is flying blind when it comes to making trade-offs among such diverse variables as initial project cost, operating cost, risk of late completion, extensiveness of landscape treatment, and so on.

Influences on Project Goals - In some cases, project goals are dictated by a clear hierarchy within the owner organization, with priorities firmly set. It is not uncommon, however, for projects to have diverse influences, such as political pressures, local community interests, and labor or construction industry interests. These influences are often in conflict and must be synthesized into a consistent set of project objectives in order for alternative courses of action in design and procurement to be assessed. Civil works projects in urban areas are an extreme example of the difficulty of synthesizing a single consistent set of objectives for a project.

Interaction With Other Decision-Making Activities - ANALYSIS OF OWNER'S GOALS is connected to the other four decision areas by feedback loops. Information on specific project goals and objectives flows from ANALYSIS OF OWNER'S GOALS and feedback on the feasibility of these goals flows back, leading in some cases to further investigation and reformulation of owner's goals. These interactions are shown by the project decision-making model. The four areas owner's goals defined in the model are discussed below in some detail.

Cost - At first it might seem that the owner's cost objective is to get the project at the lowest possible price. This is actually seldom the case. First, the owner is willing to pay to meet time, quality, and social/political objectives. The owner is also willing to pay to some extent to reduce the long-term costs of operating and maintaining the facility. The owner wants to pay a reasonable cost to meet these other project objectives. Usually the cost objective is translated into a budget based on past experience with similar projects. This budget may become a statutory limit on project cost. If so, project management becomes oriented not to reducing the project cost as much as possible but rather to ensuring that the limit is not exceeded. From a procurement standpoint, minimizing the risk of exceeding a fixed budget is quite different from striving for the lowest reasonable cost.

In order for life-cycle costs to be taken into account, the owner must derive a policy regarding the present value of future costs and cost avoidance. It is as important that such future costs not be over-stated as that they not be understated. Assessment of investment in energy efficiency is an example of where specification of such financial parameters is essential. In addition, costs related to construction time require an assumed interest rate.

The owner may also have cash flow problems. Funds may not be as available at the beginning of the project as during or after construction. Such considerations have a direct influence on the procurement approaches selected. This is seen quite often in the private sector, such as with speculative developers.

Quality - The owner's quality objectives bear most directly on the development of the facility design. The specification of owner quality objectives should take the form of a building program, specifying the nature of the activities to be housed by the facility, their interrelationships, and the environmental characteristics required to support them. These programmatic statements are then a tool for evaluating alternative designs.

Owner's quality objectives bear on procurement both through the DESIGN activity and directly. The direct effect of quality objectives on procurement relate to determination of who on the building team is most qualified to make decisions in each area of design; selection of the best professional to carry out the design role; and the method and degree of control over design and construction quality. In assessing the owner's quality objectives, therefore, it is necessary at the outset to ask certain key questions: Does this facility have special design requirements that go beyond what the average A&E firm can provide? Is a design competition warranted? Is the building of such a special nature that a specialty design firm or specialty design build firm should be sought? Is the technical performance of the facility or its subsystems such that design, construction, and operation should be specified in performance terms such as rate of output, efficiency of operation, or materials consumed?

Time - A number of factors external to the project may determine the owner's time objectives. Completion of the project by a certain date may be required in order to meet statutory requirements regarding commitment or expenditure of funds. Completion by a certain date may be required in order for a preplanned event to take place, where late completion would be catastrophic, such as with an Olympic stadium. A new facility may be replacing an outmoded facility, in which case early completion shortens the time that the obsolete facility operates; this may signify an improvement in efficiency that can be translated into dollars or other measures of benefit to the owner. Early completion may also be a financial concern, in that it reduces the cost of owning a partially completed facility.

There may also be intermediate dates, such as completion of design, which are important in and of themselves; they may, for instance, relate to funding decisions taking place on specific dates.

Social and Political Goals - The owner may have important social and political goals that go beyond time, cost, and quality. Although it is beyond the scope of this report to assess these, they clearly have an impact on procurement. Concern has been expressed within the CORPS about the extent to which the construction contract has become encumbered with provisions dictating a wide range of social and political requirements. In some cases, these provisions run counter to the owner's time, cost, and quality goals. Often, these are not within the purview of project management to trade off against other goals in setting the procurement plan, since procurement decisions related to these goals are dictated by regulation or statute. Where there is latitude for project management to fashion procurement in response to these goals, areas where they appear to conflict with other project goals should force a deeper assessment of their real intent in order to get beyond the acting out of superficial and symbolic procedures. Areas where such deeper assessment might be warranted are community involvement, safety, affirmative action, and fair play with bidders.

Resource Analysis

On many projects that are executed in the traditional mode, resource analysis is no more than the A&E's continuing awareness of building products that are on the market. Little or no research is done into the contractor climate, labor situation, availability of building systems and subsystems, or effects of construction season on the project schedule or design. The owner takes on responsibility for investigating the availability of qualified A&E firms and to varying extents, investigates the field of construction contractors to determine their availability and record of performance.

On many smaller projects, this degree of resource investigation may be satisfactory; mounting a large-scale research project to assess all aspects of the resource picture would be out of scale with the requirements of the project and would not be cost-effective. It is not uncommon, however, even on smaller projects, to find that one or two key resources presented problems of either cost or availability. Long lead times were not taken into account; bids came in high because other projects were being bid at the same time; the opportunity to use a predesigned building subsystem was lost through lack of information.

It is recommended here that each project carried out by the CORPS have responsibility assigned within the project management for ongoing resource analysis. At minimum, this would include the function of cost estimating for the project. But, in addition, this activity should be responsible for identifying potential resource problems and giving feedback to the other areas of analysis and decision-making.

Data on resource costs, availability, and resource problems should be assembled by the CORPS from the experience of its construction program in order to provide a starting point for project resource analysis. In some resource areas, the CORPS might be warranted in setting up a research effort independent of specific projects to track resource availability.

Resource Areas - Resources that are of particular concern in shaping the procurement plan are as follows:

- Building technologies, including systems and subsystems
- Building contractors and sub-contractors
- Labor
- Design and management professionals, including people available within the owner organization

- The building site

- Weather conditions

Interaction Between RESOURCE ANALYSIS and Other Areas of Decision Making

RESOURCE ANALYSIS receives the owner's cost goals from ASSESSMENT OF OWNER'S GOALS and provides feedback on the feasibility of the project budget. It receives the bill of materials for the project from DESIGN, at first as a very preliminary indication of materials, products, and systems likely to be used on the project, later as quantified lists of specific items. It provides to the DESIGN activity value engineering feedback on design alternatives under consideration and design dimensions, details, and specifications that are dictated by available resources.

RESOURCE ANALYSIS receives from ACTIVITY ANALYSIS a preliminary schedule of the demand for key resources on the project so that availability problems can be assessed. Information fed back to ACTIVITY ANALYSIS includes an assessment of the need to level off the demand for major resources and an assessment of the need to fit the schedule to building seasons or the projected availability of labor and building contractors.

PROCUREMENT PLANNING identifies for RESOURCE ANALYSIS those resources areas where problems are anticipated from a procurement point of view. It also defines the requirements of the project for design, construction, and management participants. Resource ANALYSIS feeds back an assessment of where resource problems are likely to occur, evaluation of the feasibility of meeting the owner's cost goals, review of the labor and contractor climate, and assessment of the availability of design and management professionals.

Design

DESIGN is, of course, an important area of decision making in its own right. For purposes of this report, however, we are interested in the interdependence of design decisions and the four other decision areas, since all of these interactions ultimately play a role in defining the procurement plan. The initial stages of design determine overall physical characteristics of the project. These decisions may be thought of as pre-design decisions in that they usually occur before an A&E is selected. They include rough determination of project square footage, the selection of a building site, approximate determination of number of stories, and preliminary assessment of types of construction. This early design analysis is essential to provide a basis for preliminary resource and activity analysis. Together this first round of project assessment in the areas of design, resources and activities provides a review of the feasibility of the owner's cost, time, and quality objectives and provides the basis for development of the preliminary procurement plan.

As design moves into the schematic stage, resource and activity analysis can focus more sharply on issues of greatest concern, and the procurement plan can be carried into greater detail.

Design not only provides vital information for these other areas of analysis but is also directed by them. Limits on resource availability might have important design consequences. Procurement decisions based on the resource picture may dictate such fundamental design decisions as the shape of the building, major materials used, and even the site selected for its construction. The procurement plan will dictate who will make design decisions at each level of the project from overall layout, to subsystem design through the design of building components and parts. The assignment of design responsibility has a profound effect on the physical product that results.

Activity Analysis

ACTIVITY ANALYSIS develops both the logic and duration of the activities required to carry out all phases of the project. First, it produces an assessment of the feasibility of the owner's time goals. This can begin by comparison to the schedules of past projects with similar requirements but should, as early as possible, be based on assessment of the characteristics of the project at hand. This requires initial information about project design.

ACTIVITY ANALYSIS provides a starting point for RESOURCE ANALYSIS to evaluate problems with the availability of resources at the times and at the rate of flow indicated by the project schedule. Assessment of the feasibility of the owner's time goals provides the starting point for consideration of alternative procurement approaches that can deal with minimizing project design and construction time.

As the project schedule takes shape, it becomes a tool for project management to control the execution of design and construction activities on the project. It allows project management to focus its effort at controlling project activities on the areas where problems are most likely to occur.

Procurement Planning

As indicated by the discussion of the other four decision areas and by the model itself, PROCUREMENT PLANNING is based on the weighing of owner goals against availability or resources that occurs in RESOURCE ANALYSIS, DESIGN, and ACTIVITY ANALYSIS. Only through this feasibility assessment of owner's goals can the problem areas be identified on which the procurement plan will be based. The tables on pages 24 through 33 indicate the range of procurement approaches that are appropriate in response to problem areas deriving from owner's goals and the construction environment. These tables indicate alternative approaches to each of the four elements of procurement identified in the introduction: definition of roles, project phasing, selection procedures, and methods of control. These will now be discussed before describing the use of the procurement planning tables.

Definition of Roles The three procurement approaches discussed in the introduction get their differing characters from the roles defined for design, construction, and project management. In the traditional process, the design team is defined as separate from the construction team, each managed by a team leader, with design by the A&E firm and construction by the general contractor. In the design-build approach, a major portion of the design responsibility is allocated to the contractor, who manages both the design and the construction phases. Under construction management, the construction phase is managed by a consultant working on a fee basis for the owner. He coordinates the work of specialty contractors who have separate prime contracts with the owner. The construction manager also provides cost and time input into the design process, working directly for the owner.

These distinctions are somewhat oversimplified. Even in the traditional process, the contractor/fabricator/manufacturer team has substantial responsibility for design at the detailed level. The key ingredient here is the way in which specification of the building is expressed as a basis for contractor selection. Five approaches to building specification are defined as follows:

- The building program defines functional requirements of the facility.

- Performance specifications: Defining minimum levels of performance for building elements combined with drawings that determine their physical location.

- Prescriptive specifications: Describing materials, shapes, and physical characteristics of building elements.

- Product specifications: Naming specific products and their manufacturers.

- Construction methods: Specifying how the building elements will be assembled and installed.

These methods of specification may be applied to an entire project or may be mixed to fit particular building elements. It is the specification method that defines the role of the A&E and the building producers in terms of design responsibility.

In the traditional process, the manufacturer supplies his products to fabricators and contractors, taking no responsibility for installation. There are circumstances under which it is desirable for the owner to deal directly with the manufacturer, insisting that he take primary responsibility for installation of his products. This is often the case with building systems where the work of several trades is integrated or there is substantial assembly off-site.

Under some circumstances, the building owner may want to purchase materials directly from suppliers, redefining the role of the contractor, who would then supply labor only.

This may be the case where early purchase is necessary or quantities are not easily estimated.

Project Phasing Traditionally, the design work is completed on a project before construction begins. This gives the owner the advantage of seeing the entire cost of the project before committing to construction. It also allows selection of a single general contractor responsible for the entire project. The cost of money, increasing project complexity, and the emergence of major projects that include the renovation of existing facilities has led to the use of phased construction. In this approach, the work is subdivided into packages that can be designed, bid, and constructed before the design of the entire project is completed. Phased (or fast-track) construction often requires a construction manager to coordinate among contractors and between the design team and contractors. Sub-contractors may ultimately be assigned to a general contractor once all of the construction work is under contract. Phased construction is also commonly used in the design-build approach, where a single contractor has control over design and construction of the entire project.

Selection of Participants Once roles are defined, firms must be selected to fill them.

Traditionally, A&E firms have been selected on the basis of reputation and presentations to the owner, with fees negotiated after tentative selection. Contractors have been selected in the public sector on the basis of the lowest bid of a qualified bidder. Alternative approaches to A&E selection include fee competition and design competitions. Contractor selection may be through bidding or negotiation. The contractor proposal may include price alone or price combined with a design proposal. A two-step procedure can be used to separate price from design proposals, where designs are submitted, evaluated, and approved and then price is submitted in a second step.

Methods of Control The A&E and construction contracts form the basis for controlling the performance of these members of the building team once they are selected. Periodic payment is usually based on progress of the work, which is determined by the owner, the A&E, or the CM. Incentives may be built into these contracts to encourage cost savings, on-time delivery, or higher levels of performance. In addition to withholding progress payments, additional controls include retainage of a certain percent of the contract amount until the work is completed, the requirement that work that is found unsatisfactory must be redone, and the potential termination of the contract for nonperformance. All of these control mechanisms presume that the contract provides an adequate basis for evaluating the quality of the work as it progresses.

Constraints on Procurement Approach Consideration of alternative procurement approaches on individual CORPS projects is constrained by federal statute, Department of the Army regulation, and CORPS policy at OCE, division, and district levels. Assessment of these constraints is beyond the scope of this report. Procurement decisions that have been made at organizational levels higher than the individual project can be based on more thorough assessment of owner goals than starting from scratch on each project. Such decisions provide a procurement framework within which the procurement plan for individual projects can be developed. Such pre-project procurement decisions are advisable *if* they truly reflect the owner's goals on every project to which they apply and if they are not in conflict with owner's goals, which change from one project to another.

Owner's goals are often pulling in opposite directions with respect to specific aspects of procurement. The relative importance of these goals may vary from one project to another, suggesting that a judgment must be made in such areas on each specific project. For example, the use of time and materials contracts is suggested where the extent of work cannot be known in advance of construction, but such contracts carry the risk that construction cost might exceed the construction budget; there is no lump-sum contract for the complete project. To decide whether or not to use this type of contract requires an assessment of the relative importance of the two independent variables – poorly defined construction work versus risk of cost overruns. On some projects, such as major excavation projects with unknown conditions underground, the high cost of getting a lump sum bid might outweigh the risk of running over budget on a time and materials contract. This is the kind of assessment that must be made on a project-by-project basis; however, the types of projects on which such approaches should be considered could, perhaps, be identified in advance.

Selection of Procurement Techniques The tables that follow indicate appropriate procurement responses to ten problem areas that grow out of owner's goals, and the construction environment of the project. The ten areas are:

1. OWNER'S COST GOALS

(a) Minimize overall project construction cost; minimizing project cost is of equal or greater importance than optimizing other project goals

(b) Minimize risk that initial investment in design will be wasted on unfeasible

design; feasibility of cost goals is a concern

(c) Minimize risk that construction cost will exceed fixed construction budget

(d) Minimize overall project life-cycle cost, including cost of operation and maintenance

2. OWNER'S QUALITY GOALS

(a) High architectural standard required for building with ceremonial or symbolic purpose

(b) Specialty building requiring special design expertise

(c) High-performance facility is required, (i.e. power plant, processing plant)

3. OWNER'S TIME GOALS

(a) Completion by a specific date appears to be difficult using traditional procedures; high priority on early completion

4. OWNER'S POLITICAL AND SOCIAL GOALS

(a) Objective selection of participants that is beyond the possibility of favoritism

(b) Community involvement - project design, schedule, or construction method may impact the community as a whole or special interests (includes environmental and economic impacts)

(c) Affirmative action

5. AVAILABILITY OF BUILDING TECHNOLOGIES

(a) Production/construction firms are available to provide design/build package for entire building or for building subsystems.

package builder
precaster
building systems producer
building subsystems producer
special equipment supplier
(b) Long lead times on key items
(c) Certain building materials or products are not available at a reasonable price at the location of the project

6. CONTRACTOR CLIMATE

(a) Substantial trough or peak in local contractor workloads is forecast (i.e. other major projects scheduled at the same time)

(b) Availability of contractors in important trades is a major concern (i.e. foreign projects or where highly specialized trades are required)

(c) Bid shopping is a recognized problem with local general contractors

(d) Local contractors are poorly capitalized

7. LABOR CLIMATE

(a) Major increase in labor rates is anticipated

(b) High potential has been identified for disruptive strikes

8. AVAILABILITY OF PROFESSIONALS

(a) Owner's staff for project management is limited

9. SITE AND WEATHER CONDITIONS

(a) Project is renovation of existing facility that must remain in use during construction

(b) Limited site access and site storage; remote site

(c) Temperature and precipitation affect construction trades during specific seasons

10. DESIGN

(a) Innovative technologies will be required in order to meet project goals

(b) Quantity requirements are difficult to estimate (i.e. pipeline renovation)

Procurement approaches that follow from these problem areas are identified in the tables that follow. The tables are set up in an *if...then* format as a reminder that the procurement technique is a response to the identification of the problem area.

The objective in using the tables is to find that set of procurement techniques that is a common denominator of the problem areas that characterize the project. Note that for many areas, there are several procurement approaches cited under each procurement heading. Certain of these alternatives will be eliminated when the procurement implications of other problem areas are traced. An owner goal might indicate that design and construction should overlap, while a resource consideration might suggest strict sequential phasing. This leads necessarily to prioritization of owner goals. The relative importance of owner goals and the severity of resource considerations will determine which procurement technique should be used. Many of the recommended procurement techniques that are related to problem areas are actually good practice even when the area is not a particular problem. For instance, establishing a scheduling function at the beginning of the project and assigning it to a professional with construction expertise makes sense, even when rapid completion is not a concern. The ability of the project management team to allocate its attention and resources to such procurement practices will, however, be determined by its perception of the priority of the problem area.

It is not intended that the tables that follow present a comprehensive listing of problem areas and procurement approaches that respond to them. The research required for such an exhaustive listing is beyond the scope of this report. It is intended to suggest in detail the link between a broad range of significant problem areas and many of the common approaches to the four elements of procurement that have been defined.

Conclusion and Recommendations

Nature of Procurement Planning The procurement plan for a project cannot be dictated simply and automatically by project characteristics defined at the outset. A process of assessing the feasibility of owner goals within the project's construction environment must take place in order to determine where the tough parts of the procurement problem lie. For example, an owner's very strong feelings about meeting a completion date points to accelerated or fast-track scheduling only if activity analysis indicates that completion of the project through normal contracting practices will be a problem. But activity analysis depends on preliminary design information and an assessment of contractor, labor, and materials availability. Only after these interrelated areas of analysis and decision-making have moved through several feedback cycles can we know if there is a problem requiring a special approach to procurement. Unfortunately, by pinning down the procurement approach before a thorough exploration of the feasibility of the owner's goals has been made, procurement approaches required by as-yet-undiscovered problem areas may be locked out. Procurement planning is, therefore, an ongoing process that parallels design development, resource and activity analysis, and the analysis of owner's objectives throughout the course of a building project.

Definition of Project Management Responsibilities With the exception of design, the areas of analysis and decision making defined in this report are the responsibility of the project management team. These responsibilities must be clearly assigned whether they be kept within the owner organization, assigned to professional consultants, or packaged with the overall responsibilities of a design-build contractor. In whatever fashion these decision areas are ultimately assigned, there must be, at the outset of the project, a project manager who is able to lay the foundation for making the procurement decisions that result in such assignments.

Use of the Procurement Planning Format The format presented in this report for linking perceived problem areas with procurement alternatives can be used as a guide for compiling case study experience within the CORPS. We recommend that the approach suggested here be applied to a mix of projects that are currently underway, using the resulting experience to amplify and extend the procurement options presented in the report.

PROCUREMENT PLANNING GUIDE

IF.... PROBLEM AREA	THEN.... I. Definition of Roles	II. Project Phasing	III. Participant Selection	IV. Methods of Control
1. OWNER'S COST GOALS (a) minimize overall project construction cost; minimizing project cost is of equal or greater importance than optimizing other project goals.	(a) In preliminary planning stage, consider widest range of solutions, including not building, rehab., prefab, etc. (b) define constructability assessment role during design phase. Could be CM, design/build contractor, A&E firm strong in construction, or owner personnel (c) give maximum design latitude to contractors	(a) schedule job to fit optimal construction crew sizes (b) avoid overtime (c) avoid bad construction seasons (d) allow work with float to be performed late to reduce finance charges (e) take wage increases into account when determining project schedule	(a) allow for competitive negotiation (b) avoid expectation of bid shopping either through listing of sub-contractors on bids or by pre-selection of general contractors with reputations for no bid shopping (c) encourage buildability recommendations by bidders, allow bidders to submit alternative items (d) use bid bond to insure serious bidding	(a) establish unit prices on items where change orders are probable in order to insure fair pricing of changed items (b) establish contractor incentives for value engineering (c) be flexible on design changes requested through shop drawing process (d) require performance and payment bonds (e) carefully review requests for progress payments (f) pay contractors on time (g) consider A&E fee which gives incentive for value engineering. Traditional fees based on percent of total cost actually rewards the A&E for higher construction cost.
(b) minimize risk that initial investment in design will be wasted on unfeasible design; feasibility of cost goals is a concern	(d) use design/build contractor with fixed overall price for design and construction			(h) A&E contract should require redesign if project cost is not on budget
(c) minimize risk that construction cost will exceed fixed construction budget	(e) define single overall construction contract with fixed or maximum price	(f) complete all design before construction begins	(e) be certain that there are no contractor errors in bids, select on basis of lump-sum overall price for construction. (f) carefully consider contractors record of on-budget performance	(i) establish claims management procedure (j) minimize change orders
(d) minimize overall project life-cycle cost including cost of operation and maintenance	(f) assign responsibility to designers for assessing life cycle cost of items with substantial operating and/or maintenance costs. (g) define responsibility for design, construction, operation, and maintenance of key annual cost systems under single contract		(g) select contractors on basis of present value of construction, operating and maintenance costs for a period of 5 to 10 years	(k) include maintenance contract and operating cost guarantees as part of construction contract, maintenance contract may be executed at owner's option.

339

PROCUREMENT PLANNING GUIDE

IF.... PROBLEM AREA	THEN.... I. Definition of Roles	II. Project Phasing	III. Participant Selection	IV. Methods of Control
2. OWNER'S QUALITY GOALS (for quality of construction as pertains to the cost of operation and maintenance, see section 1d).				
(a) High architectural standard required for building with cerimonial or symbolic purpose	(a) use A&E firm which is independent of construction contractor (b) establish panel of experts to review the design (c) establish clear authority in owner organization for design review and approval. (d) conduct frequent design reviews with A&E firm	(a) complete design prior to start of construction in order to avoid forcing undesirable detailed design decisions (b) organize architectural competition in one or two phases.	(a) select A&E firm on the basis of review of past work on similar building type. (b) involve design experts in the A&E selection process (c) select architect on basis of one or two step competition	(a) require samples and mock-ups of all critical materials (b) establish contractor quality control procedures, (c) require on-site decision-making capability by the A&E firm on quality issues. (d) use retainage system to insure proper completion of the work by contractors.
(b) Specialty building requiring special design expertise	(e) hire specialty design firm (f) consider specialty design/build firm (ie. clinics, banks highly technical buildings)		see (a)	(e) with specialty design/build firm, use quality of past work as standard
(c) high performance facility is required. (ie. power plant, processing plant)	(g) use design/build approach on systems delivering critical performance characteristics.		(d) select design/build contractor on basis of cost per unit of performance (e) use two step selection procedure to verify facility performance if (d) is not possible	(f) require engineering verification of engineering projections prior to construction (g) withold substantial retainage until actual performance is verified.

PROCUREMENT PLANNING GUIDE

IF.... PROBLEM AREA	THEN.... I. Definition of Roles	II. Project Phasing	III. Participant Selection	IV. Methods of Control
3. OWNER'S TIME GOALS (a) completion by a specific date appears to be difficult using traditional procedures; or high priority on early completion	(a) consider design/construction overlap with close coordination between design and construction through either: –design/build with overall control of design and construction by one contractor –CM approach with CM authority to coordinate A &E team and contractor team (b) establish scheduling function at the beginning of project and assign this role to professional with construction expertise (c) minimize red tape in communication between design engineers and specialty contractors (d) clearly define owner decision making responsibility, authority, procedure and time constraints	(a) overlap design and construction activities (b) compress design and construction activities	(a) select contractors with substantial forces in order to man the work heavily (b) avoid technology with sole source of supply (c) carefully evaluate contractors' past record of on-time performance	(a) build time incentives into design and construction contracts (b) monitor progress of critical design and construction activities (c) maintain project schedule as planning and control tool (d) streamline owner and A&E review procedures (e) consider time and materials or unit price contracts so that construction may begin early (f) structure incentives/penalties to reflect real costs to owner

PROCUREMENT PLANNING GUIDE

IF.... PROBLEM AREA	THEN.... I. Definition of Roles	II. Project Phasing	III. Participant Selection	IV. Methods of Control
4. OWNER'S POLITICAL AND SOCIAL GOALS				
(a) objective selection of participants which is beyond the possibility of favoritism	(a) design/build role is difficult to fill with totally quantitative proposal evaluation with the private sector through lease or other arrangement. this would open the door to private sector procurement practices such as design/build and negotiated contracts.		(a) if design build approach is indicated for other reasons, objectify the selection process by use of evaluation points, independent evaluation panels and/or two step selection process	
(b) Community involvement – project design, schedule, or construction method may impact the community as a whole or special interests. (includes environmental and economic impacts)	(c) plan a community involvement process from the outset			
(c) Affirmative action	(d) assess availability of minority firms to fill roles in procurement alternatives under consideration		(b) as per regulation	
(There are many other owner goals under this heading including safety, wage rates, and other requirements of federal statutes. Assessment of these requirements is not within the scope of this research contract)				

342

PROCUREMENT PLANNING GUIDE

IF.... PROBLEM AREA	THEN.... I. Definition of Roles	II. Project Phasing	III. Participant Selection	IV. Methods of Control
5. AVAILABILITY OF BUILDING TECHNOLOGIES (a) Production/construction firms are available to provide design/build package for entire building or for building sub-systems. - package builder - precaster - building systems producer - building sub-systems producer - special equipment supplier	(a) consider design/build process (b) if there is only one potential bidder for design/build, consider hybrid process with conventional design competing with design/build proposal (c) negotiate with sole source package supplier and compare price to past projects and/or A&E estimates on schematic design (d) use two step process with quality level of building sub-systems verified in first step, prices submitted in second. (e) if major subsystems are selected by one of the above methods, owner should select directly and assign to general contractor, use CM, or coordinate separate primes with owner's staff (f) require fabrication and installation under one contract (g) in general, A&E should leave design latitude where producers have design capability	(a) selection of major systems or subsystems may be warranted in advance of design development for remainder of project (b) technology assessment phase may have to be built into process.	(a) request proposals which include price and design. establish formal or informal evaluation procedure for weighing quality against cost (b) set up two step selection procedure with quality acceptability established in first step and price in second step. (c) where appropriate, include samples, mock-ups, and reference to existing buildings in quality proposals (d) separate procurement of major systems from procurement of conventional work	(a) base approvals on samples, mock-ups, or other existing facilities where possible (b) require accurate construction documents before construction begins
(b) long lead times on key items (c) certain building material or products are not available at a reasonable price at the location of the project	(h) consider owner purchase (i) define CM role during design to assess lead times (j) consider designs which reduce dependence on these items (k) assign designer responsibility of avoiding such materials	(c) early bid on key items	(e) direct owner purchase of key items	(c) provide for early payment for partially or wholly fabricated items not yet delivered to the site (d) make provision for inspection of work at point of manufacture

343

PROCUREMENT PLANNING GUIDE

IF.... PROBLEM AREA	THEN.... I. Definition of Roles	II. Project Phasing	III. Participant Selection	IV. Methods of Control
6. CONTRACTOR CLIMATE				
(a) substantial trough or peak in local contractor workloads is forecast (ie. other major projects scheduled at the same time)	(a) consider CM approach to insure that construction schedule is sensitive to contractor climate	(a) adjust project schedule to reflect contractor availability		
(b) availability of contractors in important trades is a major concern. (ie. foreign projects or where highly specialized trades are required.)	(b) create close design/construction link either through CM or design/build approach. (c) assign responsibility to designers to avoid where possible use of trades which have availability problems	(b) confront design decisions in these areas early to accomodate long lead times or need for design changes in response to contractor availability.		
(c) bid shopping is a recognized problem with local general contractors			(a) require listing of subcontractors (b) contract directly with key subcontractors	
(d) local contractors are poorly capitalized	(d) consider use of labor only only contracts with materials supplied by owner. (e) package construction into smaller contracts so that more than one contractor can be used in each trade		(c) take bids on the work in such a way that more than one contractor can be selected within particular trades (d) labor only contracts may be either lump sum or time and materials	

344

PROCUREMENT PLANNING GUIDE

IF....	THEN....			
PROBLEM AREA	I. Definition of Roles	II. Project Phasing	III. Participant Selection	IV. Methods of Control
7. LABOR CLIMATE (availability problems - see 6a, b)				
(a) major increase in labor rates is anticipated		(a) consider accelerating project schedule to shift work into period with lower wage rates		
(b) high potential has been identified for disruptive strikes	(a) consider use of non-union labor (b) consider use of owner employees			

PROCUREMENT PLANNING GUIDE

IF.... PROBLEM AREA	THEN.... I. Definition of Roles	II. Project Phasing	III. Participant Selection	IV. Methods of Control
8. AVAILABILITY OF PROFESSIONALS (a)Owner's staff for project management is limited	(a) assign coordination responsibility to design and construction professionals. (ie. CM, design/build contractor). Do not rely on traditional process if owner has demanding time or cost goals. (b) hire professional to assist with project planning prior to hiring A&E.	(a) do not overlap design and construction unless CM is available in whom the owner has substantial confidence.	(a) minimize need for owner evaluation of proposals.	(a) assign responsibility for time, cost, and quality control to professionals working under fee arrangement with the owner. CM may be needed even with a general contractor approach.

PROCUREMENT PLANNING GUIDE

IF.... PROBLEM AREA	THEN.... I. Definition of Roles	II. Project Phasing	III. Participant Selection	IV. Methods of Control
9. SITE AND WEATHER CONDITIONS (a) Project is renovation of existing facility which must remain in use during construction	(a) construction logistics must be carefully considered in conjunction with the development of schematic design. This suggests CM or design/build approach. (b) Design/build contract may be appropriate for some trades or for whole job if detailed design and quantity measurements must await demolition to determine existing conditions. (c) establish liaison between project management and facility management personnel	(a) construction schedule must be developed which is compatible with building operations and the provision of temporary relocation may be necessary.	(a) may require selection of some contractors on unit cost or time and materials basis since information on existing conditions may be limited	(a) Establish quick response relationship between contractors and owner. This must be an "on site" communications for day to day decisions.
(b) Limited site access and site storage; remote site	See (a) above.	(b) consider need for site access and site storage in establishing the project schedule.		(b) clear management authority over site access and site storage in the hands of the owner (beware of claims for owner initiated delays), CM, or general contractor.
(c) temperature and precipitation affect construction trades during specific seasons	(d) if construction time is a concern, construction professional should assess compatibility between preliminary schedule and seasonal weather conditions	(c) may require phased construction in order to avoid weather related delays.		

IF.... PROBLEM AREA	THEN.... I. Definition of Roles	II. Project Phasing	III. Participant Selection	IV. Methods of Control
10. DESIGN (a) Innovative technologies will be required in order to meet project goals	(a) consider performance based procurement, with substantial design responsibility in the hands of the producers	(a) consider separation of conventional part of the project from the part requiring new technologies and schedule on separate tracks	(a) consider two step selection process (b) consider design/build approach where cost is weighed against quality in evaluation of contractor proposals	(a) require single contract responsibility for production and installation (b) consider feasibility of mock-up to test performance and serve as a standard for controlling construction quality
(b) quantity requirements are difficult to estimate (ie. pipeline; renovation)	(b) use CM approach to closely monitor quantities installed		(c) select contractors on the basis of unit prices	(c) clearly define responsibility for security of materials delivered to the site but not yet installed. (d) CM or owner staff must carefully monitor quantity of materials installed.

Appendix 8   WPAP Process Model: Milwaukee Water Pollution Abatement Program

The Milwaukee Water Pollution Abatement Program (WPAP) required a major overhaul of Milwaukee's sewage collection system and treatment plants. Regulatory agencies required a program delivery analysis as a framework for the many aspects of the program. The discussion of the process model presented in this appendix was part of the program delivery analysis prepared in 1979. The goal of the model was to provide a map of the many considerations that had to be integrated in the program.

Why a Model?

The Milwaukee Water Pollution Abatement Program is a highly complex process. The program passes through several phases with differing characteristics as it evolves. In order to develop a program-wide implementation plan, it is necessary to identify and anticipate these phase characteristics so that good decisions are made at the proper time. The plan should consider the activities performed, resource needs, and personnel requirements within each phase and the manner of transition between phases. The use of a model allows program management to simulate the process, thereby anticipating future requirements and activities. The model defines a framework for the process.

The Structure of the Model

The process model is made up of four matrices. As time passes, the program moves from one matrix to the next, from the definition of objectives through facilities planning, on to design, and finally to implementation.

Each of these matrices can be thought of as an activity center, the function of which is to define the program in a particular way -

349

the decisions of each activity center build on the decisions of the previous one and become the input into decisions of the following activity center. The activity in the first matrix is definition of objectives. The inputs to this activity include all program influences, from court orders to public opinion. The output is a clear and consistent statement of program objectives, which becomes the foundation for facilities planning. The facilities planning activity center transforms program objectives into plans for physical elements. In the third matrix, design converts facilities plans into projects, contracts, and specifications that are the basis for implementation. Finally, in the fourth matrix, available resources are brought together to meet the requirements of contract documents. Implementation can be viewed as an exchange of resources among program participants. Contractors, manufacturers, suppliers, engineers, and managers bring their expertise, time, materials, and equipment, and leave with dollars. The Milwaukee Metropolitan Sewerage District (MMSD), local government, EPA, the Wisconsin Department of Natural Resources (DNR), and the community bring dollars and leave with facilities that will improve water quality.

This description of the WPAP process model follows the flow of decisions. However, information required to make informed decisions requires a reverse flow. This requirement will be discussed in the descriptions of the individual matrices.

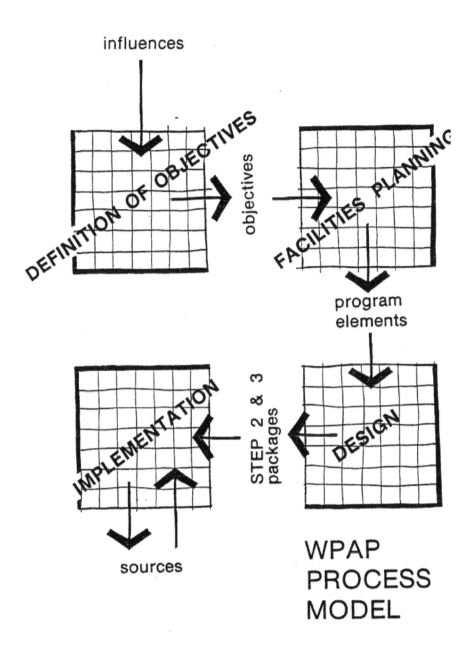

Step 0

In the first matrix, the objectives of the program are defined after considering and resolving the various influences on each objective. The output of this phase of activity should be a clear set of attainable objectives that in effect is a statement of the program. It becomes the charge that the MMSD places on the Program Management Office (PMO). The influences upon an objective will, in many instances, be conflicting. It is necessary in this phase to resolve those conflicts so that an attainable objective emerges. The goals of all the influences upon a particular program objective should be first identified, the conflicts noted, and a method of resolution determined so that an attainable objective can be stated.

After objectives determined to be attainable are stated, the concept of "management by objectives" is applied, and the appropriate individual in the PMO is assigned the responsibility for attaining each objective. In like manner, a member of the staff of the MMSD is assigned responsibility for its part in attaining the objective.

Although *definition of objectives* is shown as the first activity of the program, it can occur throughout the process. New influences may be identified, the goals of the influencing organizations may change, and some program objectives may be deemed unattainable as time passes and more information becomes available. As these events occur, objectives affected should be restated and republished. Since the objectives define the program and are the underpinnings of the entire PMO effort, any change in their direction requires the approval and concurrence of the MMSD. Program objectives fall under four general categories: physical, community, timing, and cost.

Example of conflicting influences: two courts, federal and Dane County, have conflicting quality and time requirements. These influences must be resolved before a clear objective can be implemented. Presently, Facilities Planning has received and is planning for conflicting objectives. Before the Step 1 process is completed, conflicts must be resolved and attainable objectives determined.

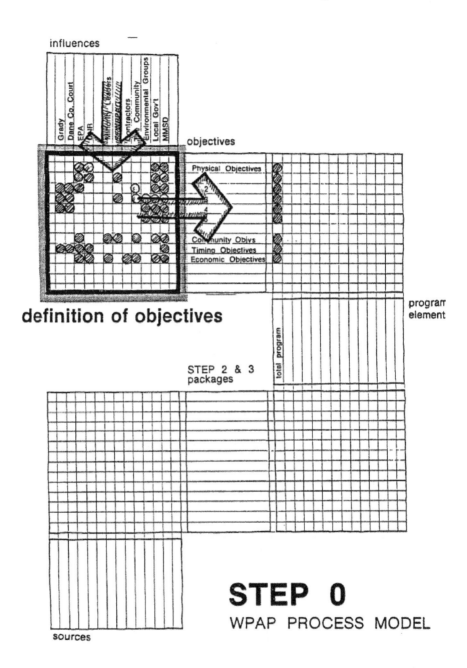

definition of objectives

STEP 0
WPAP PROCESS MODEL

Step 1

The major activity occurring in Step 1 is facilities planning, shown as the second matrix. The process of facilities planning receives all of the program objectives and converts the physical objectives into facilities plans. The other objectives, community, timing, and cost, are taken into account in facilities planning but have program-wide implications that cannot be fully attained in Step 1. Therefore, they will pass into succeeding phases, whereas the physical objectives are converted into and embodied in the facilities plans in Step 1.

It is necessary for a program of this magnitude and diversity to be divided into its physical elements and facilities plans developed for each element. A project manager has been assigned the responsibility of preparing facilities plans for each of the physical elements. A responsibility matrix developed for this activity, facilities planning, shows the project managers along the vertical axis and the persons responsible for the attainment of each objective along the horizontal axis, both program-wide and for the physical elements of the program. This form of matrix management with clearly defined responsibilities can provide assurance of facilities plans that encompass the full range of objectives.

In order for facilities planning to take place with proper cognizance given to all factors, there must be information provided from the preliminary activities that occur in the design and implementation activity centers (matrices three and four). Resource availability, for example, can have an important effect on the feasibility of a facilities plan. The information flow required in Step 1 will be discussed later.

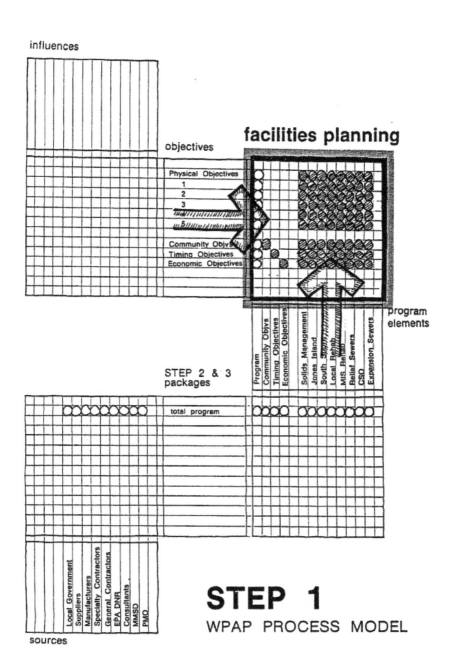

influences

objectives

facilities planning

Physical Objectives
1
2
3

Community Objvs
Timing Objectives
Economic Objectives

program
elements

STEP 2 & 3
packages

total program

STEP 1

WPAP PROCESS MODEL

sources

Step 2

In the third matrix, design, the facilities plans generated in Step 1 must be converted into designs that can be implemented. This activity, once again, involves repackaging the program in a manner that will assure the most effective conversion into design. It receives element facilities plans as input from Step 1 activities, and resource information as input from the implementation activity center. Before design activities can begin, there must be project definition. It cannot be assumed that the element facilities plan should be broken into sub-elements classified as projects. Other factors might indicate that a horizontal project organization would be more effective than the vertical organization a sub-element project might suggest. Three such factors might include demand for resources in limited supply, activities that must take place in the same location, or the functional interaction among activities that must be closely coordinated.

Example 1: Downtown might require a new interceptor line under MIS Rehabilitation and sewer separation under the Combined Sewage Overflow Project (CSO). A downtown sewer project might be more feasible than two projects (Metropolitan Interceptor Sewer System (MIS) Rehabilitation-downtown and CSO-downtown), which could conceivably tear up the same downtown street twice.

Example 2: The availability of tunneling machines might make the creation of a tunneling project organized around the scheduling of this piece of equipment, perhaps owner purchased, more feasible than sub-element CSO and collection sewer projects.

Example 3: Central purchasing of pumps or concrete pipe on a program-wide basis might be advantageous from a cost and availability standpoint. This kind of project (central purchasing) would constrain the sub-element project manager from functioning in his normally pure entrepreneurial role.

After a project has been defined, project delivery analysis begins. The purpose of this analysis is to develop a project delivery plan - to select the best delivery approach from the many options available. After the plan has been developed, construction drawings, specification, and contract preparation can proceed and are the output of this activity center.

356

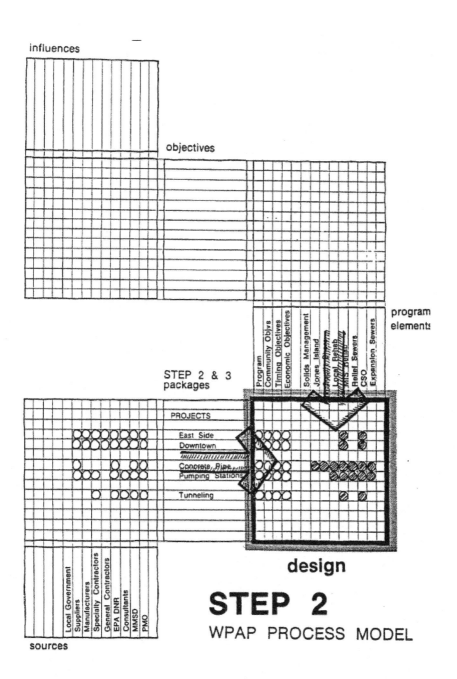

influences

objectives

program elements

STEP 2 & 3 packages

Program
Community Objvs
Timing Objectives
Economic Objectives
Solids Management
Jones Island
Local Rehab
MIS Relief
Relief Sewers
CSO
Expansion Sewers

PROJECTS

East Side
Downtown
Concrete Pipe
Pumping Stations
Tunneling

Local Government
Suppliers
Manufacturers
Specialty Contractors
General Contractors
EPA DNR
Consultants
MMSD
PMO

sources

design

STEP 2
WPAP PROCESS MODEL

Step 3

The last activity center (matrix four) is the implementation phase. Inputs from matrix three - construction drawings, specifications, and contracts - meet the source input of the community outside the PMO - contractors, labor, equipment, materials. If the projects have been properly planned, the meeting of the two inputs will be harmonious without surprises. The entire effort of the program has been directed to this overall objective and its success will be measured in this final phase.

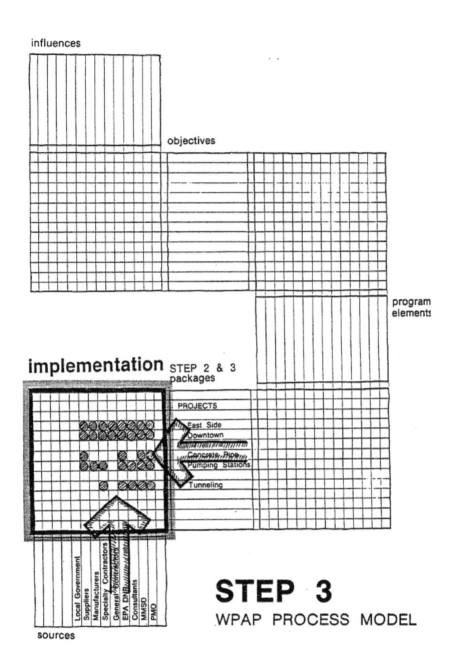

influences

objectives

program
elements

implementation STEP 2 & 3
packages

PROJECTS

East Side
Downtown
Concrete Pipe
Pumping Stations
Tunneling

Local Government
Suppliers
Manufacturers
Specialty Contractors
General Contractors
EPA DNR
Consultants
MMSD
PMO

sources

STEP 3
WPAP PROCESS MODEL

359

Step 1 – Resource Analysis

In order for informed decisions to be made in facilities planning, information on resources, the timing of their requirements, and the possible delivery alternatives should be developed. This information is likewise important as planning input for the activities that will be performed in Steps 2 and 3. A dynamic flow of information should occur among the three activity centers during Step 1. It is shown on the adjoining model for resource analysis in five steps.

- As facilities plans are developed, their resource needs should be identified. At the beginning of the Step 1 process, resource estimates will necessarily be gross and should be made for the viable alternatives of each element facilities plan. As the plans progress, these estimates can be refined and confined to the most viable alternatives. The model shows resource categories of personnel, contractors, materials, equipment, energy, funds, etc.

- As the demand side of the equation is estimated, a parallel effort occurs on the supply side. The source of the required resources must be identified, located and quantified.

- The cost and availability information developed in the preceding steps is then fed back to the facilities planning activity, where it can have an important impact on the plan itself or the determination of the most viable alternative. For example, the cost information generated is crucial to alternative selection. Likewise, the unavailability of a certain kind of process or construction equipment could affect the actual plan being developed.

- The supply and demand information should be assembled for the total program and the resulting analysis assessed against the program cost, time, and community objectives.

- The information generated in this process may require a review of, and perhaps a change in, the attainability status of a particular objective. If the resources are not and cannot be made available for the attainment of a particular objective, that information needs to be known and acted upon.

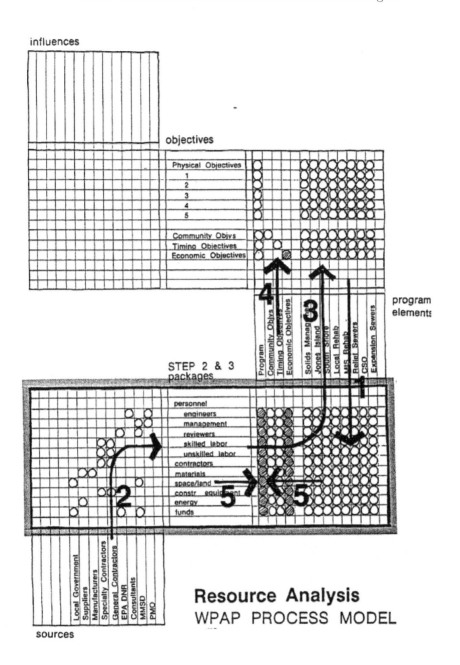

influences

objectives

Physical Objectives
1
2
3
4
5

Community Objvs
Timing Objectives
Economic Objectives

program
elements

STEP 2 & 3
packages

personnel
engineers
management
reviewers
skilled labor
unskilled labor
contractors
materials
space/land
constr equipment
energy
funds

Resource Analysis
WPAP PROCESS MODEL

sources

Step 1 – Activity Analysis

At the same time that resource analysis is occurring, activity analysis is required. Supply and demand factors are dependent on timing - the availability of a resource cannot be determined until the time requirements for its use are known. The sequence for this kind of analysis is shown on the adjoining model in the following steps:

- For each element facilities plan, the sequence of each activity in the design and construction process is determined. At the beginning of Step 1, sequence estimates will be approximate. As time passes, the estimates can be refined and further developed by dividing the element facilities plan into logical scheduling components.

- For each activity group (i.e., design, EPA, DNR review, contractor selection, etc.), the time required for completion is estimated assuming a manning level. For example, a particular design activity may require four months to complete, assuming a manning level of three designers.

- The data from bullet points one and two above are assembled into a program-wide schedule, assuming certain manning levels and an overall scheduling strategy (perhaps a percentage overlap of design and construction).

- The resulting schedule is checked against the time objectives of the program.

- The timing and manning information is fed back to facilities planning for possible redesign.

- Finally, the need for program-wide coordination is assessed. Imbalances between the time demands of facilities plans and the availability of resources will require program-wide management decisions.

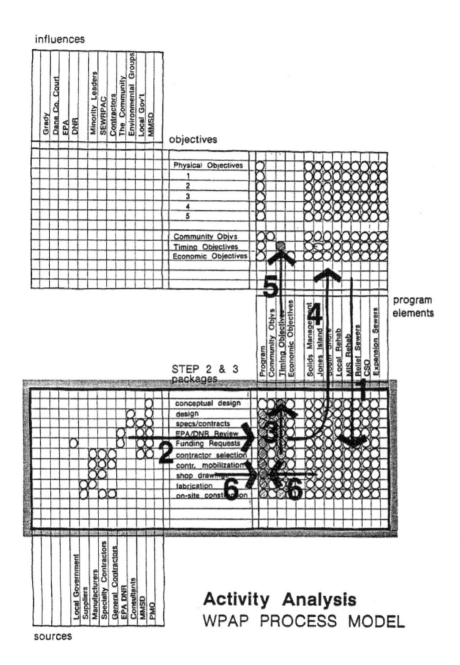

Activity Analysis
WPAP PROCESS MODEL

Step 1 – Evaluation of Alternative Step 2 and Step 3 Packaging Approaches

As resource and activity information is being developed, various approaches to packaging design and construction activities should be explored. These approaches will have an effect on timing and resources that must be studied. It is necessary to cycle through the three analyses (resource, activity and alternative packaging) several times to finally arrive at the optimal solution.

The alternative packaging evaluation process is shown in three steps on the adjoining model.

- Packaging alternatives are developed based on resource and activity analysis. Alternatives might range from projects based on a subdivision of elements to projects that are location or resource oriented (downtown sewers or central purchasing of concrete pipe).

- Packaging alternatives are assessed in terms of program objectives and the anticipated resource and activity constraints.

- The packaging approach is selected that best meets the program objectives within the anticipated constraints.

When this process is completed near the end of Step 1, program projects are defined. At this point, project objectives are stated, a project manager is assigned, and project delivery analysis begins. This procedure follows, in a more specific fashion and in greater detail, the process of resource analysis, activity analysis, and package selection just described. The guidelines for project delivery analysis outline this process.

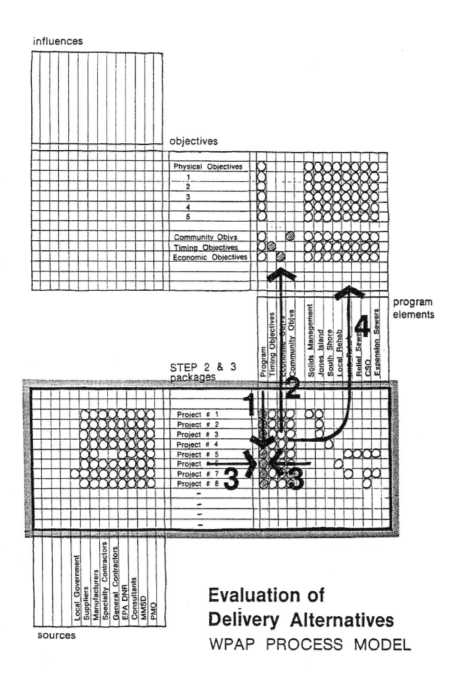

Evaluation of
Delivery Alternatives
WPAP PROCESS MODEL

List of Scenarios

Business

Construction

Design

Everyday Life

Fiction

Finance

Games & Puzzles

intended. The puzzle is used here to illustrate the need to explore beyond the presumed scope of the problem. 107

Law

Some class action suits present a serious challenge for problem decomposition. Claimants often have multiple causes of action, and these causes differ from one claimant to the next. In a class action, common causes of action are tried, leaving the remaining causes of action to be bifurcated into second trials. Complicating the decomposition of these cases into primary and secondary

Legislation

Manufacturing & Industry

Math

Science

Bibliography

Alexander, Christopher. *Notes on the Synthesis of Form.* Cambridge: Harvard University Press, 1964.

Amador, Jose, Miles, Libby, and Peters, C.B. *The Practice of Problem Based Learning, A Guide to Implementing PBL in the College Classroom.* Bolton Mass: Anker Publishing Co., 2006.

Ariely, Dan, and Wertenbrock, Klaus. "Procrastination, Deadlines, and Performance," in *Psychological Science*, Vol 13, No 3. May 2002.

Asimov, Isaac. *The End of Eternity.* New York: A Tor Book, 1959.

Axelrod, Robert and Cohen, Michael. *Harnessing Complexity.* New York: The Free Press, 1999.

Barrows, Howard. "Problem Based Learning in Medicine and Beyond: A Brief Overview." in Wilkerson and Gijselears, *New Directions for Teaching and Learning*, No 68. *Bringing Problem-Based Learning to Higher Education: Theory and Practice*, San Francisco; 1996.

Brunyé, Tad, Rapp, David, and Taylor, Holly. "Representational Flexibility and Specificity Following Spatial Descriptions of Real-World Environments," *Cognition* 108, 2008. pp. 418-443.

Camerer, Colin F. and Lovallo, Daniel. "Overconfidence and Excess Entry: An Experimental Approach," in *Choices, Values and Frames*, edited by Kahneman and Tversky. Cambridge, UK, Cambridge University Press, 2000.

Carnegie Commission on Science, Technology, and Government, *New Thinking and American Technology*, Second Edition, 1993.

de Bono, Edward. *The Mechanism of Mind.* New York: Penguin Books, 1969.

deSessa, Andrea A. "Phenomenology and the Evolution of Intuition," p. 15 in *Mental Models*, edited by Dedre Gentner and Albert L. Stevens. Hillsdale, New Jersey: Lawrence Erlbaum Associates, 1983.

Dewey, John. *Democracy and Education, an Introduction to the Philosophy of Education*, Macmillan Company, 1916. Republished as an e-document by the Penn State Electronic Classics Series.

Dörner, Dietrich. *The Logic of Failure.* Cambridge, Mass: Perseus Books, 1989.

Flavell, John H. "Metacognition and Cognitive Monitoring, A New Area of Cognitive-Developmental Inquiry," *American Psychologist*, October, 1979.

Ford, David N. and Sternman, John D. "Expert Knowledge Elicitation to Improve Mental and Formal Models," in *System Dynamics Review*, Vol 14 No 4, Winter 1998.

Fritz, Robert. *The Path of Least Resistance*. New York: Fawcett Columbine, 1984.

Gardner, Howard. *The Disciplined Mind. New York:* The Penguin Group, 1999.

Hawkins, Jeff. *On Intelligence*. New York: Times Books, 2004.

Hegarty, Mary. "Mechanical Problem Solving," Chapter 8 in *Complex Problem Solving*, edited by Sternberg and Frensch. Hillsdale, New Jersey: Lawrence Erlbaum Associates, 1991.

Kahneman, Daniel and Frederick, Shane. "Representativeness Revisited: Attribute Substitution in Intuitive Judgment," in *Heuristics of Intuitive Judgment: Extensions and Applications*. New York, Cambridge University Press, 2002.

Kincade, Scott. "A Snapshot of the Status of Problem-Based Learning in U. S. Medical Schools, 2003-2004," in *Academic Medicine*, Vol 80, No 3, March 2005.

Klayman, Joshua and Ha, Young-Won. "Confirmation, Disconfirmation and Information in Hypothesis Testing," in *Psychological Review*, Vol 94, No 2, 1987. pp. 211 – 228.

Kuhn, Thomas S. *The Structure of Scientific Revolutions*. Chicago: The University of Chicago Press, 1962.

Lovallo, Dan and Kahneman, Daniel. "Delusions of Success: How Optimism Undermines Executives' Decisions." *Harvard Business Review,* Vol 81, No 7, Cambridge, Mass. July 2003.

Maslow, A. H. "A Theory of Human Motivation." Originally Published in *Psychological Review*, Vol 50, 1943.

Meehan, Eugene. *Explanation in the Social Sciences, a System Paradigm*. Homewood, Illinois: The Dorsey Press, 1968.

Mendonca, Andrea, de Olieira, Clara, Guerrero, Dalton, and Costa, Evandro. *Difficulties in Solving Ill-defined Problems: A Case Study with Introductory Computer Programming Students*. 39th ASEE/IEEE Frontiers in Education Conference, San Antonio Texas, October 2009.

Miller, George, "The Magical Number Seven, Plus or Minus Two: Some Limits on Our Capacity for Processing Information." Originally published in *The Psychological Review*, 1956, Vol 63, pp. 81-97.

Minsky, Marvin. *A Framework for Representing Knowledge*, Artificial Intelligence Memo No 306. Cambridge, Mass: Massachusetts Institute of Technology, Artificial Intelligence Laboratory, 1974.

Munger, Charles. *The Psychology of Human Judgment*, A speech at Harvard Law School, 1995.

Newell, Alan and Simon, Herbert. *Human Problem Solving*. Englewood Cliffs, New Jersey: Prentiss-Hall, 1972.

Nickerson ,Raymond S. 'Confirmation Bias: A Ubiquitous Phenomenon in Many Guises," in *Review of General Psychology* 1998, Vol 2, No 2, pp. 175-220, 1998, Educational Publishing Foundation.

Pawley, Martin. *Terminal Architecture*. London: Reaktion Books Ltd, 1998.

Peña, William M., and Parshall, Steven A. *Problem Seeking: An Architectural Programming Primer*. New York: John Wiley and Sons, 2001.

Pólya, G. *How to Solve It; A New Aspect of Mathematical Method*. Princeton, New Jersey: Princeton University Press, 1945.

Reason, James. *Human Error*. Cambridge: Cambridge University Press, 1990.

Roberts, Jacqueline R., Xiao, Jun, Schliesman, Brian, Parsons, David J. and Shaw III, C. Frank. "The Kinetics and Mechanism of the Reaction Between Serum Albumin and Auranofin (and its Isopropyl Analogue)In Vitro," in *Inorganic Chemistry*, 35 (2) 1996. pp. 424-433.

Schoenfeld, Alan H. "Learning to Think Mathematically: Problem Solving, Metacognition and Sense-Making in Mathematics," in *Handbook for Research on Mathematics Teaching and Learning*. New York: MacMillan, 1992.

Simon, Herbert A. "Rational Choice and the Structure of the Environment," in *Psychological Review*, March 1956; Vol 63 No 2, pp. 129-138.

Sternberg, Robert J. and Frensch, Peter A. *Skill Related Differences in Game Playing*, Chapter 11 in *Complex Problem Solving*, edited by Sternberg and Frensch. Hillsdale New Jersey: Lawrence Erlbaum Associates, 1991.

Strobel, Johannes and van Barneveld, Angela, "When is PBL More Effective? A Meta-Synthesis of Meta Analyses Comparing PBL to Conventional Classrooms," in *The Interdisciplinary Journal of Problem-based Learning*, Vol 3 No 1, 2009.

Thompson, Andy. *From Butler to Blunkett and Beyond, School Building in England and the Role of the A&B Branch*. Web publication at: http://www.oecd.org/dataoecd/41/42/2675804.pdf.

Torp, Linda and Sage, Sara, *Problems as Possibilities: Problem-Based Learning for K-16 Education*. Association for Supervision and Curriculum Development, Alexandria, Virginia. 2002.

Tversky, Amos and Kahneman, Daniel, "Intuitive Prediction: Biases and Corrective Procedures," in *TIMS Studies in Management Science* 12, June 1977. pp. 313 – 327.

Tversky, Amos and Kahneman, Daniel, *Rational Choice and the Framing of Decisions, in Choices, Values and Frames*, edited by Kahneman and Tversky. Cambridge, UK: Cambridge University Press, 2000.

Tversky, Amos and Kahneman, Daniel, "The Framing of Decisions and the Psychology of Choice," in *Science*, Vol 211. January 1981.

Tversky, Amos and Kahneman, Daniel, *The Psychology of Preferences*, in *Scientific American*, Vol 246, No 1, 1982.

U. S. Army Materiel Command, *Guide for the Preparation and Use of Performance Specifications*, 1999.

Wolfram, Stephen, *A New Kind of Science* Champaign Illinois: Wolfram Media Inc, 2002.

Index

386

Made in the USA
Las Vegas, NV
16 August 2021

28279590R00223